University of London Historical Studies

XXXVII

IMPEACHMENT AND
PARLIAMENTARY JUDICATURE
IN EARLY STUART ENGLAND

This volume is published with the help of
grants from the late Miss Isobel Thornley's
Bequest to the University of London
and from the Twenty-Seven Foundation

Impeachment and Parliamentary Judicature in Early Stuart England

by

COLIN G. C. TITE

UNIVERSITY OF LONDON
THE ATHLONE PRESS
1974

Published by
THE ATHLONE PRESS
UNIVERSITY OF LONDON
at 4 Gower Street London WC1

Distributed by Tiptree Book Services Ltd
Tiptree, Essex

U.S.A. and Canada
Humanities Press Inc
New York

0 485 13137 4

Printed in Great Britain by
T. AND A. CONSTABLE LIMITED
Edinburgh

To my Parents

PREFACE

In writing this book, I have been quite unusually fortunate in the advice and encouragement which I have received. I owe a great deal to Mr Roger Lockyer who, first as supervisor of my Ph.D. research and later as co-editor for the University of London Historical Studies series, showed indefatigable kindness to me. I have benefited enormously from his conscientious guidance—whether on matters of major interpretation or on the most detailed applications of English grammar. Mr Robert Latham guided my research in its earlier stages and made many invaluable comments on the final version. Without the help of these two scholars this book would never have been completed. Professor Jocelyn Otway-Ruthven first inspired in me the interest in medieval English history which provided the starting-point of this work. Her example and her friendship have been of great importance to me ever since I was an undergraduate. She introduced me to Professor May McKisack who directed my attention to the parliaments of Edward III and patiently supervised my work on some of these. When my prime interest turned to the seventeenth century, Miss McKisack generously supported me. My bibliography and footnotes reveal the extent of my obligation to many distinguished historians. I should particularly like to thank Mr Conrad Russell for much acute advice and a number of interesting and useful references, and Mrs D. C. Spielman, whose work in this field I found to be of considerable assistance and who has kindly allowed me to make reference to it. Professor J. P. Kenyon made some very helpful criticisms of my original thesis and gave me much support in arranging for publication of this book. I have benefited from a number of conversations with Professor Clayton Roberts, who greatly assisted my work by giving me a page-proof copy, before publication, of his book, *The Growth of Responsible Government in Stuart England*. Dr Valerie Pearl in 1964 and Dr Henry

Roseveare in 1969 both gave me valuable encouragement. After this book had been accepted for publication, Dr Ian Roy agreed to act as co-editor and made some very pertinent suggestions. I am most grateful to him for undertaking this responsibility.

I am greatly indebted to Mr J. L. Jervoise, the earl of Leicester and Lord Sackville for permission to examine and make reference to manuscripts in their possession. Mr W. O. Hassall kindly guided me through the manuscript collection at Holkham Hall, Mr A. J. Taylor provided me with useful information about seventeenth-century parliamentary records, and Mr Christopher Thompson generously lent me a photocopy of Sir Nathaniel Rich's parliamentary diary of 1628 in the Huntingdonshire Record Office.

Much of the work for this book was done in the British Museum, the Institute of Historical Research of the University of London, the House of Lords Record Office, and the Inner Temple Library. I owe much to the kindness and expert guidance of their staffs. I am also grateful to the following libraries and institutions for permitting me to examine and refer to papers in their collections: the Public Record Office, the National Register of Archives, the Bodleian Library, the libraries of Royal Holloway College, London, Trinity College, Dublin, and of the universities of Cambridge, Chicago, Cornell, East Anglia, Harvard, and Yale; and the county record offices of Hampshire, Huntingdonshire, Kent, Northamptonshire, Staffordshire, Warwickshire, and Wiltshire.

Finally, I should like to thank the Governors of the Polytechnic of North London for giving me remission from some teaching, and my colleagues, Brenda Bolton, Kathryn Kreisky, and Frances Smith, for help in numerous ways. This short preface is in no way adequate as thanks to so many people.

C.G.C.T.

CONTENTS

ABBREVIATIONS

Add. MSS	Additional Manuscripts, British Museum, London
Bull. Inst. Hist. Res.	Bulletin of the Institute of Historical Research
B.M.	British Museum, London
Bodl.	Bodleian Library, Oxford
C.D.	*Commons Debates 1621*, ed. W. Notestein, F. H. Relf and H. Simpson (New Haven, 1935)
C.F.R.	*Calendar of Fine Rolls*
C.J.	*Commons Journals*
C.P.R.	*Calendar of Patent Rolls*
C.S.P.Dom.	*Calendar of State Papers Domestic*
C.S.P.Ven.	*Calendar of State Papers Venetian*
D'Ewes	Sir Simonds D'Ewes Journal of the Parliament of 1624: Harl. MS 159
D'Ewes, *Autobiography*	*The Autobiography and Correspondence of Sir Simonds D'Ewes, Bart., during the Reigns of James I and Charles I*, ed. J. O. Halliwell (London, 1845)
D.N.B.	*Dictionary of National Biography* (London, 1908-9)
E.H.R.	*English Historical Review*
Erle	Diary of Sir Walter Erle: Add. MS 18597
Grosvenor	Diary of Sir Richard Grosvenor, 1626: typescript of Trinity College, Dublin, MS 611
Grosvenor, 1628	Diary of Sir Richard Grosvenor, 1628: typescript of Trinity College, Dublin, MS 612
Harl. MSS	Harleian Manuscripts, British Museum, London

H.L.R.O.	House of Lords Record Office, London
H.M.C.	*Historical Manuscripts Commission*
Holland (Rawlinson)	Diary of Sir Thomas Holland: Bodl. Rawlinson MS D.1100
Holland (Tanner)	Diary of Sir Thomas Holland: Bodl. Tanner MS 392
Holles	Diary of John Holles: Harl. MS 6383
L.J.	*Lords Journal*
Lowther	*H.M.C. Thirteenth Report* (London, 1891-3), App. vii (Notes in Parliament, 1626 and 1628, compiled by Mr Lowther)
MS(S)	Manuscript(s)
Nicholas, Diary	Diary of Edward Nicholas: S.P.Dom. 14/166
Nicholas, *Proceedings*	*Proceedings and Debates of the House of Commons in 1620 and 1621* (Oxford, 1766)
Petyt MSS	Petyt Manuscripts, Inner Temple Library, London
P.R.O.	Public Record Office, London
Pym	Diary of John Pym: Add. MS 26639
Rot. Parl.	*Rotuli Parliamentorum ut et Petitiones, et Placita in Parliamento* (n.p., n.d.)
S.P.Dom	State Papers Domestic, Public Record Office, London
Spring	Diary of Sir William Spring: Yale University Library, New Haven, microfilm transcript of Harvard College Library, Cambridge, Massachusetts, MS Eng. 980
Trans. Royal Hist. Soc.	*Transactions of the Royal Historical Society*
Whitelocke, Diary (12.20-1)	Diary of Sir Bulstrode Whitelocke: Cambridge University Library MSS Dd. 12.20-1
Whitelocke, Diary (12.22)	Diary of Sir Bulstrode Whitelocke: Cambridge University Library MS Dd. 12.22

Introduction

During the reign of James I, the two houses of the English parliament joined together to exercise a power of criminal jurisdiction which had lain unused since the middle of the fifteenth century. The revived power claimed its initial victims in 1621, when Giles Mompesson was the first, and Francis Bacon the most prominent, of the men to be ruined. Three years later, the same weapon was employed to destroy the career of the Lord Treasurer, the earl of Middlesex. In 1626 it was used to attack the duke of Buckingham, Charles I's favourite and chief adviser; and in 1628 the process was turned against an ecclesiastic, Roger Manwaring. From 1621 onwards there was constant resort to this type of criminal jurisdiction and parliament found in it a potent means of attacking its enemies. It brought members face to face with one of the central constitutional problems of the early seventeenth century— the need to criticise ministers appointed by a king who could do no wrong—and, ultimately, it assisted in weakening the foundations of the Stuart monarchy.

This type of jurisdiction, in which the Commons act as accusers and the Lords as judge and jury, has long been given the name 'impeachment'. It is widely believed that 'impeachment' was evolved in the Good Parliament of 1376 as a means of punishing William Latimer, Richard Lyons and a number of other men influential and important in the closing years of the reign of Edward III. Subsequently, it was used on a number of occasions in the reigns of Richard II and his three immediate successors, but towards the end of Henry VI's reign it sank into obsolescence, replaced by other methods, such as attainder, which, although achieving similar results, did so by rather different processes.

It will be immediately apparent that the political circumstances which prevailed in the seventy-five years after 1376 bear some similarity to those in the early seventeenth century. In both periods monarchs were often ineffective and their governments were subjected to damaging political attack. It is also clear that parliament's criminal jurisdiction was frequently used as an instrument in such conflict, and was, in large part, a product of it. However, it is not the purpose of this study to attempt a comparison of two sets of political circumstances, separated from each other by almost two centuries. Such a comparison would, in any case, have a strictly limited value, and such similarities as do exist can readily be observed without a detailed examination. Nor is it intended to explain in any detail the political situation in either the one period or the other. The broad outlines of this situation are well enough known, and will provide a sufficiently adequate background to this study. Instead, my main purpose is to examine, largely in terms of procedure, the revival and development of the joint criminal jurisdiction of both houses of parliament in the early seventeenth century. Naturally, the ultimate explanation for this revival is to be found in the politics of the reign of James I—which determined the type of procedure which was adopted—but it has also been my aim to show this revival in the light of the practice followed in the late fourteenth and early fifteenth centuries.

A temptation to achieve simplicity would have led me to entitle this book, more briefly, *Impeachment in Early Stuart England*, yet to have succumbed would have been dangerous. There is ample evidence that, when Sir Edward Coke and his colleagues re-introduced parliament's criminal jurisdiction, they did not confine their search for guidance to those pre-cedents which the medieval records and later historians describe as 'impeachments'. Their search took in what are, apparently, other types of case, and this work will necessarily examine other forms of parliamentary procedure upon which they bestowed their attention. Moreover, whether by accident or design, the cases of the earlier 1620s are rarely, if at all, described in the contemporary accounts as 'impeachments'. In order, therefore, to avoid pre-judging the character of the jurisdiction revived in those years, I have avoided using this term except where it can clearly be justified from the records themselves. Naturally, such a course contains its own danger: it may implicitly attach to 'impeachment' a significance it did not possess—although the evidence suggests otherwise. As Coke referred to the judicial powers of the Houses, both when they collaborated and when they operated separately, as their 'judicature', I have in consequence used the phrase 'parliamentary judicature' to describe the joint criminal jurisdiction of the early Stuart parliaments. While it is possible that, in the early seventeenth century, 'impeachment' may have been a synonym for 'parliamentary judicature', it is more likely that it formed one part of that judicature. Yet whatever name is eventually given to it, parliamentary judicature was undoubtedly both complex and flexible in the early seventeenth century. The truth of this will become manifest when the cases themselves are examined; and, with the intention of distinguishing the wood from the trees, an attempt has been made to show, in tabular as well as descriptive form, the chief procedural characteristics of each of the cases studied.

The development of parliamentary judicature in the early Stuart period forms part of the same story as the growth in those years of the unicameral judicature of each House acting separately from the other. The Commons' decision in 1621 to revive parliamentary judicature stemmed, at least in part, from a realisation of the limited nature of their own unicameral judicature. It therefore follows that, in describing the evolution of parliamentary judicature in the 1620s, it will be necessary to pay some attention to the growth of both Lords' judicature and Commons' judicature in James I's reign.

This study begins with an examination of the medieval inheritance available in the early seventeenth century, and ends with the trial of Manwaring in 1628. That trial did not, of course, mark the demise of parliament's power of criminal judicature: it flourished and remained effective long after 1628. Yet it operated subsequently in circumstances very different from those prevailing in the 1620s, and Manwaring's trial forms a fitting conclusion to the developments of those years.

CHAPTER I

The Medieval Heritage

When, in 1621, the house of commons co-operated with the house of lords to bring to judgment six men who had offended them, they were employing forms of procedure whose halcyon days lay in the period from 1376 to 1459. Clearly, the urgency of affairs in 1621 did not allow the Houses to embark on flights of historical fancy for their own sake: parliament behaved as it did because of the conditions of the time and if it employed a medieval process this was because it seemed appropriate to those conditions. The Commons, in particular, were led by lawyers well versed in precedents: good use was made of these but the House did not become the slave of precedents and the lack of them merely provided it with an opportunity to exercise its procedural imagination. Nevertheless, the medieval influences upon both Commons and Lords were considerable, at least potentially, and any examination of the judicial proceedings of early seventeenth-century parliaments must explore this heritage.

To conduct such an investigation and to relate what we find to what the lawyers of the seventeenth century would have found is not an easy task. A twentieth-century analysis of medieval parliamentary judicature is unlikely to bear much similarity to the deductions made from the records by the politicians and antiquaries of the seventeenth century, despite the revolution in historical processes of thought that was then in progress. Not only do our motives for making such an enquiry differ fundamentally from those which inspired the parliaments of the early Stuarts, but our own view of the medieval procedure is likely to be coloured by our knowledge of its further development in the seventeenth century.

In addition, the inheritance is a complex one. It can be explored only by studying the parliamentary cases of the period,

but these reveal a variety of procedure which is often bewilder-
ing. In consequence, it is very difficult to make statements
about procedure which are not so hedged about with exceptions
and provisos as to be rendered almost valueless. Moreover,
even when classifications are devised, these normally will not
fit into the seventeenth-century context. On occasion, for
instance, Coke and his colleagues in the 1620s illustrated a
point of procedure with precedents which appear to us to
have little in common with each other, and we are left to guess
at the basis upon which they were chosen.

Nevertheless, despite—or even because of—the variety and
complexity of the medieval inheritance, some attempt to
identify and describe procedure must be made in order to
show the range of precedents available to seventeenth-century
politicians and the selectiveness of their choice.

It is often stated that in 1621 parliament revived the medieval
process of impeachment. As this study progresses, it will be
shown that this statement cannot be accepted without qualification, but for the moment two points must be made about it.
First, it is perfectly true that many of the medieval cases
quoted as precedents in 1621 to support the revival of parliamentary judicature are described in the records of the fourteenth and fifteenth centuries as impeachments. Yet it is also
true that some of the cases cited in 1621 are not identified
in the medieval records as impeachments, and seem to differ
significantly from those which are given this name. The second
point is that historians are by no means agreed upon an exact
definition of the medieval impeachment. It is, for example,
not clear whether the term refers to a distinct judicial procedure
or to a particular characteristic common to a variety of judicial
procedures. Nevertheless, the word cannot be ignored in an
examination of the medieval heritage, and, before considering
the variety of procedure bequeathed to the seventeenth
century, it will be as well to summarise what are at present
generally regarded as the distinguishing features of impeachment.

Until recently, historians have always set impeachment
within the framework of parliament, regarding it as essentially
a parliamentary procedure. It appears first in connection with

the trial of Edward III's chamberlain, William Latimer, in the Good Parliament of 1376; it then reappears frequently in the parliamentary records of the next seventy-five years but fades away in the middle of the fifteenth century. From the beginning, impeachment was associated with moments of political crisis and was often enough used as a weapon in factional rivalry. Whether it would be correct to conclude from this that it was regarded as primarily a political procedure is another matter, but it certainly has claims to be considered in this way and it was employed by both the king and his opponents.

To many historians, one of the primary features of a medieval impeachment derives from the parts played by the house of commons and the house of lords: in the words of Professor Wilkinson, the 'essence of Impeachment was, as it has always been considered, accusation by the Commons and judgment by the Lords'.[1] The Commons might base their charge upon evidence supplied to them by private individuals, but the case was presented to the Lords not on behalf of such individuals but by the Commons as a whole, representing the interests of the community. The charge was then maintained in common before the peers, and without any naming of individual accusers. However, the prosecution was conducted in the name of the crown, even where the monarch himself was an unwilling observer of the proceedings. A hearing took place before the upper House—normally in accordance with due legal form, however politically inspired the charge might be—and judgment was eventually pronounced by the Lords.[2]

Some historians of the medieval process of impeachment have also laid stress upon the terminology of the records, pointing to the occasions upon which 'impeached' or 'impeachment' is, or is not, used, and relating this evidence to the procedural characteristics of the cases under examination. One of the problems of this type of approach is that the word

---

[1] B. Wilkinson, *Constitutional History of Medieval England 1216-1399* (London, 1948-58), ii, 205.

[2] G. Lambrick, 'The Impeachment of the Abbot of Abingdon in 1368', *E.H.R.* lxxxii (1967), 268-9, 270, 273, 275; Wilkinson, *Constitutional History of Medieval England*, ii, 214; T. F. T. Plucknett, 'The Impeachments of 1376', *Trans. Royal Hist. Soc.* 5th ser. i (1951), 161-2; T. F. T. Plucknett, 'State Trials under Richard II', *Trans. Royal Hist. Soc.* 5th ser. ii (1952), 167.

was in general use both in the middle ages and later, signifying 'hindrance' or 'embarrassment'. Nevertheless, the more technical meaning of an accusation in a court of law appears in the reign of Edward II, and in the records of the Good Parliament of 1376 the word is used in connection with charges brought by the whole Commons in parliament. It is therefore possible that, when contemporaries described a case as an impeachment, they recognised that it conformed to a particular type of judicial procedure.[3] Yet whether or not this is true, and whatever differences there were in the details of procedure, there can be no doubt that a precise linguistic formula was invariably employed whenever a case of impeachment arose. The Commons 'accuse and impeach' or 'impeach and accuse' their victim, and these words appear, harnessed in exactly this manner, again and again from 1376 to 1459.[4]

So far we have examined those aspects of impeachment upon which some measure of agreement has existed among historians. However, we must now turn to consider three theories which extend or modify parts of what has been said.

The first concerns the character of the Commons' accusation in an impeachment. Maude Clarke maintained that these accusations were treated as indictments and that, in this respect, impeachment marked an important break with the past. Previously, judgments by the Lords had been given upon petitions presented to parliament, often by private citizens, and the Commons were only loosely, if at all, associated with this procedure. Impeachment, however, brought the Commons to the centre of the stage to present an indictment to the Lords, and Miss Clarke contrasted 'procedure by indictment, which is an assertion of right' with 'procedure by petition, with all its implications of grace and favour'. She saw the change in procedure as taking place between the trial of Sir John Lee in 1368 and that of William Latimer in 1376. Lee, who was steward of the household, was accused of various malpractices.

---

[3] M. V. Clarke, 'The Origin of Impeachment', *Fourteenth Century Studies*, ed. L. S. Sutherland and M. McKisack (Oxford, 1937), 243; Plucknett 'State Trials under Richard II', 164-5. Miss Clarke's terminological approach has, however, been challenged by J. P. Collas, ed. *Year Books of Edward II*, xxv (Selden Society, lxxxi: London, 1964), pp. lxvi-lxvii.

[4] On very few occasions 'impeach' or 'impeachment' stands alone: see Table I.

The accusation was presented to parliament in the form of five petitions, four of them anonymous and the fifth from an inhabitant of Dorset. The charges were examined in the presence of the king, the Lords and some members of the Commons. Lee's defence proved inadequate and he was sentenced, presumably by the Lords, though at a later stage the fifth petition was the subject of a separate judgment by the Council. The whole case has its obscurities, but Miss Clarke emphasised the limited character of the Commons' part in it.

On the other hand, the Commons' part in Latimer's trial was considerable. Latimer was the most prominent of a group of people, all associated in one way or another with the king, who were tried in the Good Parliament of 1376. As will be seen, the cases of the others—men like Bury, Ellis, Lyons, Neville and Peach—show variations, but they are all described in the records as impeachments and Latimer's case may serve as a model to show the part of the Commons.

As was true of so many impeachments, Latimer's trial took place in an atmosphere of political uncertainty. In 1376 Edward III was old and his heir, the Black Prince, was dying, and half way through the trial a council of reform was appointed. Latimer, closely connected with one party in the political struggle, was accused by the Commons of indulging in treasonable and fraudulent activities. The House, as a body, took a vital part in initiating proceedings, collecting evidence against him and drawing up a schedule of charges which ended by accusing him of 'notoriously accroaching royal power'. Then, in the presence of the Lords, he 'was impeached and accused by the clamour of the commons', following which the lower House demanded his arrest until he had given satisfaction to the king for his misdeeds. The Commons were present during part of Latimer's defence before the Lords, and made a reply. They evidently suggested a punishment, and when judgment was given they were apparently present.[5]

Although the cases of Lee and Latimer were both quoted in 1621 in support of the revival of parliamentary judicature, without any indication that the one might be more relevant

[5] Clarke, 'Origin of Impeachment', 243, 258-60, 262ff; Plucknett, 'Impeachments of 1376', 162; *Rot. Parl.* ii, 324-6.

than the other, there are clearly substantial differences between them. Moreover, while Latimer's case has frequently been regarded as the archetype of impeachment, that of Lee is not, apparently, an impeachment at all. If the latter case has to be categorised, it must be placed in a class of non-impeachment cases in which the Commons were, nevertheless, involved. However, be that as it may, Miss Clarke's opinion that, in the transition from the one case to the other, procedure on petition gave way to procedure on indictment has been challenged, notably by Professor Plucknett. Plucknett has argued that the existence of this development cannot be substantiated from the evidence, since there is nothing either in the language of the medieval records or in the particular circumstances of Latimer's case to suggest that the Commons ever made an indictment.[6] He has received support from Professor Wilkinson: 'It could, indeed, be plausibly argued that the idea of Impeachment as an indictment and not a petition by the commons before the lords (and not before the king) was, like the idea of a Feudal System, a legal invention of the seventeenth century.'[7] The exact character of the Commons' accusation in cases described in the records as impeachments must, therefore, remain at present an open question.

The second of the three theories which necessitate some modification of what was said earlier about the nature of impeachment strikes at the assumption that it was a distinct judicial procedure, suggesting that it was instead one of a number of methods of instituting criminal proceedings. This theory—the work of Plucknett—was derived from a study of the trial of Latimer. Plucknett drew attention to the fact that this impeachment was based upon 'the clamour of the commons', and he suggested that the use of the term 'impeachment' in this context implied that it 'was not a jurisdiction of the Lords, nor

[6] T. F. T. Plucknett, 'The Origin of Impeachment', *Trans. Royal Hist. Soc.* 4th ser. xxiv (1942), 49-50, 54-5. Plucknett says (p. 55): 'In the fourteenth century, as now, 'indictment' means an allegation of crime made by a jury before a royal officer.'

[7] B. Wilkinson, *Studies in the Constitutional History of the Thirteenth and Fourteenth Centuries*, 2nd edition (Manchester, 1952), 87. Professor Wilkinson believes that the alteration in procedure occurred because the source from which the Commons were seeking redress was changing—from the king to the Lords: p. 87.

a mode of trial, but a means of initiating criminal proceedings, based not on indictment, information or appeal of felony but on "clamour".[8] Although Plucknett's theory has received little support from other historians, it cannot be ignored in any attempt to investigate the essence of impeachment.

The last theory to be considered recognises impeachment as a distinct judicial procedure but questions the assumption that it could operate only in a parliamentary context. In 1967 Gabrielle Lambrick published an account of a trial, described in the records as an impeachment, which did not take place in parliament and in which the Commons were not, therefore, the accusers. The case is that of the abbot of Abingdon who, in 1368, was impeached before justices of *oyer* and *terminer* for levying certain dues and for usurping royal privileges.[9] As was normal in parliamentary impeachments, the prosecution was in the name of the crown, but the accusation was instigated by a single local community—the townsmen of Abingdon— and had nothing to do with parliament, although as in parliamentary impeachments, the charge was maintained in common. Moreover, whereas parliamentary impeachment was a criminal judicature, the case of the abbot hovered in an indeterminate way 'between criminal and civil jurisdiction'.[10]

One of Miss Lambrick's suggestions is that impeachment was already an established procedure before 1376, and that Latimer's case of that year represented the transfer of the process to parliament. She concludes her study:

The Abingdon case shows us impeachment in a light so different from the traditional aura of parliamentary procedure that it becomes necessary to take a very much broader view of this versatile form of medieval legal action. It seems that it could embrace many different permutations and combinations of procedure, while resting on firm foundations of legal principle; and that it was primarily evolved to fulfil a need for a legal yet efficient method of dealing with various kinds of difficult case, arising from various kinds of special circumstance, where the interests of king and community

---

[8] Plucknett, 'Impeachments of 1376', 159.
[9] Lambrick, 250-76. The abbot was not, apparently, 'accused and impeached' but merely 'impeached'.
[10] Lambrick, 257, 268.

were equally at stake and for which satisfactory remedies could not usually be provided at common law.[11]

The case of the abbot of Abingdon clearly strikes at the root of the traditional view of impeachment as essentially a parliamentary process,[12] even though it may be possible to regard impeachment in parliament as having a political significance which impeachment outside parliament lacked. Miss Lambrick's work, together with that of Miss Clarke and Professor Plucknett, demonstrates the difficulties of arriving at a precise definition of medieval impeachment.

We may now turn to consider the variety of judicial procedure bequeathed by the medieval parliaments to their seventeenth-century successors. In theory, such a task involves a survey of all the records of all the medieval parliaments; but as in practice the parliamentarians of the early seventeenth century selected the vast bulk of their precedents from the years between the middle of the fourteenth and the middle of the fifteenth centuries, this examination will be confined to procedures used during that period. An attempt will be made to construct a composite model, to show the variety of methods which might be adopted to deal with a case as it passed through the main stages in parliament.[13] Such a model must, of course, be based upon all cases which appear to have relevance in the context of 1621, whether or not they were actually quoted as precedents then. Some of these cases are described in the records as impeachments, some of them are not; and it must,

[11] Lambrick, 270, 275-6.

[12] Lambrick, 270, 275. Miss Lambrick comments (p. 275): 'In fact, even when it is recognised to be wrong-headed, the seventeenth-century lawyers' view of impeachment as essentially a parliamentary affair, an indictment by the Commons before the Lords, has so influenced subsequent thought on the subject that it has been all too easy to ignore the significance of medieval impeachments which did *not* take place in parliament, or in which the Commons were *not* the accusers and prosecutors.' This is not perhaps entirely fair, at least to the lawyers of the early years of the century. Although they maintain that impeachment was a parliamentary process, they do not, at any point, state that it was exclusively parliamentary.

[13] To prevent this exercise from appearing too theoretical, reference will be made to the specific cases from which the model has been derived; but as far as possible, this information will be confined to the footnotes unless the case was one quoted as a precedent during the revival of parliamentary judicature in 1621.

in any case, be remembered that the parliament men of 1621 did not select their precedents merely from among cases which are called impeachments.

Our procedural model must necessarily start with a consideration of the various methods employed during the century after 1350 for introducing criminal proceedings into parliament. Such proceedings might be based upon the notoriety of the crime, upon the clamour of the community, upon petitions or bills presented to parliament, or upon appeal of treason or felony.[14] Appeal was confined to the Lords and seems to have concerned the Commons little: it need not, therefore, be discussed.[15] However, the first three methods formed the foundation for proceedings which often involved both Houses, and each must be examined.

At one time, a statement by the king that the facts in a crime were notoriously known had been sufficient to secure a conviction.[16] By the middle of the fourteenth century this was no longer true, but the concept of notoriety survived as a basis for an accusation. In 1376, Latimer was accused by the Commons of having 'notoriously accroached royal power', and the lower House used similar language in its case against Lyons in the same year,[17] while the concept appears again in subsequent trials.[18]

Judicial proceedings in parliament might also be based upon clamour. Latimer was 'impeached and accused by the clamour of the Commons' and similar phraseology was used in the trial

[14] Plucknett, 'Origin of Impeachment', 51, 55-6; Lambrick, 269.

[15] For appeal, see M. V. Clarke, 'Forfeitures and Treason in 1388', *Fourteenth Century Studies*, 133ff; T. F. T. Plucknett, 'Impeachment and Attainder', *Trans. Royal Hist. Soc.* 5th ser. iii (1953), 145ff; A. Steel, *Richard II* (Cambridge, 1962), 141ff; S. Rezneck, 'The Early History of the Parliamentary Declaration of Treason', *E.H.R.* xlii (1927), 511; J. G. Bellamy, 'Appeal and Impeachment in the Good Parliament', *Bull. Inst. Hist. Res.* xxxix (1966), 43; J. G. Bellamy, *The Law of Treason in England in the Later Middle Ages* (Cambridge, 1971), 141ff.

[16] Mortimer, 1330. See also Plucknett, 'Origin of Impeachment', 58-9, 64ff.

[17] Plucknett, 'Impeachments of 1376', 158-60; *Rot. Parl.* ii, 323, 325; Lambrick, 269; Plucknett, 'Origin of Impeachment', 71.

[18] For example, the trial of Henry Despenser, bishop of Norwich, in 1383. See also Lambrick, 275; Plucknett, 'Impeachment and Attainder', 150-1; Plucknett, 'Origin of Impeachment', 70; Plucknett, 'State Trials under Richard II', 163; *Rot. Parl.* iii, 153-4, 378; E. M. Thompson, ed. *Chronicon Angliae* (London, 1874), p. lxxviii.

of Bury in the same Parliament.[19] Yet it is difficult to know exactly what meaning should be placed upon the word—which appears again in the seventeenth century. Plucknett considered that the clamour of the Commons was 'the old theory of conviction by notoriety with the sole difference that it is the Speaker instead of the King who asserts that the misdeeds are notorious'.[20] Miss Lambrick suggests that it lies somewhere between 'the suit of an identifiable local community ... and ... the expression of general public opinion in the "notoriety" of the crimes with which the accused was charged'.[21] Neither of these theories seems capable of positive proof, and it may be that we are doomed to perpetual uncertainty about the meaning of 'clamour'; but Miss Lambrick's work, taken in conjunction with Professor Plucknett's, prompts us to ask whether we have not tried to find too deep a meaning in this word. It is possible that, as two methods of initiating proceedings, clamour and notoriety were barely distinguishable, and that it was the clamour of the people, or of the Commons, which made the facts in a case notorious.

The third method of initiating judicial proceedings in parliament was by petition or bill—the terms are often interchangeable at this time. A petition might be presented to parliament by an individual or a group of people from outside it, or it might originate within parliament. Procedure by petition necessarily contained implications of grace and favour, and a recognition that the petition might be rejected. (In this connection it is as well to bear in mind the suggestion made by Miss Clarke, though not generally accepted, that the Good Parliament of 1376 translated procedure by petition into procedure by indictment—'an assertion of right'—thereby establishing one of the characteristics of impeachment.)[22] It appears that a petition might become the basis of judicial proceedings in parliament in one of two ways. In the first of these the Commons would adopt a petition as their own cause. This occurred in Lee's case of 1368, when the lower House

[19] *Rot. Parl.* ii, 324, 330.

[20] Plucknett, 'Impeachments of 1376', 159. The similarity between the concepts of notoriety and common fame is noted below, p. 79.

[21] Lambrick, 274.

[22] Clarke, 'Origin of Impeachment', 265. See above, p. 8.

made a direct accusation cast in the form of petitions which it had received.[23] In the Good Parliament itself, the Commons certainly seem to have been less inclined than previously to adopt petitions as a means of instituting proceedings. However, at least part of their attack on Latimer took this form, and there is some evidence of a similar procedure during the case of Bury who, like Latimer, is recorded as having been impeached.[24] But such evidence is lacking in the trials of Ellis and Peach, a fact which, as these are also described as impeachments, supports Miss Clarke's interpretation. Nevertheless, one of the grounds upon which Professor Wilkinson has challenged this interpretation is that procedure on petitions adopted by the Commons continued after 1376. He thinks 'it might even be argued that the idea of petition was still implicit in the "complaint"' by the Commons of 1386 against Michael de la Pole.[25]

Another way of proceeding by petition was for the Commons to deal with it without actually taking it over themselves. The best-known example is probably the petition brought against the Chancellor, Michael de la Pole, in 1384, two years before his greater ordeal in the Wonderful Parliament. The petition was presented to the Commons by John Cavendish, a London fishmonger, and de la Pole had to defend himself, first before the Lords and subsequently before the Lords and Commons together. His defence succeeded and Cavendish was fined for defaming him.[26]

[23] Plucknett, 'Origin of Impeachment', 65ff; Clarke, 'Origin of Impeachment', 257-9; *Rot. Parl.* ii, 297-8. See also above, p. 9.

[24] Wilkinson, *Studies*, 88 and n. 1, 91; V. H. Galbraith, ed. *The Anonimalle Chronicle 1333-81* (Manchester, 1927), 88, 90.

[25] Wilkinson, *Studies*, 86-7. He appears to ignore the fact that Miss Clarke noted the use of procedure by petition against Despenser in 1383, perhaps because Miss Clarke herself did not seem to regard this case as a genuine impeachment: Clarke, 'Origin of Impeachment', 265. Ellis was eventually complained of in petitions, but only after his impeachment had failed: Plucknett, 'Impeachments of 1376', 163.

[26] Plucknett, 'State Trials under Richard II', 164-5; *Rot. Parl.* iii, 168. Plucknett pointed out that the Roll is 'careful not to call this an impeachment'.

The process of turning petitions presented to the Commons into private bills for enactment by parliament became quite well established in the reign of Henry IV. Private bill procedure was distinctly judicial in character: T. Erskine May, *A Treatise on the Law, Privileges, Proceedings and Usages of Parliament*, 13th edition (London, 1924), 609.

It is possible that the fourteenth century recognised other methods of instituting judicial proceedings in parliament. Perhaps to impeach somebody was, or became, one of these methods, instead of being some kind of procedure originated in one or more of the three ways which have been discussed. But enough has been said to show that several means existed for beginning proceedings, that they might all co-exist in one case, and that none of them was totally excluded from a case described as an impeachment.

Before concluding this survey of the means by which a case might be introduced into parliament, it should be noted that attainder—a parliamentary and judicial process which was to reach its climax in a later period—seems to have had some of its origins in the century after 1350. Professor Tout saw, in the doctrine of the high court of parliament enunciated in 1388, a foundation for acts of attainder, and elements of this process have been observed in the case of Sir John Mortimer in 1423.[27]

We must now consider the procedure followed once a case had been brought before parliament. This shows as much variety as the methods used to originate an action. It will be discussed from various angles. First of all, the fact that an accusation was introduced into parliament did not necessarily mean that every stage of the case would be conducted there. It was possible for part of a trial to take place before the Council outside parliament. Lee's case is an example of this, while the Council may have taken a separate part in the hearing of Latimer's trial, even though the house of lords dominated the later stages of it. Both the Lords and the Council heard the reply of William Weston in 1377, while the ill-defined body of 'Seignurs et Baronage', whom the Commons asked to punish him and his companion in misfortune, John de Gomeniz, possibly included the Council. However, by 1386 the Council no longer receives a mention in such trials, and the Lords and

---

[27] Also in the case of Lord Stanley in 1459: T. F. Tout, *Chapters in the Administrative History of Mediaeval England* (Manchester, 1920-33), iii, 432; Rezneck, 506; Plucknett, 'Impeachment and Attainder', 157. See also Wilkinson, *Constitutional History of Medieval England*, ii, 258ff; Steel, 152, 178-9; L. W. V. Harcourt, *His Grace the Steward and Trial of Peers* (London, 1907), 388; and the full discussion in Bellamy, *Law of Treason*, 177-205.

king alone gave judgment on Michael de la Pole—like Latimer, described as having been impeached.[28]

Central to much of the discussion of parliamentary judicature in the late fourteenth and early fifteenth centuries has been the position and function of the house of commons, and its part in these procedures will now be considered. Towards the end of Edward III's reign, the practice had arisen of the Commons' sending a deputation to the Lords to ask for a committee to confer with them,[29] and this, together with favourable political conditions, may well have assisted the development of the Commons' part in judicature. The extent of their share fluctuated considerably. It appears to have been small in Lee's trial, where some of the Commons seem merely to have been present during part of the examination, and then only as listeners.[30] But in 1376 it expanded considerably, doubtless assisted by the lack of a Court initiative at the very end of Edward's reign. In that year, and particularly in the impeachment of Latimer, the Commons mounted a collective action through their Speaker, who demanded that all, and not merely some, members should be present during the hearings. Furthermore, the House established an effective 'coalition' with the Lords, and insisted in fact if not in words, that Latimer's trial should be held in full parliament.[31] Acting through the Speaker, the Commons dealt in detail with the charges against Latimer, asked for the sworn evidence of witnesses to be given to their House, and demanded his arrest. During the trial itself, the Commons assumed corporate responsibility for their accusation and undertook the duties of prosecutor, although maintaining that they were acting on behalf of the king. In addition, while part of the defence seems to have taken place in their absence, they are recorded as having been responsible

[28] Clarke, 'Origin of Impeachment', 243; Wilkinson, *Studies*, 89, 98 and n. 1, 99; Plucknett, 'Origin of Impeachment', 53; *Rot. Parl.* ii, 298; iii, 10-11, 216ff.

[29] H. G. Richardson and G. O. Sayles, 'The Parliaments of Edward III', *Bull. Inst. Hist. Res.* ix (1931), 15 n. 3.

[30] *Rot. Parl.* ii, 297-8; Clarke, 'Origin of Impeachment', 258.

[31] Galbraith, *Anonimalle Chronicle*, 84; Wilkinson, *Constitutional History of Medieval England*, ii, 209; A. F. Pollard, 'The Authorship and Value of the *Anonimalle Chronicle*', *E.H.R.* liii (1938), 588.

for securing Latimer's removal from office.[32] The surviving
records for the other cases of 1376 are less substantial than those
for Latimer's trial, but they suggest that the Commons took a
fairly prominent part in these cases, too. The House preferred
charges in parliament against Lyons, demanded his arrest and
prayed for judgment upon him. It conducted its own examination of Ellis and asked for judgment upon him and Neville.
It accused Peach on behalf of the king and of the injured
parties simultaneously.[33] All these men are, of course, described as having been impeached.

The case of Alice Perrers, Edward III's mistress, is altogether
more obscure, even though it was, at one stage, referred to as
an impeachment. After hearing of her great influence over the
king, the Commons of the Good Parliament of 1376 petitioned
for her removal. She was unable to reply to many of the charges
against her and, having been declared guilty, apparently in the
Lords, 'by the judgement of many', she was banished from
Court by an ordinance made in parliament. But she had been
restored to her place by the following spring and the attack
on her was renewed in Richard II's first parliament. She was
'caused to come' into parliament—by whom was not stated—
and brought before the Lords. The ordinance and charges
against her were read out; she was given a day to answer; and
witnesses were sworn and examined. There is no indication
that the Commons took any part in the proceedings, but she
was eventually found guilty on the articles 'contained in the
impeachment'.[34]

In the early years of Richard's reign, the Commons' part in
parliamentary trials seems to decline. They made a supplication
against Gomeniz and Weston, and the latter, at least, addressed

---

[32] Plucknett, 'Impeachments of 1376', 156, 158, 161-2; Wilkinson, *Studies*,
88, 89, 91; Clarke, 'Origin of Impeachment', 243; *Rot. Parl.* ii, 326. One of the
witnesses for whose sworn evidence the Commons asked was a member of the
Lords. The lower House recognised that to examine peers on oath was beyond
its competence, and it therefore obtained the king's approval to do this:
Plucknett, 'Impeachments of 1376', 156.

[33] Plucknett, 'Origin of Impeachment', 69-70; Plucknett, 'Impeachments of
1376', 156, 158, 163-4; Galbraith, *Anonimalle Chronicle*, 89-90; Clarke, 'Origin of
Impeachment', 243; *Rot. Parl.* ii, 327-9.

[34] Thompson, 95ff; Plucknett, 'State Trials under Richard II', 160-1; Wilkinson,
Constitutional History of Medieval England, ii, 220; *Rot. Parl.* iii, 12-14.

his reply to them as well as to the Council and Lords; but in a trial of 1383,[35] at the prayer of the Commons, the Chancellor conducted the proceedings and presented the charges.[36] In 1386, however, 'All the commons together and of one accord came before the king, prelates and lords in the hall of Parliament to complain grievously against Michael de la Pole . . . and there present to accuse him . . .'[37] When de la Pole made his defence, the Commons replied to it and demanded judgment. In his turn, de la Pole responded to the Commons' reply, and his arrest is recorded as having been at their request.[38]

Later trials serve largely to confirm some of the Commons' functions. In 1423 the House is reported to have endorsed the accuracy of the indictment of Sir John Mortimer, but in 1450 it encountered difficulties in the early stages of its case against the duke of Suffolk. The duke, a member of the Council, had admitted that rumour accused him of scandalous misconduct, and on the strength of his acknowledgement the Commons asked the Lords to commit him to prison. The peers refused to do so without a specific accusation. In fact, the Commons soon provided this, charging Suffolk with making treasonable overtures to the French. Accordingly, the Lords sent him to the Tower and formal articles of impeachment were presented a few days later[39]—an order of events which was to be followed two centuries afterwards when Strafford was impeached.

Some understanding of judicial procedure in medieval parliaments may also be gained by examining the requests made by the accused and the replies these received. For, although many of the trials were blatantly political and parliament, on occasion, doubtless made up the rules as it went along, those on trial normally seem to have received a full and seriously conducted hearing, with due attention paid

---

[35] Despenser, bishop of Norwich.
[36] *Rot. Parl.* iii, 10, 152-3; Clarke, 'Origin of Impeachment', 265; Plucknett, 'State Trials under Richard II', 163-4.
[37] *Rot. Parl.* iii, 216.
[38] *Rot. Parl.* iii. 216ff; Plucknett, 'State Trials under Richard II', 165.
[39] *Rot. Parl.* iv, 202; v, 176-7; Harcourt, 383-4; Rezneck, 506.

to legal form.[40] Latimer made at least five requests or complaints during his trial. He first asked for the charge in writing,
but it is likely that he was forced to plead to each article as it
was read to him. Such treatment was probably not untypical
and oral proceedings seem to have been common, though in
1377 Weston was allowed to make a written answer. Latimer
also asked for the presence of counsel, but he was allowed no
more than expert assistance behind the scenes, and de la Pole
fared no better in 1386. Latimer's complaint that there was
no accuser for him to answer was hardly met when the
Commons accused him as a body, but when de la Pole faced
the same situation he raised no objection—and this practice,
which most historians believe to be a characteristic of impeachment, became common. Latimer also asked for time to prepare
his answer, a concession which would, however, have been of
little use without written charges, and which was apparently
refused. However, his fifth demand—that he should be tried as
a peer—was satisfied by the form of the trial.[41] Finally, while
discussing the pleas made by the accused, it is interesting to
note that two of the men 'impeached and accused' in 1388
tried to defend themselves on the ground that what they had
done had been at the king's express command. Although the
two were convicted, the Lords reached no decision on this
defence, and the point was not determined until the trial of
Danby.[42]

Normally the judgment in the parliamentary trials of the
late fourteenth and early fifteenth centuries was given by the
Lords, but some exceptions should be noted. In 1376, Lyons,
Ellis and Peach were judged or punished with the assent of,
or on the advice of, parliament; and in de la Pole's case of
1386 the Commons asked for 'the judgment of Parliament'.

---

[40] For example, careless drafting prevented some of the charges against de la
Pole from being pressed. For this and other cases, see M. V. Clarke, 'The Lancastrian Faction and the Wonderful Parliament', *Fourteenth Century Studies*, 48;
M. Aston, 'The Impeachment of Bishop Despenser', *Bull. Inst. Hist. Res.* xxxviii
(1965), 130; Wilkinson, *Constitutional History of Medieval England*, ii, 263-4.

[41] For these and other cases, see Plucknett, 'Impeachments of 1376', 158-61;
Plucknett, 'Origin of Impeachment', 70; Plucknett, 'State Trials under Richard II',
165; Clarke, 'Forfeitures and Treason', 138; Clarke, 'Origin of Impeachment',
262, 265; Thompson, p. lxxviii; *Rot. Parl.* ii, 324ff; iii, 10, 216.

[42] Plucknett, 'Impeachment and Attainder', 146-7.

It is difficult to know how significant such phraseology is, though Professor Wilkinson, basing his view on two of the chronicles, believes that its use in 1386 indicates that the Commons had advanced beyond 'the simple . . . judgement by Lords of 1376'. In the event, however, judgment on de la Pole seems to have been given by the king and Lords.[43] Yet de la Pole's earlier case, in 1384, suggests that participation of the Lords was not absolutely essential at every stage of a judgment. On that occasion, the Lords, having cleared de la Pole, delegated to the judges the task of dealing with the man who had wrongfully accused him, though it should be added that this was not a case which the Commons had taken upon their own shoulders.[44]

As for the punishments inflicted in trials before parliament, these ranged from enforced restitution of property to execution, and included forfeiture, banishment and imprisonment. On occasion, as in Latimer's case, the Commons suggested penalties, and these were sometimes adopted. Furthermore, a sentence, once awarded, could be increased—a fate which befell Lyons when the Lords decided that they had been too lenient.[45]

It is difficult to be certain of the theoretical position occupied by the crown in parliamentary trials, but it seems probable either that the proceedings were *ex parte regis*, or that, at the least, the king's assent was required or assumed. It has already been observed[46] that prosecution by the crown appears to have been a consistent feature of impeachment, but this characteristic does not seem to distinguish such cases from cases which are not described in the records as impeachments. In the case of Lee, for instance, in 1368, the prosecution was apparently conducted *ex parte regis*, but there is no suggestion in the contemporary records that this was regarded as an impeachment: as for Latimer's case, which was, the Commons' repeated

---

[43] *C.P.R. 1374-7*, 439-40, 448, 455; *C.F.R. 1369-77*, 350; *Rot. Parl.* iii, 218; Wilkinson, *Constitutional History of Medieval England*, ii, 234-5 and n. 19; Wilkinson, *Studies*, 98.

[44] Plucknett, 'State Trials under Richard II', 164-5. For de la Pole's case of 1384, see p. 15, above. The punishment of his accuser should perhaps be regarded as an action distinct from that against de la Pole himself.

[45] Plucknett, 'Impeachments of 1376', 163.

[46] See p. 7, above.

C

protestation that they were prosecuting on behalf of the king speaks for itself. When Richard asked the judges in 1387 whether the Lords and Commons might impeach the king's officers and justices without the king's permission, he was told that they could not; and when, in the following year, these judges were themselves impeached, the king is said to have given his consent to the judgments passed upon them. Furthermore, the Commons of 1397 sought the crown's permission before bringing the impeachments of that year.[47]

Although part of the difficulty in categorising the procedures of the medieval parliament in judicial cases arises from the fact that these procedures were so flexible, this very flexibility enabled it to deal with potentially difficult situations. For instance, the presence of the accused was not always necessary. In 1388 the judges were probably sentenced in their absence, while in 1397 Sir Thomas Mortimer was accused, even though he was a fugitive. A day was appointed for the hearing of his case, writs were issued for his arrest, and penalties laid down if he defaulted.[48] In addition, parliament showed itself quite prepared to punish people who misled it either with evidence which they later contradicted, as in Neville's trial of 1376, or with false accusations, such as those against de la Pole in 1384.[49]

We may conclude this survey of judicial procedure by speculating upon the theoretical basis of the law administered by parliament. During 1388, great use was made in the Lords of the procedure known as the appeal, a process with which the Commons were barely connected. At that time the Lords declared that 'in so high a crime as is alleged in this appeal . . . the process will not be taken anywhere except to parliament, nor judged by any other law except the law and court of parliament . . .'[50] We do not know whether this *lex parliamenti* was thought to operate in any other trials than the appeals of

---

[47] Plucknett, 'Impeachment and Attainder', 147, 153; Plucknett, 'Impeachments of 1376', 162; Clarke, 'Origin of Impeachment', 258-9; *Rot. Parl.* iii, 233.

[48] Clarke, 'Forfeitures and Treason', 136-7; Plucknett, 'Impeachment and Attainder', 147, 151; Harcourt, 358.

[49] Plucknett, 'State Trials under Richard II', 164-5; *Rot. Parl.* ii, 329.

[50] Wilkinson, *Constitutional History of Medieval England*, ii, 280; Plucknett, 'State Trials under Richard II', 168-9; *Rot. Parl.* iii, 236.

1388, but it is a concept which reappears in the seventeenth century in the broader context of judicature in parliament.

This survey of late-medieval judicial practices may show, if nothing else, the considerable variety and lack of definition that prevailed. It is not at all certain that impeachment was considered by contemporaries to be a special type of procedure, markedly different from other procedures—though this may have been the case. Virtually the only feature common to all cases described as 'impeachments' is the use of the formula 'accuse and impeach', or some variation of it, and it may be as well to observe, at this point, that such a formula was not employed in the seventeenth century until the trial of the duke of Buckingham. It is not, of course, surprising that procedures overlapped and became confused. Like their seventeenth-century successors late-medieval parliaments had to deal with the crises of the moment and adapted their procedures accordingly. It may be that early Stuart parliaments did the same, and that to refer to 'the revival of impeachment in 1621' is to over-simplify what was in fact a complex inheritance and a tentative process.

CHAPTER II

The Early Stuart Inheritance

The enquiry, conducted in the previous chapter into medieval procedure, included cases which were ignored, as well as cases which were quoted, in the parliaments of the early seventeenth century: for this reason, if for no other, it would be dangerous to assume that Stuart England received unaltered the heritage which appears to us to have been available. It is, therefore, now important to make some attempt to understand what the men who assembled in James I's parliaments chose to regard as their inheritance. Such an enquiry must start at the records which were available in the early seventeenth century.

These were the primary source of guidance—whether to those who initiated parliament's attacks, to their victims, to the monarch whose prerogatives stood to suffer from parliamentary pretensions, or to the Lords threatened by the Commons' encroachments. For while it may be fantasy to imagine the agents of opposing parties confronting each other across a pile of records, it is nevertheless true that those under attack made good use of precedents, sometimes formulating their theories of the Commons' power with more accuracy, if with less lasting effect, than their assailants. The story of the records is closely linked with the work of the antiquarian scholars: both will now be considered.

The seventeenth century was, of course, by no means the first to realise the value of records. A search for precedents had been going on since the days of Bracton, and during the middle ages faith in the past led men to take good care of what, sometime during the fourteenth century, they came to regard not merely as the royal records but as the public records.[1] As this

---

[1] F. S. Fussner, *The Historical Revolution; English Historical Writing and Thought 1580-1640* (London, 1962), 31; V. H. Galbraith, *Studies in the Public Records* (London, 1949), 84, 87.

notion of public ownership developed, so too did demand for right of access. In 1372 Edward III granted a Commons' petition that the records should be accessible to anyone, whether to be used in favour of or against the king's interests, and on 7 March 1621 the House of Commons remembered this concession.[2] However, in the interim, enthusiasm for looking after the records waned and by the early seventeenth century their condition had deteriorated.[3] Coke protested to James I that the Ordnance Office had stored gunpowder beneath the records in the Tower. In July 1620 James ordered its removal— though whether out of concern for the records or for the crown jewels which were stored nearby and therefore equally vulnerable, we have no means of knowing. In fact, nothing was done and the gunpowder was still there more than a century later.[4] Nevertheless, the collections of public records had by this time been centralised in four main groups of repositories, all within easy reach of the parliamentary committees which were appointed to search them, and in about 1606 the zealous and energetic Thomas Wilson was appointed Keeper of the Records.[5] In the early seventeenth century increased use was made of the records and this must have led not only to a wider knowledge of their organisation, assisted by Thomas Powell's publication in 1622 of the first guide, but also to a greater

[2] Galbraith, *Studies*, 85, quoting from *Rot. Parl.* ii, 314; *C.D.* iv, 132. The concession made in 1372 did not last long as a similar petition was presented in 1384, and in 1439 the king refused a Commons' petition that King's Bench and Common Plea records be made available for reference: Galbraith, *Studies*, 85; *Rot. Parl.* iii, 202.

[3] Galbraith, *Studies*, 87; R. B. Wernham, 'The Public Records in the Sixteenth and Seventeenth Centuries', *English Historical Scholarship in the Sixteenth and Seventeenth Centuries*, ed. L. Fox (London, 1956), 12-16; H. Mirrlees, *A Fly in Amber* (London, 1962), 101; J. Butt, 'The Facilities for Antiquarian Study in the Seventeenth Century', *Essays and Studies*, xxiv (1938), 64-79. Marc Friedlaender takes a somewhat more optimistic view: 'Growth in the Resources for Studies in Earlier English History 1534-1625' (unpublished Ph.D. thesis of the University of Chicago, 1938), 173.

[4] *C.S.P. Dom. 1619-23*, 160; Wernham, 27. Friedlaender is wrong in stating (p. 172) that the powder had been removed as a result of James's order. His source, S.P. Dom. 14/156, f. 40, shows this quite clearly.

[5] *D.N.B.* under Wilson; Fussner, 71. Repositories had been established at the Rolls House and Tower, the four Treasuries at Westminster, the State Paper Office at Whitehall, and in various offices of the courts and departments of government. In (or possibly before) 1621 the Jewel Tower in the Palace of Westminster came into use as a storage place for Parliamentary records: A. J. Taylor, *The Jewel Tower, Westminster*, 2nd edition (London, 1965), 12.

opportunity for the medieval heritage to influence thinking.[6] In addition, abstracts and abridgements of the Parliament Rolls made a knowledge of these widely available; Selden certainly produced his during 1621 and a catalogue of them was compiled by Robert Bowyer who was Clerk of the Parliaments from 1610 to 1621.[7]

Although much of the medieval evidence used by the parliament of 1621 came directly from the Parliament Rolls, there existed at this time, in private collections but available for examination, several manuscripts of chronicles telling, *inter alia*, the story of some of the medieval trials. Unfortunately, as the *Journals* and parliamentary diaries of 1621 refer only in the briefest possible way to the precedents, it seems impossible to state categorically that such records were used by the parliament men or their opponents. But their history and ownership makes it at least possible that they formed part of the heritage. Two chronicles are of considerable value for the trials of the reigns of Edward III and Richard II, to which the men of 1621 repeatedly turned. The first is that section of the St Albans chronicles which has been edited and published as the *Chronicon Angliae* and which covers the Good Parliament and the years up to 1388. Of the manuscripts of this part of the chronicle two are basic. Both these were known in the late sixteenth century when they were owned by Matthew Parker. Foxe used one in his *Acts and Monuments* while Stow seems to have employed a translation, though probably not the Latin originals, of the other. Much of Parker's library went to Corpus Christi College, Cambridge, but although these manuscripts were included they did not stay: one eventually found its way into the Harleian library; the other turned up on the shelves of the Cottonian collection as Otto C. ii. It is listed in the manuscript catalogue of Cotton's library in 1621, and it may therefore have helped to colour the advice that its owner was to give during and after the trials of that year. For of all the surviving manuscripts of the chronicle this is the one which

[6] Fussner, 33. Nine years after publishing his *Direction for Search of Records*, Powell, until 1622 solicitor-general in the Marches of Wales, published the much fuller *Repertorie of Records: D.N.B.* under Powell.

[7] E. R. Foster, ed. *Proceedings in Parliament 1610* (New Haven, 1966), i, p. xxii and n. 9.

adopts the line most vehemently critical of John of Gaunt, and it was Gaunt's inability to protect his dependants that opened the way to success in the impeachments of 1376.[8] The second chronicle, a record of fundamental importance for the history of the Good Parliament, is the *Anonimalle Chronicle*. Although its ownership in the seventeenth century is in doubt, and it subsequently disappeared from view until rediscovered forty years ago, this chronicle was known to Stow who used it in the later editions of his *Annals*.[9] In recounting the story of the impeachments of 1376 it places much more emphasis than do the Parliament Rolls on William Latimer, who has not only been traditionally regarded as the first man to be impeached, but whose trial was probably the precedent most commonly used in 1621. Further, this chronicle is the only source of the proceedings and debates of the Commons before they came into full parliament to demand the impeachments.[10]

[8] Cotton's catalogue, which should be better known, is now Harl. MS 6018. It is entitled Catalogus Librorum Manuscriptorum in Bibliotheca Roberti Cottoni 1621. Otto C. ii is entered on f. 114v. For the history and character of the manuscripts of the chronicle, see Thompson, pp. xii-xxx. Of the less important manuscripts of this part of the chronicle, one, Bodl. MS 316, bears what appears to be a seventeenth-century monogram, and another is the Cottonian Faustina B. ix (which, however, does not appear in Cotton's catalogue). The latter, which was found by Leland in Tynemouth Priory, is later in date and more guarded in its views than Otto C. ii. For a passage, found only in Otto C. ii, showing Gaunt in a bad light, see pp. 74-5 of Thompson's edition of the Chronicle.

[9] Galbraith, *Anonimalle Chronicle*, pp. v, xix. Galbraith believes that it had passed into the possession of the Ingilby family before the seventeenth century but this is disputed by Pollard, who, however, makes no alternative suggestion: 'Authorship and Value of the *Anonimalle Chronicle*', 604.

[10] J. G. Edwards in his review of Galbraith's edition of the *Anonimalle Chronicle* in *E.H.R.* xliii (1928), 106, 107; Pollard, 'Authorship and Value of the *Anonimalle Chronicle*', 587. This account of the chronicles available in the early seventeenth century makes no claim to be exhaustive. It merely indicates the major sources accessible to, or probably accessible to, members in 1621 for the precedents which they most frequently used. It could be multiplied, but with little profit. It is perhaps worth noting, however, that several Tudor chroniclers, whose work was printed and therefore easily available, referred to many of the medieval impeachments, but did so only briefly. Furthermore, although the *Historia Anglicana* gives more space than the *Chronicon Angliae* to the case of de la Pole in 1386, it adds little to the information provided by the latter and there is no evidence that the manuscript (now B.M. Royal 13E ix) of this section was available to the parliament men of the early seventeenth century. For a detailed study of the St Albans chronicles, see V. H. Galbraith, 'Thomas Walsingham and the Saint Albans Chronicle 1272-1422', *E.H.R.* xlvii (1932), 12-30; and the same author's introductory essays to his edition of *The St Albans Chronicle 1406-1420* (Oxford, 1937).

If the men of the early seventeenth century required further evidence of the peculiar relevance of the reign of Richard II to their own time it could be found, in easily digestible form, in the theatre. At least two plays, apart from Shakespeare's, dealt with Richard's reign;[11] Shakespeare dramatised only the last eighteen months of the reign but he makes one reference to what is almost certainly the power of judgment of the Commons and to their hostility to the king's servants.[12] However, the judicial conflict with which the play is chiefly concerned is the appeal, a process in which the Commons were not involved, and which died out in 1399, to be revived, unsuccessfully, by Charles I in his attempt to 'impeach' the five members.[13]

But it is unlikely that such uncertain literary evidence played any substantial part in the reign of James I. For active in these years were some of the very best of English antiquaries. We shall probably never know exactly how far the influence and knowledge of these men guided the development of parliamentary judicature, but there is no doubt that their expertise was made available for use, that they were prepared to embroil themselves in the feud and that their skills were regarded as sufficiently dangerous for the government to be provoked into retaliation in and after 1621. Antiquarianism had, of course, emerged particularly strongly late in the reign of Elizabeth

[11] One, in production in 1611, began with Wat Tyler's rebellion and introduced Gloucester's death, but not, apparently, Richard's deposition and death. The second, probably written in the period 1620-30, was *The Tragedy of Richard II concluding with the Murder of the Duke of Gloucester*: A. W. Verity, ed. *King Richard II* (Cambridge, 1899), p. xiv.

[12] Act II, scene 2, ll. 125ff. Bushy, Bagot and Green are discussing their predicament after the king's departure for Ireland and the news of Bolingbroke's invasion:

> Green: ... our nearness to the king in love
> Is near the hate of those love not the king.
> Bagot: And that's the wavering commons: for their love
> Lies in their purses, and whoso empties them,
> By so much fills their hearts with deadly hate.
> Bushy: Wherein the king stands generally condemn'd.
> Bagot: If judgment lie in them, then so do we,
> Because we ever have been near the king.

The first quarto of *King Richard II* was published in 1597.

[13] Clarke, 'Origin of Impeachment', 270. The five members were not, of course, impeached—at least, not in the traditional sense of the word as defined above (p. 7)—for the Commons did not present charges against them to the Lords.

with the foundation of the Society of Antiquaries: but members were concerned with the collection of facts, rather than with problems of explanation and historical context. Despite its relative harmlessness the Society had ceased to meet in about 1608 because of the disfavour of the king, and attempts in 1614 to revive it, with its sharper teeth drawn, were again blocked by James. But the torch was carried into the seventeenth century by men such as Spelman, Camden, Ussher, Cotton and Selden. Their work led to a vastly more critical approach to English historical scholarship which ultimately helped to undermine notions of the unchanging character of institutions and the common law on which many of the claims of the parliament of 1621 rested.[14] But meanwhile, of this group of men, Cotton and Selden made their knowledge readily available for use as ammunition in the legal-cum-political disputes of their day and it is hard to believe that the historical revolution was not helped forward by the increasing demand for precedents and expert advice which arose from such phenomena as the development of parliamentary judicature.

In 1621 Cotton was less committed to one side than was Selden although later in the 'twenties he was to become increasingly the adviser and friend of the parliamentary leaders. His interests were well rooted in the past: William Camden, himself a friend of Stow, had been his schoolmaster and friend, and Cotton was a member of the Society of Antiquaries—one of the few who was not a lawyer. He was a member of James's first and last parliaments and as early as 1607 was supplying information for use in parliament. During the following years he was employed by both king and parliament in searching records, opportunities which he used to

[14] P. Styles, 'Politics and Historical Research in the Early Seventeenth Century', *English Historical Scholarship*, 52; J. H. M. Salmon, *The French Religious Wars in English Political Thought* (Oxford, 1959), 66-7; Fussner, 94-102, 114. On p. 95, Fussner suggests that James's refusal in 1614 to permit the Society to reform was due to the growing use of precedents in relation to contemporary constitutional issues. If so, it is curious that James did not raise objections at their first appearance in the Parliament of 1621, as he was to do later in the same Parliament. For the date of cessation of meetings of the Society of Antiquaries, see D. S. Berkowitz who maintains that formal sessions ended in 1604: 'Young Mr Selden; Essays in Seventeenth-century Learning and Politics' (unpublished Ph.D. thesis of the University of Harvard, 1946), ch. VI, 48.

augment his own library.[15] It is likely, too, that he was at this time engaged in collecting what was later published as *An Exact Abridgement of the Records in the Tower of London*. With friends who were influential enough to gain him access to collections of records without payment of the normal fees, with a library splendidly organised and strategically placed in his house close to parliament, and with a wealth of knowledge of his own, he must, by 1621, have been without rival as an expert guide and adviser. Nevertheless, while he was undoubtedly of use to parliament, there is less evidence than one would need to claim that he had any great influence upon its activities. Shortly after the first session opened the Commons asked for his help in solving an election dispute and, later, when the lower House became entangled in its own extravagant claims to jurisdiction over Floyd, he wrote *A Briefe Discourse Concerning The Power of the Peeres, and Commons of Parliament, in point of Judicature*; but his identification with the Commons was not so strong as to prevent the king from appointing him a few months afterwards to the committee of enquiry to search Coke's papers.[16] Indeed, it is highly probable that Cotton was too impartial for the liking of the parliamentary leaders, that searching the records was still, for him, an academic exercise. He was not prepared to accept the precedents blindly: there is, in the *Abridgement*, a note condemning as an 'Injustice in Parliament' the process there against Alice Perrers, Edward III's mistress.[17] The case against her was one of the precedents that the parliament men of 1621 were inclined to quote. Furthermore, he was ready to give some encouragement to

[15] *D.N.B.* under Cotton and Stow; Mirrlees, 149, 365-6; Fussner, 132; British Museum, *A Guide to a Select Exhibition of Cottonian Manuscripts* (Oxford, 1931), 33.

[16] *C.D.* iv, 54; Fussner, 126, 133. Cotton, whose authorship of this work has now been conclusively settled by Berkowitz, dedicated *A Briefe Discourse* to Sir Edward Montagu, a supporter of the crown who was, nevertheless, prepared to join in the search for precedents and talk to Cotton in an attempt to justify the Commons' action over Floyd: *C.D.* iii, 191; *C.J.* i, 619; Berkowitz, App. E; Fussner, 133-4. Fussner also points out that Cotton's *The Antiquity and Dignity of Parliaments* was much used as a source of precedents during the debates of December 1621.

[17] R. Cotton, *An Exact Abridgement of the Records in the Tower of London* (London, 1657), 158. The note concludes that Perrers' 'mishap was, that she was friendly to many, but all were not so to her. The Record is strange and worthy of sight.' The article on Cotton in the *D.N.B.* suggests that the *Abridgement* was written by William Bowyer, assisted by Robert Bowyer, but gives no reason for this opinion.

parliament's victims. In July 1621, Michell, who had been accused in the spring, heard that Cotton had spoken in his favour at the hearing before the king which led to his discharge from prison and the remission of his fine. He hastily wrote to Cotton asking for confirmation and further help, thereby inaugurating a correspondence which, despite the discouragement of its apparent one-sidedness, was remarkable for the persistence with which its author justified himself. Shortly before this Cotton received a letter from Sir John Bennet, who had recently been attacked. Bennet asked for precedents from the Parliament Rolls of cases similar to his, adding a request that if Cotton could not supply these he should provide directions to enable Bennet to conduct his own searches in the Tower.[18] However, if Cotton himself sat on the fence in 1621, the contents of his library, with which he was always generous, were available to help transmit the medieval inheritance and it was presumably through fear of the use to which Bacon might put it that the government forbade him access to Cotton's library after his fall.[19] But if the library was closed to Bacon it was readily available to John Selden, who had his own key, and there can be no doubt of the importance of Selden in the trials of 1621.[20]

Selden was, of course, a lawyer and was probably friendly with Cotton by 1605 when Cotton was thirty-four and Selden twenty-one. It was a friendship which lasted well and which, increasingly as the years passed, was placed at the service of parliament. Less cautious in his views than Cotton, Selden probably found Cotton's help invaluable in overcoming official resistance to his requests to examine records,[21] and by 1621, having published his *History of Tithes*, he had become a scholar of the first rank. Yet although Selden realised the weaknesses exhibited by the previous generation of antiquaries in its

[18] For Michell's letters, see Cottonian MS Julius C. iii, ff. 253, 254, 256. It is possible, of course, that Cotton replied to Michell but that his letters have not survived. For Bennet's letter, f. 23. This letter was written on 24 June, 1621, not, as Fussner states (pp. 138-9), on 24 July.

[19] *D.N.B.* under Cotton.

[20] E. N. Adams, *Old English Scholarship in England 1566-1800* (London, 1917), 66. By a judicious marriage, to a former countess of Kent, Selden had money enough to build up his own remarkable library: ibid. 68.

[21] Fussner, 135.

approach to the past and although he was never so crudely unhistorical as his associates, his own analysis of the medieval legacy did not wholly escape the distorting effect of current political pressures.[22] The conjunction in Selden of outstanding scholarship and a committed point of view leads to the conclusion that, in hiring his services in 1621, the house of lords, and indirectly the house of commons, acquired an employee of peculiar quality.

In or about 1621 Selden's knowledge took shape in two pieces of writing, the treatise *Of the Judicature in Parliaments* and the collection *The Priviledges of the Baronage of England*. The first will be discussed later in this chapter; the second was without doubt composed during the first session of the parliament of 1621, at the request of the house of lords. As early as mid-February seven peers had inaugurated a search by William Noy of the Tower records, and towards the end of March, probably at the instance of the same peers, the investigation was stepped up and a committee appointed to look for precedents for judicature, accusations and judgments in parliament.[23] This committee was doubtless responsible for recruiting Selden, who was certainly in the employ of the Lords by 27 March.[24] He must have worked hard, for his collection of privileges, covering more than 150 sheets, was apparently completed by the beginning of June.[25]

[22] Salmon, 66. See also Fussner, 277.
[23] Carte MS 78, ff. 495, 501. Thomas Knyvett was appointed, on 30 March, to make notes of the records in the Tower and elsewhere, paying no fee: *H.M.C. Third Report* (London, 1872), App., 21. The committee consisted of Huntingdon, Warwick and Haughton, three of the seven peers: *L.J.* iii, 65. Huntingdon was especially interested in Lords' procedure and privileges. From 1607 to 1621 he sat regularly in the house of lords and wrote accounts of the parliaments of 1610, 1614 and 1621. Later certainly, and possibly in 1610, he received reports from the Commons of their activities: Foster, *Parliament 1610*, i, pp. xxxff.
[24] *Notes on the Debates in the House of Lords, officially taken by Robert Bowyer and Henry Elsing, Clerks of the Parliaments, A.D. 1621, 1625, 1628*, ed. F. H. Relf (Camden Society, 3rd ser. xlii: London, 1929), 48, which tells us that Hakewill was also employed by the Lords at this time. Selden was associated with the Lords earlier still, though less directly: the first roll of Standing Orders for the Lords was produced in March 1621 by Elsynge with Selden's help: M. F. Bond, 'The Formation of the Archives of Parliament 1497-1691', *Journal of the Society of Archivists*, i (1957), 156.
[25] This is inferred from a letter of 23 June, 1621, which indicates that as soon as parliament went into recess in June Selden's parliamentary papers were seized. It is most unlikely that he could have continued his work in these circumstances

The Lords paid Selden for his services, so they presumably made the maximum use of his work. For their money they received what was very largely merely a translation without comment of those sections of the Parliament Rolls containing the precedents most frequently quoted in the debates on judicature in 1621. The precedents translated are similar to those Coke gave when he made his speech on judicature in March 1621. This makes it likely that Selden's work was designed to enable the Lords to weigh up, and if necessary refute, Coke's assertions, a guess which receives backing from Selden's inclusion of the case of Sir John Lee, tried in 1368. Coke said that Lee was 'punished by the Lords, at the Prayer of the Commons', a claim unsupported by the Parliament Rolls which merely indicate that some of the Commons were present in the earlier stages of the examination but apparently only as listeners.[26] Despite its inadequacy, for many men[27] in 1621 the case seems to have held all the magic of a relevant precedent. Selden was stretching the record less harshly than Coke when he translated Lee's case omitting all mention of the Commons.[28]

Selden's collection of privileges contains one considerable mystery. For the most part it is a word-for-word translation of

and, when the second session opened, the efforts of both Selden and the peers were concentrated on recovering the papers and filling the gaps found to exist on their return, preparatory to having them bound: *L.J.* iii, 176; *H.M.C. Third Report*, App., 25; R. F. Williams, ed. *The Court and Times of James the First* (London, 1848), ii, 260-1. While engaged on these historical researches Selden also seems to have been regarded by the Lords as a proper recipient of the records of their current judicial activities. At the command of the sub-committee Elsynge lent his records of the proceedings against Mompesson: Petyt MS 538/7, f. 336. He doubtless used this material when he wrote *Of the Judicature in Parliaments*.

[26] *C.J.* i, 545-6; *Rot. Parl.* ii, 297, 298. Reference has already been made to the case, but for a full discussion of it and its place in the development of impeachment see Clarke, 'Origin of Impeachment', 258-9, 267-8, and Plucknett, 'Origin of Impeachment', 53-4. Coke repeats the mistake in *The Fourth Part of the Institutes of the Laws of England*, 5th edition (London, 1671), 23: 'Sir John at Lee adjudged by the Lords and Commons'. For Lee's case see above, p. 8. For Selden's precedents see Table I.

[27] Including Bacon: *The Letters and the Life of Francis Bacon* (London, 1861-74), vii, 232-4. It was also one of the precedents reported to the Lords by the committee appointed in late March to search for precedents: Braye MS 11, f. 105.

[28] J. Selden, *The Priviledges of the Baronage of England when they sit in Parliament* (London, 1689), 34-6.

the Parliament Rolls without abbreviation or editing.[29] But when he reaches the case of Michael de la Pole, the ex-Chancellor who was impeached at the complaint of the Commons in 1386, wholesale omission and abbreviation take place. The editing is extremely spasmodic and if this were our only record of the case parts of the proceedings would be virtually incomprehensible. Selden omits or summarises part of de la Pole's defence, though he gives his most successful plea, but he prints in full the Commons' reply to the defence he has suppressed. When he comes to the judgment he omits one of the charges which went against de la Pole and he leaves out the record of the dropping of three charges brought against him. Now, when Coke discussed judicature in March 1621, he quoted de la Pole's case in substantiation of the first of his four types of judicature, that exercised by the king and magnates, and Bacon listed it as possibly relevant to his own situation when he was considering this round about Easter 1621.[30] As it was evidently regarded as a case of some significance, the reasons for Selden's editing are worth examination. The simplest explanation is that the omissions are due to the king or his servants' failure to return all Selden's papers which had been seized during the summer of 1621;[31] but if so it is strange that confiscation afflicted only this translation whose missing portions can hardly be construed as adversely affecting the royal prerogative. A man less scholarly than Selden might be accused of carelessness but this cannot possibly account for all the omissions, nor does it explain why he should summarise here when he normally translates *verbatim* elsewhere. These con-

---

[29] He does not translate the whole of the record of Ellis's case but this was relatively unimportant, occupying little space in the Parliament Rolls. He makes a minor change in the record on Latimer by translating '... Latymer estoit empeschez & accusez par clamour des ditz Communes' as 'Latimer was impeached and accused by the Vote of the said Earls', but as he later renders '... Latymer y estoit empeschez par le dit Commune' as 'Latimer was impeached by the Commons' this change is unlikely to be due to anything more than an innocent mistake, even if one favourable to the Lords. He also mistranslates part of the section recording Latimer's punishment: *Rot. Parl.* ii, 324 par. 20, 325 par. 24; Selden, *Priviledges*, 42, 46, 53.

[30] Spedding, vii, 232. Coke does not seem to have mentioned de la Pole's case until the debate itself. His views on judicature will be discussed below, pp. 43ff.

[31] *L.J.* iii, 176.

siderations, together with the fact that Selden concealed his omissions by not translating the words used in the Parliament Roll to number de la Pole's pleas, make it clear that the alterations were deliberate. The explanation of intentional falsification of the record can surely be found only in the circumstances of 1621.

If, as was suggested earlier, Selden made his collection to assist his employers, the Lords, to defend themselves against the Commons, it is possible that he altered this record in an attempt to weaken the Commons' position; but it is difficult to see how the changes he made could have achieved this. Furthermore, Coke, in his speech on judicature, had not claimed—surprisingly enough—that de la Pole's case supported the Commons' claims to participate. The explanation must lie elsewhere. It may very well be that Selden was translating the Parliament Rolls during the very weeks when Bacon was being tried. It was vital to parliamentary judicature that this attack should succeed, as Selden knew better than most. The Lords' will needed strengthening when it was on a collision course with the Lord Chancellor,[32] and this could perhaps be achieved by judicious alteration of the record of what might appear to be the most relevant of all precedents, the impeachment of a previous Chancellor. For the overall effect of Selden's alterations was to weaken de la Pole's very successful defence, leaving a picture of a man unable to answer charges of fraud and receiving draconian punishment from the Lords.[33] This explanation cannot be wholly satisfying because Selden's translation fails to eliminate completely hints that de la Pole was not as great a fool as he is made to appear. Nevertheless,

[32] According to F. H. Relf Coke too believed in the need to strengthen the Lords' will: see below, p. 101. It is fascinating to note that, in Wilkinson's view, the impeachment of de la Pole took place at a time of great assertion of the power of the Lords in Parliament: *Studies*, 99; and above, pp. 16-17.

[33] As already indicated, de la Pole's impeachment has been discussed by Clarke, 'Origin of Impeachment', 265; Clarke, 'Lancastrian Faction', 48-52; Plucknett, 'State Trials under Richard II', 165-6; Wilkinson, *Studies*, 98; N. B. Lewis, 'Article VII of the Impeachment of Michael de la Pole in 1386', *E.H.R.* xlii (1927), 402-7; J. J. N. Palmer, 'The Impeachment of Michael de la Pole in 1386', *Bull. Inst. Hist. Res.* xlii (1969), 96-101. Steel (p. 123) also discusses the case but he has misread Lewis's article and fastens on to de la Pole charges of usury which Lewis was discussing (p. 403) with reference to Lyons.

if Selden was less able as a forger than as a historian, he obviously felt that his part-time occupation was worth the effort involved.[34] It would seem that he, as an antiquary, believed that his knowledge was so relevant to the events of 1621 that it could be used to guide them; it would also seem that he felt that the house of lords, or part of it, shared his belief.

In compiling *The Priviledges of the Baronage of England* Selden was writing propaganda and his influence was evidently regarded as sufficiently dangerous for his arrest and examination to follow the conclusion of the first session of the 1621 parliament.[35] But that his influence was not confined to parliament is shown by his correspondence with Bacon in February 1622 about the latter's sentence. Paradoxically if the explanation suggested for Selden's alterations of the record of de la Pole's case is correct, he told Bacon that he questioned the validity of his sentence because of inadequacies in the recording of the judgment.[36] Selden, the historian, had re-emerged.

It is clear, from this examination of medieval records possibly available in the early seventeenth century and of the work of Stuart antiquaries in summarising and explaining their contents, that lack of information hardly circumscribed the range of procedures open to those who looked for guidance to their medieval predecessors. Early Stuart England seems to have been well provided with case histories of medieval parliamentary judicature. It is therefore necessary to look elsewhere to discover what James I's parliaments regarded as their proper authority in judicial matters. There are two main sources of this information—treatises written on the subject in the early seventeenth century, and occasional references in speeches delivered in parliament at the time.

Two treatises survive—a book, *Of the Judicature in Parliaments*, and a manuscript pamphlet, The moderne forme of the Parliaments of England—and they must be discussed in some detail. The first, probably by John Selden, was written

[34] Fundamentally Selden rated the value of precedents lower than his use of them in 1621 would suggest: Fussner, 288-9; B. M. Lansdowne MS 173, ff. 50v-52.
[35] Nicholas, *Proceedings*, ii, App.
[36] Spedding, vii, 332-3.

long before it was published, and cannot be dated precisely.[37] Hargrave, in his preface to Hale's *The Jurisdiction of the Lords House*, suggested that it was written while Selden was employed by the Lords in 1621; if so, as Hargrave realised, sections dealing with the parliamentary trials of 1624 and 1626 must have been added later. But the whole work was certainly completed no later than 1626.[38]

In introducing his subject Selden set himself a formidable task. He states that six different types of judicature belong to parliament: judging delinquents, both for capital crimes and for misdemeanours; reversing erroneous judgments given in parliament; reversing erroneous judgments given in the King's Bench; deciding difficult or long delayed suits; hearing private petitions; and enforcing various parliamentary privileges. Selden says that each of these types involves several clearly defined stages, and he implies that he will consider every type in all its stages. In fact, what survives—possibly all that he wrote—is his study of the first type, but this requires a book of nearly two hundred pages. As he makes each point, he illustrates it by reference to precedent: it is difficult to fault him on his use of many of these and he makes no attempt to conceal his occasional inability to understand a particular case.[39] The result is a manual whose author speaks with conviction.

This is equally true of the pamphlet, The moderne forme of the Parliaments of England, whose probable author was Henry Elsynge. Elsynge became Clerk of the Parliaments in March 1621, holding the appointment until 1635 and dying in 1636.[40]

---

[37] Selden's authorship is not established beyond question though the probability favours this attribution: Berkowitz, ch. V. The printed edition bears no date of publication.

[38] Berkowitz, ch. V, 42, 44; F. Hargrave's preface to M. Hale, *The Jurisdiction of the Lords House* (London, 1796), pp. xxx-xxxi.

[39] Not surprisingly he found some difficulty with the cases of Alice Perrers and Sir John Mortimer: J. Selden, *Of the Judicature in Parliaments* (London, n.d.), 22, 59-61. For Perrers, see p. 18, above; for Mortimer, see Rezneck, 506. For Selden's precedents, see Table I.

[40] M. F. Bond, 'Clerks of the Parliaments 1509-1953', *E.H.R.* lxxiii (1958), 83. The pamphlet has been printed, with an introduction, by Miss C. S. Sims, in *American Historical Review*, liii (1948), 288-305. The use of the words 'moderne forme' in the title is interesting: this appears to be the only case of a statement by an early seventeenth-century man that he regarded his period as modern. I am indebted to Mr Conrad Russell for drawing this to my attention.

D

He was thus in an unrivalled position to gain an expert knowledge of parliamentary procedure and the pamphlet was doubtless written during his tenure of office. Whether it preceded or followed Selden's work is unknown, but the section entitled 'Proceedings in Judicature' covers almost exactly the same ground and occasional similarities of phraseology suggest a degree of plagiarism. In dealing with parliamentary judicature, Elsynge is very brief, quotes few precedents and admits to no uncertainties. Neither work undermines the assertions of the other.

What Selden categorises as 'Judgments against Delinquents' and what Elsynge entitles 'Proceedings in Judicature' involve six distinct stages which both authors identify.[41] These are the accusation, the answer of the accused, the replication by the party accusing, the proofs of the witnesses, the judgment, and the execution. The form of the first stage, the accusation, determines much of the procedure in the subsequent stages. Selden says that there were four kinds of accusation—by the Commons, by information *ex parte regis*, by private persons, and by appeal by members of the Lords. The last two may be dealt with quickly: Selden recognises that the appeal was abolished shortly after Henry IV's accession and Elsynge states that it was 'beyond the Law'. Private persons proceed either by petitions or by articles in writing exhibited in parliament, and Selden correctly quotes precedents, which include the private bills against Ellis in 1376 and the petition of Cavendish against de la Pole in 1384, as examples of this procedure.[42]

The first two kinds of accusation are more complex and overlap each other to an extent. The Commons may accuse either by making a complaint or by introducing an impeachment. If they impeach the suit is theirs, but if they complain the suit is the king's.[43] As for the second kind of accusation—information *ex parte regis*—it appears that this may be based on information provided directly by the king or by the Commons when they 'as any other private Person accuse any man unto

---

[41] Selden, *Of Judicature*, 8; Elsynge, 301.
[42] Selden, *Of Judicature*, 11, 66ff; Elsynge, 302, 303.
[43] Selden, *Of Judicature*, 14; Elsynge, 302.

the Lords . . .' However the information arises, the suit is always *ex parte regis*.[44] It may, perhaps, be questioned how far there is a real distinction between proceedings based on the Commons' complaint and proceedings based on Commons' information;[45] but what is important is that both Selden and Elsynge plainly indicate that impeachment procedure is only one of two or perhaps three types of accusation with which the Commons might be closely associated in cases of parliamentary judicature. This fact will be of significance to an understanding of some of the parliamentary trials of the early seventeenth century.

According to Selden and Elsynge, the procedure in an impeachment differed from that in a trial begun by information or complaint laid by the Commons. Elsynge sets out the distinction clearly and conveniently summarises procedure after the initial accusation:

If the Comons exhibite noe Articles neither in writing nor by word of mouth by their Speaker at the Barr, then it is onely a Complaint. And in such cases, the Proceedings therein are left to the Lords, and they cause it to bee proceeded in *ex parte Domini Regis*, and it is not necessary that the Comons should bee further acquainted therewith, unlesse the Comons doe in that Complaint require that the Proceedings bee in their presence, or unlesse it be for Capitall causes, for in cases Capitall, whosoever complaines, the Comons are to bee acquainted with the cause, the Answer, and the Judgment . . .

If the Comons doe impeach the party accused that is to exhibite Articles, or any other Declaracion against him in writing, or by their Speaker, then the suyte is theirs, and they are to bee privy to all Proceedings against the Party accused. They are to have a Copie of the Answer, and may reply unto the same. They are to exhibite the Interrogatories and the names of their Wittnesses to be examined, and produce such proofes as they have against him, & have Copies of the Examinacions. Judgment is not to bee given till they demand it, and then to bee done in their presence, of all which, there are divers ancient presidents.[46]

---

[44] Selden, *Of Judicature*, 33, 61.

[45] Selden is inclined to use the same precedents to illustrate both, and Elsynge does not make the distinction: *Of Judicature*, 12ff, 61ff.

[46] Elsynge, 302. See also Selden, *Of Judicature*, 14, 109, 118-9, 124, 162.

Selden provides two further details. Accusations *ex parte regis* are exhibited by the king's attorney, and the Commons are not normally to be present at the trial unless the Lords desire it.[47] Finally, both authors emphasise that, if the Commons initiate proceedings the Lords must not be associated in the accusation, and that, conversely, in cases of parliamentary judicature, the Commons have no power of judgment, which is the prerogative solely of the Lords.[48]

There is no doubt that both Selden and Elsynge were preaching counsels of perfection: they were writing treatises rather than legal reports. The cases of the 1620s cannot necessarily be fitted into the categories which they define. For it must be remembered that Selden may not have written his book until 1626, while Elsynge's work may be a product of the 1630's— when he perhaps found himself rather less busy than formerly; and it is at least possible that their definitions acquired precision only after the cases themselves had been tried. Furthermore, both men were to some extent, theorists, possessing an undoubtedly more profound knowledge of their subject than the average early seventeenth-century parliament man, to whom their definitions and distinctions may have seemed legalistic and possibly even imaginary. Of course, both were in a position to offer guidance and advice on procedure, though in 1621, when Elsynge became Clerk of the Parliaments and when Selden was employed by the Lords, such counsel is more likely to have been directed towards the upper House than to the lower. It is possible that the position changed somewhat in 1624, when Selden entered the Commons for the first time.[49]

If we are to aim at any real understanding of the views of the parliament men of the early seventeenth century on the

---

[47] Selden, *Of Judicature*, 54, 163. He does, however, also seem to suggest that the Commons may be present at a trial *ex parte regis* if they demand this: p. 163.

[48] Selden, *Of Judicature*, 11, 133; Elsynge, 301, 303. The distinction drawn by Selden and Elsynge between complaints and impeachments has received scant acknowledgement by twentieth-century historians. Maude Clarke is the only exception I have discovered: 'Origin of Impeachment', 269.

[49] *D.N.B.* under Selden. To judge by one of the questions put to Selden during his examination by the government in the summer of 1621, he was at least sus-

subject of parliamentary judicature, we can only hope to acquire it from their speeches and from the writings of a man like Sir Edward Coke, who was a practical politician as well as a legal expert. However, there are difficulties. Such sources yield isolated pieces of information, rather than a thorough exposition. This is hardly surprising: the urgency of affairs in James I's parliaments scarcely encouraged the delivery of elaborate pronouncements on theoretical subjects.

There is also a terminological problem. The precise meaning of the term 'impeachment' in the early seventeenth century is curiously difficult to comprehend. There are two main reasons for this.[50] First, although many of the parliamentary trials of the 1620s have long been described as impeachments the records themselves rarely use the word, and never, until 1626, in connection with these cases. On one of its few appearances in the records of 1621, it is used in the *Commons Journal* to describe what the lower House had done to the Catholic lawyer, Floyd, for slandering the king and queen of Bohemia. As the Commons did not charge him before the Lords, he was not, according to the traditional definition of the process, impeached at all.[51] Nor does the term appear in Coke's writings which, as will be shown, are disappointingly sketchy on the whole subject of parliamentary judicature. Secondly, it is difficult to know what meaning should be attached to the word on the occasions when it is used. In the late sixteenth century, as in the middle ages, the word was in general use, with the consequently rather imprecise meaning of 'hindrance'

---

pected of sympathising with the Commons' position then. He was asked, in connection with Floyd's case, whether he did not wish that the Commons had power of judicature in such matters. Whether this sympathy issued forth into advice in 1621 is not known.

[50] Apart, that is, from its absence from the dictionaries of the period: the word is not listed in Sir Henry Spelman's *Archaeologus in modum Glossarii ad rem antiquam posteriorem*, published in 1626, nor—except in the special instance of 'impeachment of waste'—in Dr John Cowell's book, *The Interpreter*, published in 1607. Spelman's *Glossary* claimed to deal with new meanings of words; *The Interpreter* was the best known law dictionary of the day. Cowell was Regius Professor of Civil Law at Cambridge.

[51] *C.J.* i, 608.

or 'embarrassment'. Yet it also carried a more technical meaning: both John Minsheu, in 1617, and Thomas Powell, in 1623, use 'impeach' as a synonym for 'accuse';[52] and a few years earlier, Shakespeare had used 'appeach' in *King Richard II* to mean 'denounce' or 'charge'.[53] It has already been stated[54] that some historians of the medieval parliament believe that in the parliamentary records of 1376 it is possible to distinguish the meaning of an accusation brought by the whole Commons in parliament; and they have found significance in the subsequent occasions when the word is avoided as well as when it is used—an approach which may possibly have relevance in a seventeenth-century context. Of course, it may be unrealistic to expect to understand precisely and on every occasion the meaning of a term so often used to describe a political conflict between the monarch and his opponents, when, presumably the end was more important than the means. Moreover, a word capable of bearing more than one meaning is not without value to the politician.

If 'impeachment' is conspicuous by its absence from the records of the 1620s, the reverse is true of the term 'complaint'. As will be shown, this word was frequently used to describe grievances which were brought to the Commons as well as cases which the lower House presented to the Lords. The use of the word raises problems of interpretation similar to those already mentioned in connection with 'impeachment'. Apart from its general meaning the word also refers to a formal accusation or charge, and in the seventeenth century was often embodied in the phrase 'bill of complaint'.[55] Of course, there also exists the definition which Selden and Elsynge provided for the term, but whether the Commons used it in this

[52] Clarke, 'Origin of Impeachment', 242; J. Minsheu, *The Guide into Tongues* (London, 1617); T. Powell, *The Attourneys Academy* (London, 1623). One particular instance of the use of the term should be noted. In March 1610 the servant of an M.P., Sir James Scudamore, was arrested by a sheriff and the Commons, who were of course in session, took notice of the deed, and referred the matter to the committee for privileges. On the 16th this gave advice 'Not to impeach the Sheriff, not knowing that he was Servant': *C.J.* i, 412.

[53] *Richard II*, act V, scene 2, l. 79. For other uses of the word in *Richard II* see act I, scene 1, ll. 170 and 189.

[54] See above, p. 8.

[55] *Oxford English Dictionary* (Oxford, 1888-1928), under 'complaint'.

precise way or in a more general manner is a problem which is unlikely to be solved conclusively.[56]

However, if these terminological difficulties hinder our understanding of the views on parliamentary judicature of James I's parliament men, they do not render fruitless an examination of their speeches and writings. The views of Sir Edward Coke provide the obvious starting point. Coke could dominate the Commons with his personality and his knowledge. Untroubled by the problems of interpretation and critical analysis with which the new generation of antiquaries were grappling, a scholar in the late sixteenth- rather than the early seventeenth-century mould, he accepted the precedents with little hesitation and there were few who dared to contradict him in his use of them. Although he might misapply them and refuse to be put out by the lack of them or to question the reason for this lack, he was undoubtedly one of the chief channels through which the medieval heritage could make itself felt in and after 1621.[57]

When Coke wrote *The Institutes of the Laws of England* he included in the fourth part, written during or after 1628, a chapter on parliament as a court. This has a section on judicature in which Coke declares that the Houses both separately and together have a power of judicature. However, this is not an introduction to a detailed discussion, because Coke at once adds that 'the handling hereof according to the worth and weight of the matter would require a whole Treatise of it self; and to say the truth, it is best understood by reading the Judgments and Records of Parliament . . .'[58] He then contents himself with listing precedents in a way which does very little to illuminate the subject. He records that, in the 1620s, there were divers notable judgments, at the prosecution of the Commons, by

[56] Another word which possessed two meanings, one general and the other technical, was 'grievance': E. R. Foster, 'The Procedure of the House of Commons against Patents and Monopolies', *Conflict in Stuart England*, ed. W. A. Aiken and B. D. Henning (London, 1960), 85, n. 105.

[57] Coke had a library of *c.* 1,200 volumes, particularly strong in the texts of English medieval historians: *A Catalogue of the Library of Sir Edward Coke*, ed. W. O. Hassall (London, 1950), pp. xii, xx. Coke annotated many of his books but unfortunately these notes give little or no indication of his opinions.

[58] Coke, *Fourth Part of the Institutes*, 23; C. D. Bowen, *The Lion and the Throne; the Life and Times of Sir Edward Coke 1552-1634* (London, 1957), 436.

the Lords at the Parliaments holden 18 and 21 Jac. Regis against
Sir Giles Mompesson, Sir John Michel, Viscount St. Albone Lord
Chancellour of England, the Earl of M. Lord Treasurer of England,
whereby the due proceeding of Judicature in such cases doth
appear.[59]

But he provides no explanations or classifications, and we are
left to wonder why he used a phrase like 'at the prosecution of
the Commons', which, when compared with the contemporary
record, seems to exaggerate substantially the part taken by the
lower House in these cases.

This is disappointing, but rather more information can be
gleaned from two speeches Coke made early in the first session
of 1621. These are particularly important because, unlike the
more random remarks made on judicature by his colleagues
in this parliament, they were delivered before that parliament
had progressed far in any real exercise of its judicature, and
were therefore perhaps less influenced than they might otherwise have been by the experiences of 1621 itself. The first
speech was delivered on 28 February, during a discussion in
committee of Mompesson's offences. Coke said:

The Courte of Parliament a Courte of Counsell and a Courte of
Pleas. When the Howses were devided, The indevisible things
remayned with the Lords. Pleas continued in the Upper-Howse
longe after the Stattute.

Complaints and Examinacions of greevances have been ancient
in the Howse of Commons, the matter of fact tryed there; they have
often resorted to the Lords for Judicature. The proceedings have
beene with some varietye. In some cases the Howse of Commons
made Plaintiffs and Delinquents to answere there, sometymes the
Steward of the Howse made a Complaint and the Comons were made
a partie, And sometymes the Commons would have the Connizance
alone. Never anie that was fowned guiltie hath been able to beare
out the storme of the Common Forces. There hath beene noe
iudgment in this kind since 2 H. 6.[60]

Coke is here identifying three types of procedure. In the first,
the Commons appear to be responsible for initiating the hearing

---

[59] Coke, *Fourth Part of the Institutes*, 23.

[60] *C.D.* iv, 115-6. '2 H. 6' should presumably read '28 H. 6' (the impeachment
of Suffolk in 1450), a common enough error in the diaries of the early seventeenth
century.

before the Lords; in the second, the Commons are associated with the proceedings as a party, but the 'Complaint' is instituted by an official of some sort. In speaking of the 'Steward of the Howse' Coke is presumably thinking either of the steward of the household who prosecuted Gomeniz, Weston and Perrers in 1377, or of the steward of England who performed the same function in 1397, though to both Selden and Elsynge the function of the steward, whether of England or of the household is to preside rather than to prosecute, and then only in capital cases and not in misdemeanours.[61] Coke's third type of procedure is that where the Commons in certain unspecified instances have sole jurisdiction, without reference to the Lords.

Coke may have illustrated each type of procedure with selected precedents, but the surviving records do no more than list a few at the end of the speech, without classifying them. However, some days later, on 8 March, during the preparations for presenting Mompesson to the Lords, Coke again gave his views on judicature and the precedents he used to illustrate his categories are clearly recorded.[62] On this occasion, he listed four types of judicature. Proceedings might take place before the king and the Lords, before the Lords alone, before the Lords and Commons, and before the Commons alone. Coke's elaboration of these categories shows that, although he was here looking at the subject of judicature from a slightly different angle and discussing four types rather than three, he is not contradicting his statement made a week previously.

As evidence of proceedings before the king and the Lords, Coke quotes the case of Suffolk in 1450. Although this has certainly been thought of as an impeachment, it was one in which the king's part was much greater than normal, and it may have been this characteristic which led Coke to use it as an illustration for this category.[63] Although he provides no further explanation of this first type of procedure, what he understands by it becomes clearer when he turns to the second

---

[61] Plucknett, 'Impeachment and Attainder', 148ff; *Rot. Parl.* iii, 12; Harcourt, 347; Selden, *Of Judicature*, 176-7; Elsynge, 303-4.

[62] For Coke's precedents, see Table I.

[63] *C.D.* ii, 195; v, 280; vi, 307. It is possible that he also mentioned Michael de la Pole's case in 1386, though not all accounts are agreed on this.

type. He states that, when the king is a party, the Lords judge alone. They can do so either on writs of error arising out of judgments in the King's Bench, or in cases originating before them, or on complaints of the Commons. As an example of original jurisdiction, he quotes the case of Alice Perrers in 1377. In so doing he was presumably influenced by the obscure character of this case: it will be remembered that the Parliament Roll fails to state who was responsible for presenting her to the Lords.[64] As one example of proceedings before the Lords on complaints of the Commons, Coke gives the case of Sir John Lee, but he also lists, under the same heading, the cases of Lyons, Ellis, Neville and Peach, which were among the impeachments of 1376 which Maude Clarke contrasted with Lee's case.[65]

However, Coke does not include Latimer, the most important of the men impeached in 1376, in this list. He uses this case, together with—according to one account—the cases of Gomeniz and Weston from 1377, to illustrate his third type of judicature, the type which involved proceedings before the Lords and Commons. His reason for assigning Latimer's trial to this category is evidently Latimer's pardon, which states that he was judged before the Lords and Commons; but the Commons' part in the two trials of 1377 was far less substantial.[66]

Coke's fourth type of judicature, procedure before the Commons alone, requires little discussion for the present. His precedents indicate that he is thinking largely in terms of proceedings against those who offended against the privileges of the House.[67]

These two speeches by Coke obviously contain some puzzling features in their references to the judicial powers of the Houses. It is not easy to understand the principles upon which Coke

---

[64] C.D. v, 32, 281; Rot. Parl. iii, 12. See also p. 18, above. Whether or not the Lords possessed an original jurisdiction was, of course, to be a matter of fierce argument later in the seventeenth century.

[65] C.D. ii, 195-6; v, 281; vi, 44. For these cases, see pp. 14, 17-18, above.

[66] C.D. ii, 196; vi, 44; Nicholas, Proceedings, i, 134. This is Coke's interpretation of Latimer's pardon; but see Wilkinson, Studies, 90 n. 2. As for Gomeniz and Weston, it is interesting to note that Selden states that they were arraigned before the Lords and Commons in full parliament: Of Judicature, 42.

[67] C.D. ii, 197.

allocates his precedents to their various categories, and it was
Maude Clarke's view that his use of these indicated that he
did not understand the 'special character of procedure by
impeachment'.[68] But whether or not this verdict is fair, Coke
clearly did believe that the Commons might be associated with
the Lords in more than one way in parliamentary judicature.
On 28 February, he states that the lower House might either
initiate proceedings before the Lords, or be brought in as a
party to complaints introduced by the steward; on 8 March,
he says that judicature may be jointly exercised by the two
Houses, or that it may be exercised by the Lords on complaints
brought by the Commons. It is tempting to see in these distinctions a foreshadowing of the rigid definitions of impeachment and complaint set up by Selden and Elsynge. Procedure
on complaint may have meant much the same to all three men,
for Coke does seem to use the word to describe the processes
in which the Commons had a lesser, rather than a greater,
share; but this may be accidental rather than deliberate and,
as there is no evidence that he ever used the word 'impeachment', it is not certain that he would have recognised any
procedural distinction between impeachment and complaint.
Furthermore, it would be hard indeed to establish real distinctions between Coke's various types of judicature merely on
the basis of the precedents he cites: that he genuinely believed
in these distinctions, his speeches prove as conclusively as is
ever likely to be possible, but that his precedents really support
the existence of all his distinctions is rather more doubtful.
However, it is evident that Coke understood that parliamentary judicature—the judicature resulting from the co-
operation of the two Houses—could manifest itself in two forms,
in one of which the Commons were more closely, or more
fundamentally, associated than in the other.

Whether or not other members of the Commons shared
Coke's views on procedure in judicature, there is no means of
knowing. No reports survive of other speeches on the same
theme. The confusion in some of the diary accounts of Coke's
second speech suggests that their authors found the subject

[68] Clarke, 'Origin of Impeachment', 267.

unfamiliar.[69] On the other hand, those members who were lawyers must have had an acquaintance with this procedure, and there is no reason to suppose that Coke's views were untypical of his profession. But only William Hakewill, a man who shared Coke's legal background as well as his antiquarian interests, made any comment which might be construed as being related to Coke's theme. Towards the end of April, 1621, during proceedings against Bennet, he said: 'I have observed when we have gone to the Lords it hath been by impeachment, clamor or accusation.'[70] This remark, which is not explained, probably raises more difficulties than it solves. Evidently, to Hakewill, impeachment was only one of the methods by which the Commons could approach the Lords, but it would indeed be useful to know what Hakewill regarded as the procedural characteristics of each of his three methods, especially as this is one of the few occasions before 1626 when the word 'impeachment' appears in the records. Furthermore, his remark must lead us to wonder what he would have made, or did make, of the report in the Parliament Roll of 1376, which states that Latimer was 'impeached and accused by the clamour of the Commons'.[71]

Apart from his comments about procedure, Coke made another point in his speech of 28 February. He states that when 'the Howses were devided, The indevisible things remayned with the Lords', and in the following paragraph he adds that 'Complaints and Examinacions of greevances have been ancient in the Howse of Commons, the matter of fact tryed there; they have often resorted to the Lords for Judicature.'[72] He is here referring to a division of function between the Houses which virtually compelled the Commons to depend on the Lords for the punishment of a man, unless his offence was against their

[69] Their confusion could, of course, have been the result of a poorly constructed speech, but this seems an unlikely explanation as Pym's account of Coke's speech is very clear. This very clarity, in its turn, suggests that Pym may have shared Coke's familiarity with the subject.

[70] *C.D.* ii, 314. Another account reports this speech as follows: '. . . to send theis things to the Lords. But we not to condemn him. 3 fold grounds: 1, clamor; 2, accusation; 3, impeachment by the Commons . . .': *C.D.* iii, 55.

[71] *Rot. Parl.* ii, 324.

[72] *C.D.* iv, 115.

own privileges. What Coke was saying—before the trials of 1621 had really got under way—was that the Commons' power was limited to the examination of alleged grievances and a pronouncement as to whether the allegation was valid. The Commons could not, for example, punish the author of a grievance: this was the Lords' function; and it may be noted, in passing, that it was the need to do this, rather than to persist in the ineffective condemnation of the grievances themselves, which was to lead to the revival of the process by which the Commons presented offenders to the Lords. Now, this limitation on the power of the Commons was to prove irksome in 1621 during Floyd's case, but if the intemperate speeches delivered on that occasion are recognised as untypical of the normal mood, as they undoubtedly were, Coke's statement appears to have been generally acknowledged as correct. During the course of the trials of 1621, Pym, Samuel Sandys and Noy all confirmed Coke's view, though Pym maintained that, in the past, the Commons had been present at the judgment and had influenced the terms of the punishment.[73]

As has already been pointed out, Coke's two speeches have, for us, the great advantage of having been delivered before there had been much experience of parliamentary judicature in 1621. In consequence, the interpretation which they place upon the medieval heritage cannot have been influenced by the outcome of the trials of 1621. This is not true of the contributions on parliamentary judicature made by other members during this session, which may well have been substantially influenced by the results of those trials. Nevertheless, despite the obvious dangers, it seems appropriate to attempt a summary of these views. On the other hand, opinions given in subsequent parliaments are likely to have been so influenced by the judicial developments of the 1620s that it would be unwise to include them in this section.

It has been suggested that the Commons of 1621 did not seriously quarrel with Coke's view of their dependence on the Lords in most cases of judicature, but it was also recognised that, except in matters concerning their own members and privileges, the Lords could not deal with public grievances

[73] *C.D.* ii, 303, 312, 370; iii, 136; vi, 90; Nicholas, *Proceedings*, i, 283.

unless these were presented to them by the Commons. The most forceful assertion of this doctrine occurs during and after Floyd's condemnation by the lower House—an assumption of power which it proved unable to justify—so that members' protestations may contain an element of wounded pride; but the doctrine gained the support of men like Hakewill, Pym, Sir Thomas Roe and possibly Noy, and Hakewill produced two precedents to show that judgments had been reversed in cases where the Commons had not made an accusation.[74] Hakewill also maintained that, on occasions when the Lords had not pronounced judgment, the Commons had gone to the king; while Rich asserted, very radically, that if the Lords refused to punish those complained of, the Commons should pass judgment themselves, 'which is our ancient course'.[75]

It seems to have been implicitly accepted in 1621 that accusations brought by the Commons had to be precise, rather than vague, and the consequences of the deficiencies in the first attack on Suffolk in 1450 certainly supported this view.[76] Furthermore, Pym made the point that the Commons might jeopardise their power of inquisition in parliamentary judicature unless they ensured that evidence handed to the Lords was already fully proved. An unidentified speaker in mid-May claimed that the House had some right to select punishments, and Alford, Hakewill and Pym on separate occasions declared that the Commons could demand a second judgment, if they were not satisfied with the first.[77]

One aspect of the procedure of demanding judgment caused anxiety in 1621. On 14 May, when the Lords appeared to be taking little action on the Commons' complaint against Field, Hakewill complained of the custom, which, he said, had grown up during the session, by which the Commons waited

[74] *C.D.* ii, 352, 362; iii, 166, 177, 288; iv, 361; vi, 141; *C.J.* i, 608, 610, 624. Sackville may have had doubts about the doctrine, but his position is not very clear: *C.D.* v, 162.

[75] *C.D.* ii, 371; iii, 178.

[76] Harcourt, 383-4; *Rot. Parl.* v, 176-7; Nicholas, *Proceedings*, ii, 83. The Lords refused to order Suffolk's imprisonment until the Commons made a specific accusation against him. Selden draws attention to this aspect of the case: *Of Judicature*, 29.

[77] *C.D.* ii, 303, 368, 370; iii, 250, 264; Nicholas, *Proceedings*, i, 228.

to be invited by the Lords to demand judgment before actually doing so. Alford, Roe and Sackville make it clear that the result of this habit was that cases presented to the Lords might remain there unsettled, or that the Commons might never know the details of a Lords' judgment. Hakewill provided the remedy—to demand judgment uninvited—and the implication is that this was believed to be the ancient custom.[78]

In general, there was probably little quarrel with the belief that the Commons' part in judicature was one of considerable importance, and one which had, in the past, led to attacks on some of the most prominent men in the land. In April 1621 Pym said that parliament was the 'great eye of the kingdom to find out offences and punish them', and at the end of the session he told the House that 'We have donn greate works . . . Judgment, the which hath slept theis 300 yeears and is the greatest benifit that may be, is now revived.'[79] Although his arithmetic was wrong, his confidence was probably justified. It is possible that, in the course of their searches among the medieval Parliament Rolls, members had come across two statements which helped to convince them of their own ancient worth. In a Commons' petition of 1377 the claim was made that it was 'only to parliament that men may come when they are unjustly aggrieved by the king's ministers', while eleven years later, in the Merciless Parliament, the Lords declared that high crimes could be tried only in parliament, by its law and procedure.[80]

One of the dangers inherent in making statements about the inheritance of the Commons of 1621 is that these can exaggerate the degree of certainty felt by members. Sometimes, no doubt, the House whistled loudly only to keep its courage up, and it is

[78] *C.D.* iii, 249, 271; vi, 156; Nicholas, *Proceedings*, ii, 69. It is interesting to note that, in his definition of impeachment, Elsynge says that 'Judgment is not to bee given till they [i.e. the Commons] demand it . . .': Elsynge, 302. In the case of Field, it was resolved to send a message to the Lords warning them that the Commons proposed 'in dew time' to demand judgment, though in fact they did not do so: *C.D.* iii, 271.

[79] *C.D.* ii, 303; iii, 353. The figurative meaning of 'eye' in the seventeenth century was the 'seat of intelligence' or 'light': *Oxford English Dictionary*, under 'eye'.

[80] *Rot. Parl.* iii, 23, 236; Richardson and Sayles, 1-2; Clarke, 'Forfeitures and Treason', 125.

possible to catch glimpses of uncertainties lurking beneath its perhaps too confident gestures. Maude Clarke believed that the Master of the Wards, Lionel Cranfield, was giving expression to a widely held point of view when he observed, referring largely to Coke's statement of 8 March on judicature,

Sorry, we [are] so uncertain in the Power of this House.—More puzzled this Parliament than ever before.—Told, in the beginning of this Parliament, we [are] an absolute Court: That, in some Cases, we [are] to judge alone; in others, with the Lords; in others the Lords alone.[81]

But his remarks may be less significant than they sound: Cranfield seems by this time to have retreated from the rather advanced and aggressive position he had adopted in assisting in the early stages of the parliamentary onslaught,[82] and he was speaking during the anxious days when the Commons were claiming the right to punish Floyd—a claim which many members quickly recognised as untenable. This is not of course to deny that uncertainties existed, but they were perhaps surprisingly few. Although the Commons of 1621 may not have had the assurance of their successors who, in Plucknett's opinion, framed a theory of impeachment which asserted that they were 'the grand inquest of the nation, and the whole proceeding was merely the common law trial on indictment transferred to the larger scene of parliament',[83] nevertheless they had the confidence and knowledge to carry through, relatively smoothly, proceedings against men of the stature of Bacon.

There was clearly ample opportunity for the medieval heritage to influence events in the early seventeenth century. It was a complex inheritance and there is evidence that Coke and his contemporaries were aware of its variety. Coke's influential belief that parliamentary powers were static and unalterable,[84]

[81] *C.J.* i, 602.
[82] See below, pp. 89, 110. He was also at this time (May) accused of having told the Lords that the Commons were not a court of record: M. Prestwich, *Cranfield; Politics and Profits under the Early Stuarts* (Oxford, 1966), 316-7.
[83] Plucknett, 'Origin of Impeachment', 47.
[84] Clarke, 'Origin of Impeachment', 266-7.

combined with Pym's faith in the blessings of medieval judicature, make it likely that their colleagues had some realisation of the worth of their inheritance. How far that inheritance influenced their actions cannot be precisely calculated. The men who guided the development of parliamentary judicature in 1621 lived in 1621, not in 1376 or 1386, but it is reasonable to believe that when they looked over their shoulders or studied the records, they were not doing so merely to search out convenient excuses for their present actions.

CHAPTER III

Judicature in James I's earlier
Parliaments, 1604-14

This study has so far been concerned with what Selden called 'Judgments against Delinquents', and with the antecedents of that parliamentary judicature—the process involving the co-operation of both Houses—which decisively re-emerged in 1621. But it must be remembered that 'Judgments against Delinquents' was only one of six different types of judicature which, in Selden's view, belonged to parliament. Although he did not discuss them, he listed the remaining five: reversing erroneous judgments given in parliament; reversing erroneous judgments given in the King's Bench; deciding difficult or long delayed suits; hearing private petitions; and enforcing various parliamentary privileges.[1] Now Selden was writing in about 1626, and, although his phraseology suggests that he believed that these powers resided in the Houses at that time, his list is not necessarily valid for the period preceding this date. James I's parliaments, for instance, did not necessarily possess all these powers. However, if they possessed any of them, it is worth asking whether such powers had any connection with the development of the type of judicature which is the main concern of this study. Unlike that parliamentary judicature, the exercise of these powers did not depend upon co-operation between the two Houses: the first three were the peculiar responsibility of the Lords, while the last two might be used by either House alone. Such unicameral judicature might seem to have little to do with a judicature which depended upon the joint action of both Houses, but, as will be shown, there is evidence to suggest that the exercise of unicameral judicature assisted the re-birth of parliamentary judicature. Moreover,

[1] Selden, *Of Judicature*, 8-10.

while parliamentary judicature developed, so too did certain aspects of unicameral judicature: in some ways, both form part of the same story.

The Lords and Commons of the early seventeenth century possessed the right to apply their separate judicial powers in a number of areas, which gradually became more clearly defined and, in some respects, extended. But in the century and a half which preceded the accession of James I, these powers, like those of parliamentary judicature, were little used. This was the conclusion reached in the eighteenth century, by Francis Hargrave, and there is little reason to question his findings which were based on an intensive study of the parliamentary *Journals*.[2] Hargrave acknowledged the existence of a unicameral judicature by Lords and Commons in cases of privilege, but apart from this he found only occasional instances of a Lords' jurisdiction on writs of error, arising from judgments in other courts, and only one order by the Lords for a writ of *scire facias*.[3] Later in his survey, Hargrave recalled another type of judicature, represented in the medieval records by the appointment, at the beginning of each parliament, of receivers and triers of petitions. But this judicature, too, was slumbering by the beginning of the seventeenth century.[4]

In practice, therefore, in the early years of James I's reign, the separate judicature of the two Houses was hardly extensive. In and after 1621 this was to change, and attention will be paid to these changes in subsequent chapters, but for the moment the judicature of the Commons extended only to matters concerning their privileges and their members, while the similar powers of the Lords were augmented only by their jurisdiction in cases of error.[5] Although these powers might be refined and improved in specific ways—and the Commons clearly gained a notable victory in winning the right to determine disputed elections—such jurisdictions did not necessarily point the way to the revival of a procedure involving the

---

[2] Hargrave's preface to Hale, pp. vi-viii. This preface, provided for the eighteenth-century edition of Hale's treatise, is still the most thorough work on the subject of the Lords' jurisdiction: Relf, p. x.

[3] Hargrave's preface to Hale, pp. vii-ix.

[4] Ibid. p. xxxiii.

[5] Ibid. pp. iii-iv.

co-operation of the two Houses. Judicature on writs of error concerned the Lords alone, and this was unequivocally acknowledged by Noy in 1621;[6] while matters involving members and privileges were normally settled by the House concerned, without reference to the other. As far back as 1542 the Commons had realised that, if they were to maintain their privileges, they must stand on their own feet.[7]

Yet, largely in the name of privilege, James's first two parliaments dealt with a number of cases which exhibit some unusual features, and which therefore require examination. The cases were those of John Thornborough, bishop of Bristol, in 1604, Dr John Cowell, Sir Stephen Proctor and Henry Spiller in 1610, and Richard Neile, bishop of Lincoln, in 1614. Apart from a number of detailed procedural points, these cases are of interest in two ways. First, in those concerned primarily with privilege, circumstances compelled the Houses to act together, however unwillingly. Secondly, Lord Chancellor Ellesmere thought that the Commons of 1610 usurped judicial power, citing as examples their proceedings against Proctor and Spiller,[8] and there is no doubt that, although the Commons were partly concerned with Proctor's offence against their privileges, they were also anxious to punish him for other sins. Before these five cases are examined, it is worth noting that when Robert Bowyer, Clerk of the Parliaments from 1610 to 1621, worked over his own and his predecessor's parliamentary records, compiling reports on special topics, three of the six were devoted to the cases of Thornborough, Cowell and Proctor.[9] There is no means of knowing why he chose to write

---

[6] *C.D.* ii, 338. Also by Coke, *Fourth Part of the Institutes*, 21.

[7] In the case of George Ferrers, M.P. for Plymouth, who had been arrested for debt. The Commons first turned to the Lords for help, but subsequently refused the Lord Chancellor's offer of a writ on the ground that their serjeant's mace was sufficient warrant for Ferrers' release: Petyt MS 538/1, ff. 1v-4. For the dating of this case, see H. H. Leonard, 'Ferrers' Case; a note', *Bull. Inst. Hist. Res.* xlii (1969), 230-4.

[8] He also gave other examples, but, as these suggest a different type of trespass, it will avoid confusion if they are considered separately: see pp. 80-1, below.

[9] These reports are in Petyt MSS 538/1, ff. 147ff (Thornborough), 538/2, ff. 148-55 (Proctor), ff. 158-65 (Cowell). The other three reports are of the debate in 1614 on impositions, in which Bowyer devotes a good deal of space to the complaint against Neile, and of the cases of Shirley and Goodwin in 1604. They are, respectively, in Petyt MSS 538/2, ff. 247-64v, 538/1, ff. 93-131v, ff.

up these proceedings, but he clearly regarded them as in some way significant.

The bishop of Bristol offended the house of commons because he had written a book in which he discussed a debate there on the subject of the proposed union with Scotland. In his work, he had answered objections raised against the union, as well as made public what had been discussed in the Commons. In consequence, he had, in the opinion of the lower House, increased the risk of dissension in the kingdom and dishonoured both Houses. Two proposals for action were advanced: that he should be summoned to the Bar of the Commons, as was usual in cases of privilege; or that the House should go to the king, in whose name publication of the book had presumably been authorised. But because the bishop was a member of the Lords, the Commons appointed a committee of eleven members to draw up a message about the book and their grievance for despatch to the upper House. On receiving the message, the Lords asked for time to read the book. They replied on 30 May, proposing a conference in three days' time 'at the Outward Chamber, near the Parliament Presence', in the meantime calling before them two men, Field and Chard, whom they examined and charged with offences in connection with their printing of the bishop's book.[10] The Commons next appointed a committee of fifty or more members, charged with the task of examining the book and preparing for the forthcoming conference. Sir Henry Hobart was appointed to open the Commons' statement, described as the 'Complaint of the House', to the committee of twenty-four nominated by the Lords. Having heard the objections raised by the lower House, the peers excused themselves from discussion to report to their House which, on 5 June, decided that the Commons could best be satisfied by a voluntary acknowledgement from

182-96. In the account of the first session of 1610 in Petyt MS 537/14 which differs slightly from the printed *Commons Journal* the passages relating to Proctor are frequently marked in the margin with a line (—) or a P.

[10] Petyt MS 538/1, 148-149v; *L.J.* ii, 306, 308, 309; *C.J.* i, 226-8; Spedding, iii, 208.

the bishop of his error. This, together with an apology, was eventually extracted from Thornborough, who insisted that he had acted in ignorance and without malice, having intended only to show his support for the projected union.[11] On 9 June, at a further conference, Salisbury reported the bishop's submission, declared that the Lords had rebuked him, and stated that only his rank and position had deterred them from greater severity. Several members of the Commons reacted unfavourably to Bacon's report of these proceedings: demands were made that the bishop should either submit in person to the Commons or that his written submission should be examined and incorporated in the records of the House.[12] After a further reference to the committee these rather extravagant demands were eventually reduced, and on 21 June a group of members, headed by Sir Francis Hastings, was sent to the Lords with a temperately worded message. Wishing to be more fully satisfied, the Commons asked for a copy of the account which they presumed the Lords had compiled of the bishop's acknowledgement of his error, so that they might incorporate it in their own proceedings.[13]

At this point the record begins to fail. The Lords replied to the Commons' request by proposing a conference for 30 June. This meeting certainly took place, but what happened we hardly know. The *Commons Journal* has only the slightest mention of Hastings' report: it contains words which may indicate that the Lords had handed over the bishop's submission but we cannot be sure.[14] In any case it perhaps hardly matters. The struggle between the Houses had ended in a draw: the Commons had jostled the Lords into rebuking one of their own members at the insistence of the lower House; but in doing so the Lords had preserved their dignity and protected the bishop from the worst excesses of the Commons' anger.

This case was concerned purely with a matter of privilege,

[11] *L.J.* ii, 314; *C.J.* i, 230-2.
[12] *L.J.* ii, 315; *C.J.* i, 234, 236; Spedding, iii, 208-10. The speakers in this angry debate were Sir Thomas Ridgeway, Sir John Holles, Sir Herbert Crofts, Sir Robert Wingfield, Mr Secretary Herbert.
[13] *L.J.* ii, 325; *C.J.* i, 244.
[14] *L.J.* ii, 332; *C.J.* i, 251.

but because the bishop was a member of the Lords and the issue was raised by the Commons, the two Houses were forced into some kind of collaboration in order to settle the matter. This involved them in a joint committee meeting, a practice which was to assist in the successful revival of parliamentary judicature in the 1620s; and the Lords had to acknowledge the Commons' initiative in the case by making arrangements to satisfy them on its outcome.

In addition, by preparing their case in committees rather than at meetings of the whole House, the Commons were making use of a procedure which was to serve them well in the 1620s. This procedure had been increasingly used in the last years of Elizabeth's reign, and by 1621 it had reached considerable maturity. In the 1620s, when the use of committees by the Commons materially assisted the development of parliamentary judicature, the House was employing an established procedure which, apart from minor modifications, does not seem to have required much further development in those years: there is, in the field of parliamentary judicature, little difference between the powers exercised by committees in 1621 and 1626. In the earlier years of James's reign important developments did occur in the use of committees in connection with judicature, and these will be noted, but our knowledge of them is limited by the sparse nature of the material surviving on the Commons of these years compared with the period from 1621 onwards.[15]

In between the case of the bishop of Bristol and those of 1610 an abortive attempt was made to create a special type of judicature to deal with the authors of the Gunpowder Plot. It appears that Sir Robert Wingfield and others wanted to petition the king to permit the trial in parliament of those involved, so that punishments in excess of those provided by the law might be imposed. The mind boggles at what might have been devised, but the proposal came to nothing, though

[15] J. E. Neale, *The Elizabethan House of Commons* (London, 1954), 377; W. Notestein, *The Winning of the Initiative by the House of Commons* (London, 1962), 43-4.

after the trial and execution of the conspirators a bill of attainder was passed.[16]

The cases of Cowell and Proctor began at virtually the same moment, in the last days of February 1610, but that of the latter was much the more protracted. Cowell's book, *The Interpreter*, a law dictionary, had been published at Cambridge in 1607 and the row which broke out shortly after the beginning of the parliamentary session of 1610, derived from its definitions of the words 'subsidy', 'king', 'parliament', and 'prerogative'. Cowell had emphasised the king's absolute power, thereby damaging, in the Commons' view, the authority of parliament.[17] In origin, therefore, the case was similar to that of the bishop of Bristol; but although it developed along much the same lines, the Commons' approach was both more sophisticated and more determined, and Cowell was not let off as lightly as the bishop.

The complaint against Cowell was introduced into the Commons on 23 February, probably by Hoskyns; it was at once referred to the committee of grievances, a committee of the whole House, which appears for the first time in 1610. This committee was destined to perform a function discharged, in Elizabeth's reign, by the Secretaries and other councillors, and was to have a vital share in the preparation of cases presented by the Commons to the Lords in the 1620s.[18] Even at this stage it was already very busy touting for and investigating complaints. The committee read the book but, in order to investigate it more closely, set up a sub-committee. This sub-committee reported presumably that there was a case to answer

---

[16] *L.J.* ii, 366, 367, 370, 399, 401, 404-6, 435, 445; *C.J.* i, 293, 303, 308; L. B. Osborn, *The Life, Letters and Writings of John Hoskyns 1566-1638* (New Haven, 1937), 24; *The Parliamentary Diary of Robert Bowyer 1606-7*, ed. D. H. Willson (Minneapolis, 1931), 7. On 9 November, 1605, James himself, in a speech to parliament, said that he might arrange for the trial of the conspirators in parliament: B. M. Lansdowne MS 513, ff. 10-10v. The version of the speech given in this manuscript differs from that in the *Lords Journal* which makes no mention of this proposal: *L.J.* ii, 357-9.

[17] Foster, *Parliament 1610*, i, 18, 25. In 1604, the bishop of Bristol had offended the Commons rather than the whole parliament, though the Commons claimed that he had dishonoured both Houses: see p. 57, above.

[18] Notestein, *Winning of the Initiative*, 32, 40 n. 1. The first committee of the whole House appeared in about 1610: ibid. 37.

because on the 24th it was asked to consider a charge. At the same time, the House discussed procedure: there must have been a proposal for unilateral action by the Commons alone, because Francis Bacon objected to this on the ground that Cowell's views were not merely the concern of the lower House, but of the king and the whole body of parliament. He then proposed that the Commons should 'have Conjunction with the Lords, for the Punishment of this Man'[19] and the sub-committee was asked to consider how this could best be arranged.[20] On the 27th it recommended to the House that a message be drawn up and sent to the Lords, pointing out the dangerous nature of Cowell's book and asking for their participation in examining it and punishing its author. To this the House agreed and a delegation of forty members presented the message to the Lords.

Because the Commons chose to act in this way, it might at first sight seem as though they were abandoning their own unicameral jurisdiction in the case. As the issue was one of privilege and as Cowell, unlike Thornborough, was not a member of the Lords, the Commons might well have determined to deal with him themselves. Indeed, eleven years later, the Recorder reminded the Commons of Cowell and said that 'we might have iudged him owr selves'.[21] But Bacon had made the really telling point: Cowell had offended against the privileges of parliament and not merely of the Commons. A few days later, the Lord Treasurer confirmed this view: the case concerned all parts of parliament—king, Lords and Commons—and was sufficiently unusual for him to propose a search of the precedents.[22] Yet if the reasons which now per-

---

[19] S. B. Chrimes has suggested that Bacon made this proposal to ensure that any attack on Cowell would be by both Houses, supported by the king, rather than by the Commons alone with its implications of challenge to the king and his prerogative: 'The Constitutional Ideas of Dr John Cowell', *E.H.R.* lxiv (1949), 468.

[20] *C.J.* i, 399-400; Spedding, iv, 161. Beaulieu in a letter of 1 March to Trumbull, appears to be the only source for a story that the Commons had petitioned the king for permission to proceed against Cowell. He says that if the king grants it the Commons will, it is thought, punish him severely: *Memorials of Affairs of State in the Reigns of Q. Elizabeth and K. James I; collected (chiefly) from the Original Papers of the Right Honourable Sir Ralph Winwood*, ed. E. Sawyer (London, 1725), iii, 125.

[21] *C.D.* iii, 207.

[22] Foster, *Parliament 1610*, i, 186, 189.

suaded the Commons to join with the Lords differed from those
which dictated their decision in 1604, the result was the same.
The lower House was once again associating with the peers
and venturing into unfamiliar territory in defence of parliamentary privilege.

The receipt by the Lords of the Commons' message gave rise
to some debate. The archbishop of Canterbury, embarrassed
by the fact that *The Interpreter* had been dedicated to him,
criticised the Commons for wasting time and neglecting the
king's business, and for using the opportunity to air their
prejudices against the civil and ecclesiastical law. The Lord
Privy Seal and Lord Knollys suggested that the Lords should
be prepared to hear what the Commons had to say but that
they should avoid entering into argument with them. Saye
wanted the request dealt with sympathetically, while Salisbury
warned the House not to forget the king's interest in a matter
of this kind but commended the Commons' desire as reasonable. He said that if the Commons would exhibit the cause of
offence the Lords would examine and, if need be, punish.[23]
At the end of the debate the Lords agreed to hear the Commons'
complaints and on 2 March the meeting of committees took
place.[24] In a cordial atmosphere Martin explained which parts
of the book the Commons found objectionable and the meeting
ended with the Lords stating that they could make no reply
until they had consulted their House. There, three days later,
the Lord Chancellor declared that three courses of action were
open to the Lords: they could join with the Commons as
requested, in which case decisions about procedure would be
needed; they could refuse to join, in which case the Commons
would expect an explanation; or they could hold a second
meeting with the lower House to consider what to do next.
The Lord Treasurer helped the House to make up its mind.
He again said that he approved of what the Commons had
done but he felt unable to agree to punish Cowell for a book
written 'out of parliament and not touching any particular
member, without knowing whether there have been like

[23] Ibid. 18-19, 180; *C.J.* i, 400; Petyt MS 538/2, f. 161v
[24] *L.J.* ii, 560; Foster, *Parliament 1610*, i, 19, 23, 181, 183-4.

precedents'. He therefore proposed that the clerk be ordered to search for precedents and that the Commons be asked for another conference.[25]

This conference was in fact used to announce that the king had intervened in the case. Salisbury told the Commons' committee that James rejected the views expressed in the book and would have prevented its publication if he had known of it. He now intended to have all copies suppressed.[26]

This virtually ended the matter as far as parliament was concerned. In an audience on the 21st the king reiterated his intention and four days later the proclamation calling in the book was published. The Commons were apparently satisfied because, in sending thanks to James, they abandoned the usual procedure of using the Speaker as their messenger and appointed a delegation led by the Chancellor of the Exchequer.[27] But in reality this solution was a compromise, if some of the letter-writers of the time are to be believed. Parliament had abandoned the chase out of respect for the king's wish that Cowell should not be harassed further; but James had been compelled to place him under house arrest because he had been unable to justify some of his definitions when the king had examined him.[28] The house of lords may or may not have been on the verge of collaborating with the Commons when the king intervened, but James had not been able to exercise complete control over the situation and the measures taken against Cowell and his book would doubtless not have been adopted but for the proceedings in parliament. Furthermore, the

[25] Foster, *Parliament 1610*, i, 25, 27, 186; *L.J.* ii, 561.

[26] Foster, *Parliament 1610*, i, 29-31.

[27] Ibid. i, 45; *C.S.P. Dom. 1603-10*, 594. The change in customary procedure is specifically noted in Foster, ii, 363.

[28] Winwood, iii, 131, gives Beaulieu's letter of 15 March explaining parliament's attitude. Two days earlier Edmondes had reported to Trumbull that James's first reaction to the book had merely been one of disapproval but that he had been persuaded to examine Cowell a second time. From this had stemmed Cowell's committal, until he could make answer, to the house of an alderman: Winwood, iii, 137; Foster, *Parliament 1610*, i, 189n; *H.M.C. Report on the Manuscripts of the Marquess of Downshire* (London, 1924-40), ii, 262. Cowell remained under house arrest for at least the next six weeks: on 30 April Bancroft asked Salisbury for his release: *C.S.P. Dom. 1603-10*, 605. It should, however, be noted that Professor Chrimes regarded the decision over Cowell as largely a victory for the crown and prerogative power: pp. 471-3.

circumstances of the case had compelled the Houses to associate with each other in Cowell's prosecution, and had forced them to devise procedures to combat an assault on the privileges of parliament, rather than to deal with the more normal infringements of the privileges of one chamber or the other. Furthermore, such joint action was valuable preparation for the years ahead, when the Houses would deal with cases concerning the public interest rather than their privileges. Indeed, it seems possible to observe a progression from the lesser to the greater —from a defence of the privileges of one House to a defence of the privileges of both Houses, with a concern for the public interest as the third stage.

When Ellesmere wrote his observations on James's first parliament, he drew attention to the willingness of the Commons in the fourth session to usurp judicial power. In particular, he protested that they 'did ... convent before them Sir Stephen Proctor, knight, and Henry Spiller, esq., upon private information and suggestions. A case of rare example, and if it be drawn to a precedent may have a dangerous consequence.'[29] In and after 1621 it became common practice for the Commons to 'convent' men before them, but at this date such procedure was normally associated with issues of privilege. In Proctor's case, no question of privilege arose until the hearing was already in progress; while in Spiller's case, this issue probably did not appear at all. The proceedings against both men suggest that Ellesmere's strictures were justified.

In the course of their dealings with Proctor, the Commons doubtless widened their procedural experience. In addition, by acting against a man whom James claimed was his servant,

[29] Foster, *Parliament 1610,* i, 280. Ellesmere does not elaborate and we therefore do not know his precise objections. As both Proctor and Spiller were minor servants of the king and therefore supposed to be immune from Commons' examination or punishment, he may have been objecting on these grounds. But he does not mention that the two men were the king's servants—and James did not make this point when he reprimanded the Commons for their dealings with Proctor. In fact, the implication of Ellesmere's remarks is that he was quarrelling with the methods of the Commons rather than with the category of person attacked, though the two types of criticism cannot be completely separated from each other and, probably, both worried him.

they were venturing on to unfamiliar territory and taking an important, if on this occasion largely unsuccessful, step towards the position they were to establish in the 1620s. Moreover, the case enabled them to test the strength of purpose of the Lords, as Cowell's had done.

Proctor had been employed in executing the penal laws and in collecting the resulting fines. Of course, many members regarded this as a most worthy occupation, but there is no doubt that they also believed that the laws were being insufficiently enforced. Moreover, Proctor's appointment had adversely affected the power and profits of the justices of the peace, many of whom sat in the Commons. The case against Proctor should perhaps be seen in this context, though his offence was more specific.[30]

In the course of his duties Proctor had discovered the existence of a number of abuses, including what would now be called a protection racket. Although he reported his findings and proposed remedies, he also proved unable to resist the temptations of his office and his sins provided the lower House with exactly the material it was looking for in the early weeks of the session of 1610. On 24 February the Commons heard a complaint against Proctor—we do not know from whom—and would doubtless have punished him rapidly had not the king intervened and imprisoned him.[31] Instead, they seem to have referred the matter to their committee of grievances for, on 8 March, Sir Edwin Sandys reported that in the committee's view the commission under which Proctor had acted was grievous, and had been obtained from the king by deceit. The position of the Commons at this point bears some resemblance to that of their successors eleven years later. In 1621, having condemned various patents in a manner which resembled their predecessors' treatment of Proctor's commission, the Commons had to decide how to punish the patentees. On that occasion, they resolved to go to the Lords. However, the Commons of 1610 chose to 'convent' Proctor before their

---

[30] C. Roberts, *The Growth of Responsible Government in Stuart England* (Cambridge, 1966), 12-13.

[31] Spedding, iv, 96, 104; Foster, *Parliament 1610*, ii, 33. For the view that the Commons, if left alone, would have proceeded against Proctor, see Beaulieu's letter to Trumbull of 1 March: Winwood, iii, 125.

own House. But they were faced with the difficulty that Proctor, as the king's prisoner, was beyond their reach: they therefore resolved to petition the king to release him to them for censure. At the same time a member, Sir John Mallory, who appears to have been the author of the whole attack on Proctor, declared himself ready to present detailed evidence in the case.[32] The House was thus firmly embarked on proceedings against the man, and not merely against his commission. Whether the Commons of 1610 really had jurisdiction over the latter is perhaps a moot point: no theoretical justification is to be found in the records, but in 1621 action against patents was vindicated on the ground that grievances were the special province of representatives of the realm.[33] But there is little doubt that in 1610 they had no right to deal as they did with Proctor himself, as Ellesmere pointed out.

The king assented to the Commons' petition to release Proctor to them for censure, and the House arranged for its committee of grievances to conduct the investigation, thereby delegating to it important powers which were to be used many times in the future. Little is heard of this examination in the records of the next fortnight, though on 21 March the committee heard Proctor and his accusers face to face; on the same day, in an address to both Houses, James professed that he had been ignorant of Proctor's abuses until they had told him of them, but stated that he was now willing to see them reformed.[34] At the beginning of April the Commons adjourned for a fortnight, but after Easter the examination continued, and reached a climax in the early part of May. On the 2nd Proctor was brought from the Gatehouse, where he lay as the king's prisoner, and at the Bar of the Commons was committed as their prisoner to the custody of the serjeant. A week later, after fairly intensive preparations, he was brought once more to the Bar where he was charged by the Speaker. He used the occasion to deliver an attack upon his chief accuser, Sir John Mallory, thus introducing the question of privilege, and he

[32] *C.J.* i, 407. Clayton Roberts says (p. 11) that Mallory was engaged in a personal feud with Proctor.
[33] Foster, 'Patents and Monopolies', 75.
[34] *C.J.* i, 408, 412, 415; Foster, *Parliament 1610*, i, 48; ii, 63, 361.

seems to have denied at least some of the charges, though unfortunately the record at this point is very sketchy. The proceedings certainly included a discussion of possible punishments, but Proctor appears to have remained in the serjeant's care. On 10 May he petitioned the Commons for a trial and on the 12th they debated their next step.[35] They were now faced not only with the original charges against him, but also with the breach of privilege resulting from his speech against Mallory. They debated whether they might fine him and whether for the 'abuses offered to the commonwealth' they ought not to ask the king to commit him, but the only conclusion they seem to have reached was that for his attack on Mallory they were entitled to commit him either to the serjeant or to the Tower.[36] They arranged to resume their discussion on the 14th but on that day a second intervention by the king brought matters to a head. Through the Chancellor of the Exchequer James complained that the Commons had exceeded the authority he had bestowed upon them: he had given them licence to censure Proctor; they had exceeded this by committing the king's prisoner to the custody of their serjeant. James instructed them in what he considered to be the correct procedure: they should censure Proctor and then return him to the custody of the king who would take cognisance of the Commons' censure and deliver him once more to the House. It could then proceed against him either by bill or by petition and the king would eventually deal with the one or the other in a suitable manner.[37]

[35] *C.J.* i, 423-8; Foster, *Parliament 1610*, ii, 76, 366, 368.

[36] *C.J.* i, 428; Foster, *Parliament 1610*, ii, 368. It may well have been in this debate that Moore made the speech that S. R. Gardiner printed on pp. 124-5 of *Parliamentary Debates in 1610* (Camden Society lxxxi: London, 1862). Although Gardiner could not date the speech, it presumably occurred between 9 May (when charges against Proctor were read in the Commons) and 15 May (when a committee was appointed to frame a bill against him), for Moore proposed drawing up a bill to enumerate his offences and attainting him of *praemunire*. As precedents, he gave the case of Peach and the attainder of Hugh Despenser.

[37] Foster, *Parliament 1610*, ii, 374. It has been stated (Roberts, 13) that the Commons had the right to employ procedure by bill to deal with infringements of the law, and procedure by petition to secure the redress of grievances that were merely onerous and not unlawful. However, this statement can be challenged. In 1614, a committee considering impositions recommended to the Commons that they should proceed 'first by bill to the lords and for fear itt might be thear

Before considering the debate which followed this message it is perhaps worth speculating upon the motives for James's intervention. Ostensibly he was objecting to what the Commons had done twelve days previously but if this explanation is to be accepted it is then necessary to account for his very slow reaction. It is more likely that the king had become increasingly alarmed at the growing boldness of the Commons in dealing with one of his servants and that he used this excuse to divert them in a more harmless direction. To propose to the Commons procedure by bill or petition was to do just this. Both methods involved securing the king's consent. Moreover, it is possible that, by suggesting to the Commons that they should draw up a bill, James was proposing something very like the course they should have adopted in the first place, if an order of 1621 is any guide: '. . . if a particular Man desire that his Grief should be heard and remedied in this House [i.e. the Commons] . . . he must prefer a Bill to that Purpose into the House.'[38] This order is, of course, not contemporary with Proctor's case, but it is a reference to the procedure, well established since the middle ages, by which petitions presented to the Commons were translated into private bills designed to remedy the complaint.[39] If, as seems likely, James was proposing the adoption of this procedure, he was really telling them to revert to a time-honoured practice—a practice which could probably have coped quite well with Mallory's original complaint against Proctor.

At any rate, James's intervention in the case worked, in a way rarely to be repeated, as the debate on his message showed. Proctor was returned to the Gatehouse where the king had originally imprisoned him and, for the moment, even escaped the censure which James had authorised. Furthermore, the House acknowledged that he was no longer in its hands. It

stopped as itt was the last parliament that therfore we should put up our petition to the king to, as desiring rather itt should dy att his maiesties feet then in the hands of ill nurses': Bodl. MS Eng. Hist. C. 286, p. 67. This proposal tends to blur this distinction between bills and petitions, and indicates that the House might employ both methods simultaneously.

[38] Nicholas, *Proceedings*, i, 75. This was, of course, to be altered by the judicial developments of 1621.

[39] Erskine May, 609; Relf, p. xix.

then resolved to petition the king to release him a second time for censure and execution of judgment, and it seems to have been very ready, though no decision was taken, to fall in with James's proposal of procedure by bill to deal with Proctor's abuses of his commission. On the 15th the king agreed to release his prisoner to the Commons, but explicitly told the House that it could not punish the misdemeanours against the state. Immediately after receiving this answer the Commons set up a committee[40] to frame a bill and then debated how they should punish Proctor for his speech against Mallory. They dismissed a proposal that he should be required to submit personally to Mallory, on the ground that he had committed contempt of the whole House; and they concluded this phase of the case by resolving to censure him for the contempt and imprison him in the Tower.[41]

On 6 June the Commons received the bill from their committee, and during the next month passed it through all its stages. They refused the petition of Proctor for counsel to plead for him on that part of the bill dealing directly with the abuses in the exercise of his commission, but they agreed that he should have legal advice for the section which concerned the sale of his lands, from which it was intended to repay his creditors and those he had wronged. Private bill procedure required that the supporters and opponents of the bill should be heard: though the record at this stage is scanty, there is evidence that some such hearings took place. On 5 July the house of lords entered the case for the first time when it received the bill from the Commons.[42]

The bill is to be found in the house of lords' records under the date on which it was received from the Commons.[43] It

[40] Mallory was not a member, so that even if the Commons were reverting to correct procedure by having a bill framed, Mallory, as the person accusing, was apparently not being required to undertake the work.

[41] *C.J.* i, 428; Foster, *Parliament 1610*, ii, 374-5.

[42] Petyt MS 537/14, f. 97v; *C.J.* i, 436, 440, 442-3; *L.J.* ii, 635; Foster, *Parliament 1610*, ii, 149, 381. Private bills have long been recognised as judicial or semi-judicial in character. Parties appeared by counsel and witnesses were examined: Erskine May, 609; A. F. Pollard, *The Evolution of Parliament* (London, 1920), 118; C. H. McIlwain, *The High Court of Parliament and its Supremacy* (New Haven, 1910), 222-4; Foster, 'Patents and Monopolies', 75, 84 n. 95.

[43] It is printed by Foster, *Parliament 1610*, ii, 412-4.

F

begins by reciting Proctor's offences and says that having been 'openly convented and heard at large in parliament, [he] was censured to be most faulty and deserving to be punished in some other degree than such as by ordinary course of justice could be laid upon him, the offences being so exorbitant'. Among its subsequent clauses it cancels his patents and commissions, disqualifies him from office, degrades him from knighthood, makes provision for the payment of his debts and debars him from the presence of the king, queen and heir apparent.

Having failed to influence the Commons, Proctor now turned his attention to the house of lords. On the day of the bill's second reading he petitioned the peers to hear him with his counsel and drew their attention to the Commons' rejection of this request. The Lords then debated the reasons for the Commons' refusal, decided to accede to Proctor's petition, and appointed 17 July for hearing him and 'those that could object against him'.[44] On that day, Proctor and his counsel were duly heard at the Bar, though what they said we do not know. The bill was certainly read out and Mallory and his supporters were present to put their case, but matters cannot have progressed very far when the Lords interrupted proceedings. Explaining that they had insufficient time for the case, they referred the whole question, including the bill, to a committee which was appointed to meet on the following day. One wonders—with little hope that the issue can be resolved—whether this was an excuse, designed to withdraw the weaknesses in the Commons' case from the glare of publicity and to make the proceedings more palatable to the king who was on that very day being petitioned by both Houses to allow his servants to be arrested and sued as freely as other men.[45] For, having examined the bill in the presence of the parties, the committee reported that Proctor had committed no

[44] Foster, *Parliament 1610*, i, 137-8; *L.J.* ii, 644. In the debate on the petition Lord Saye showed most sympathy for the Commons' point of view, but he declared himself in favour of hearing Proctor.

[45] Foster, *Parliament 1610*, i, 146; *L.J.* ii, 647; Roberts, 1. There is a 'Breviate of the Bill and Answer' in S.P. Dom 14/54, ff. 63-64v. The answers are merely brief rejections and denials of the charges and there is no indication when they were made.

offence which would justify passing it.[46] However, this conclusion failed to commend itself to a group of peers, of whom Salisbury was the most prominent. Some members wondered whether evidence had been suppressed and felt that the Commons would not have passed the bill without justification. Presumably as a compromise, it was decided to ask the Commons for a conference, but although this was held the Commons had previously resolved to withhold their reasons for passing the bill. At the last minute, the lower House did produce supplementary evidence against Proctor, but the peers were unconvinced and the bill failed to secure their approval. In consequence, as the session ended, the only consolation available to the Commons and their sympathisers in the Lords was the exemption of Proctor from the scope of the general pardon which was then being proclaimed.[47]

The proceedings against Proctor were obviously unusual in certain respects. The early attempts of the Commons to deal with the case implied claims to a judicature they did not possess, and, if private bill procedure was subsequently followed, it did not start in the orthodox way. The substantial part taken initially by the Commons dictated their interest in the subsequent proceedings, and the Lords' refusal to pass the bill was a rebuff to them as well as to Mallory, who can probably be regarded as the bill's sponsor. The bill itself was concerned with punishing the man, rather than with remedying the situation he had exploited: in effect, as Professor Clayton

[46] It was doubtless influenced in reaching this conclusion by the character of the witnesses against Proctor: Roberts, 11; B. M. Lansdowne MS 167, f. 27v.

[47] C.J. i, 452-4; L.J. ii, 650-1, 655, 657; Foster, Parliament 1610, i, 156-8, 165-6; ii, 287, 386; Petyt MS 538/2, ff. 151v-152. Clayton Roberts expresses surprise at the persistence of the Commons in pressing the charges after their failure before the Lords' committee on the 18th. In explanation of this persistence he suggests three highly sophisticated reasons, based on the nature of Proctor's activities and the threat these implied to the position of J.P.s, and upon the desire of the Commons to proceed against royal officials on common fame: Roberts, 12. The third reason seems to be much more relevant to the situation in 1614 (see pp. 75 ff. below) and the explanation here to be much simpler—that the Commons persisted because the Lords encouraged them to do so, by rejecting their own committee's conclusion and by asking the lower House for a conference.

Roberts has pointed out, it was a bill of attainder, though the description is not used in the records of the case.[48]

The failure of the bill doubtless influenced members' views on the effectiveness of this procedure. The king had successfully protected his servant, hardly losing the initiative in the case, and even if the bill had passed the Lords, James could still have refused his consent. If Ellesmere's comments on the Commons' aspirations are correct, this procedure was unlikely to assist the development of their judicial powers, however respectably medieval its ancestry. It is interesting to notice that in February 1621 Coke was objecting to private bill procedure:[49] perhaps the case of Proctor helped to eliminate from the Commons' repertoire one process bequeathed to them by their ancestors.[50]

Ellesmere also drew attention to the case of Henry Spiller as another example of usurpation of judicial authority by the lower House.[51] The case began in much the same way: a private petition on behalf of one Felton was presented to the house of commons by Sir Francis Hastings, one of the knights of the shire from Somerset. It alleged that Spiller, a clerk of the Exchequer, had used his position to protect recusants from fines. The House referred the matter to the committee of grievances, making arrangements for both parties to be heard, together with counsel. But Felton proved unable to substantiate his charges and, as a false accuser, was imprisoned

[48] Roberts, 13 n. 2. Although, as he indicates, it was never called this it is interesting to note the precedent for attainder given by Moore (above, p. 67 n. 36). The process of attainder was presumably fairly well understood from what followed the trial and execution of the Gunpowder Plot conspirators (above, p. 59) though in the case of Proctor (as in that of Strafford) the bill was resorted to when other means of punishment had failed. Bills of attainder are, of course, a variety of private bill.

[49] Relf points out Coke's dislike of the method: p. xix. He objected to it because too often those sponsoring the bill were not well enough known to the Commons: Nicholas, *Proceedings*, i, 89. Even if his real objection was that it gave the Commons inadequate scope, he could hardly say so.

[50] It seems to have had few supporters as a possible alternative to the exercise of parliamentary judicature in 1621, but it may be noted that it was suggested as a way of resolving the Commons' difficulties over Floyd (below, see p. 124). In this case, perhaps an ineffective procedure was better than none at all.

[51] Foster, *Parliament 1610*, i, 280.

in the Fleet.[52] So far, the House seems to have been following correct private bill procedure, and with the failure of Felton's petition the matter should, presumably, have ended.[53] Yet a fortnight later, early in July 1610, Hastings made an attempt to have the House re-examine the matter. Not surprisingly, this gave rise to a debate concerning the extent of the Commons' authority; but although it was resolved to resume the examination little came of this and doubtless the failure of the case against Proctor played its part in causing the collapse of proceedings against Spiller.[54]

The attack on Spiller demonstrates the Commons' determination to press forward proceedings on their own responsibility, and it seems probable that it was this feature of the case which particularly worried Ellesmere. Yet in the end they failed, as they had failed against Proctor. The circumstances were different, but the two cases served to highlight weaknesses which were fundamentally similar. The Commons could not justify the powers on which they were depending, and legitimate procedures were inadequate to secure the desired results. On their own authority, they could not punish men who were not members and who had not violated their privileges, whether or not they were the king's servants. It was to be their successors in 1621 who found a way out of the impasse with the aid of an upper House which was prepared to co-operate and thus to assist the revival of parliamentary judicature. On the other hand, in addition to the wisdom produced by disillusionment, the case against Spiller provided a further opportunity to test the inviolability of royal servants, and it revitalised the medieval concept of punishment of false accusers—a notion

[52] The committee's opinion was that Spiller was a knave, but a crafty one: Foster, *Parliament 1610*, ii, 131.

[53] One manuscript has, at this point, '. . . the matter laid to sleep': Foster, *Parliament 1610*, ii, 131.

[54] Foster, *Parliament 1610*, ii, 128-31, 377-8; Williams, *James I*, i, 116; *C.J.* i, 435, 437, 440, 446-8; B. M. Lansdowne MS 486, ff. 148-148v; Spedding, iv, 47n; Roberts, 11-12, 14. There is evidence that Spiller's behaviour continued to cause anger after 1610. In 1614 a complaint against him was presented to the Council, while in 1621 the Commons grumbled about him and in 1626 resolved to present him to the king as a recusant: *C.S.P. Dom. 1611-18*, 239; Nicholas, *Proceedings*, i, 143-4; *C.J.* i, 838. I am grateful to Mr Conrad Russell for this last reference.

which may partly underlie the penalty inflicted on Davenport in 1621 for his accusation against Field.[55]

As the fourth session of James's long parliament drew to its close negotiations over the Great Contract became increasingly difficult, and in the fifth session, in the autumn of 1610, broke down altogether amid considerable acrimony. James declared himself tired of parliament's insolence, but during the next three years he did little to remove the underlying grievances which in part explained parliament's attitude. When therefore the assembly which was to become known as the Addled Parliament met in 1614, reasons existed for criticism of the government which the row over the undertakers aggravated. This tension should be remembered when one considers the case of Bishop Neile, who was known to be a member of the high-church party. This case was confined to matters of privilege, but the Commons were noticeably more belligerent than before and the hearings led to the raising of two issues which were to be of significance in the 1620s.

Impositions were a subject which generated great passion in 1614 and it was in connection with these that Neile uttered the intemperate remarks which caused the Commons to turn on him in fury. By the middle of May a committee of the lower House had reported that impositions not authorised by parliament were illegal, and it recommended that the Commons should confer with the Lords on what was clearly an issue of fundamental importance.[56] The request was duly sent to the Lords who debated it on 21 May, first as a House and then as a committee. Opening the debate the bishop spoke against the proposed conference on the ground that those who had taken the oaths of allegiance and supremacy had sworn to

[55] See below, pp. 137-8.
[56] T. L. Moir, *The Addled Parliament of 1614* (Oxford, 1958), 110, 112. In the previous month the Commons had begun to take action against patentees holding a glass monopoly and a monopoly in trade with France. They ordered the patentees to appear before them with their patents, and prepared for a committee to examine these. The cases of Lyons and Peach were quoted as precedents for proceeding against monopolists and, as Clayton Roberts points out, the Commons might well have embarked on the path they took in 1621. However, nothing seems to have come of these preliminary investigations, partly because the House became much occupied with impositions: Roberts, 21; *C.J.* i, 469-70, 472, 475.

uphold the privileges of the crown, one of which the conference would be questioning. However, the committee decided that the House should meet the Commons to listen to their point of view but not to discuss it with them. Yet when this was reported to the House on the following Monday, the 23rd, the decision was altered: the Lord Chancellor repeated a suggestion he had made on the previous Saturday, that the House should first consult the judges upon the legality of impositions. Neile emphatically supported this proposal and it was adopted, but in the course of his speech he said that if the Lords met the Commons the latter would probably deliver 'vndewtyfull and seditious speches vnfitte for us to heare'.[57] Consulting the judges proved to be a fruitless exercise because, through Chief Justice Coke, they excused themselves from giving an opinion. Moreover, implicit in Coke's speech was the conviction that the Lords should hear the Commons. On the 24th the peers therefore had to discuss the proposed meeting once more. For the third time Neile spoke against it and finally, on the 26th, the Lords replied to the Commons' request, turning it down.[58]

By this time reports had already reached the Commons of the bishop's speeches and the reaction which stemmed from these was to occupy a great deal of members' time right up to the dissolution early in June. The House began with a lengthy debate on 25 May, opened by Sir Mervyn Audley and Sir Robert Phelips, who were jointly responsible for reporting the

[57] *H.M.C. Report on the Manuscripts of the late Reginald Rawdon Hastings* (London, 1928-47), iv, 249-53; Moir, 118-9; *C.S.P. Ven. 1613-15*, 133; B. M. Lansdowne MS 513, ff. 146-150v.

[58] *H.M.C. Hastings*, iv, 256-65; Spedding, v, 58; Moir, 120-2; Petyt MS 537/8, ff. 285v-286 (which here is either part of, or a copy of, Bowyer's last scribbled book for 1614: cf. f. 285 and Foster, *Parliament 1610*, i, p. xxiv). Some of the speakers in these debates are of interest in the light of the development in the Lords of a party sympathetic to the Commons. Chandos, De la Warr, Dorset, Knyvett, North, Rich, St John, Saye, Sheffield, Southampton, and Spencer spoke in favour of hearing the Commons. They were opposed by the Lord Chancellor, the Lord Chamberlain, the archbishop of Canterbury, the bishops of Bath, Durham, St Asaph, and Winchester, and by Howard de Walden, Knollys, Nottingham, Worcester, Zouch, and rather lukewarmly by Pembroke. Of this second group, all but Howard de Walden and the four bishops were privy councillors. In the division on the 23rd almost all the privy councillors and bishops supported the proposal to consult the judges.

offensive speeches and naming the bishop as their author. The Commons then found themselves face to face with a difficulty which was to haunt them during the coming days: Neile's speeches were not to be found in the Lords' official *Journal*, so that their knowledge of them derived merely from rumour, or common fame, not a satisfactory basis for a reasoned complaint. Indeed—though this never came to the surface—the fact that the bishop's words were reported to the Commons at all was a breach of the Lords' privileges.[59] However, the more hot-headed members contributed to the debate in a manner uninhibited by the nature of their information. Hoskyns indulged in a typically violent outburst and another member, possibly Thomas Crew, speculated on the very different treatment that would have been meted out to one of their members for an attack on the Lords. In his view the Lords should have considered handing Neile over to the Commons. On the other hand Sir Dudley Digges and Edward Alford advised caution, the latter suggesting a search of the precedents for guidance about the best course of procedure. Finally, after a discussion of the relative merits of an approach to the Lords or to the king, the House set up a select committee to consider the bishop's words and the basis of the Commons' case, and to advise on procedure.[60]

The following day, with Hakewill as its spokesman, the committee reported that, as the words were spoken in the Lords, common fame was 'certain Ground enough' for considering Neile's remarks. It had discussed three courses of procedure: to ask the Lords to confirm the accuracy of the rumours; to complain to them of the wrong and to ask them for redress; and to go to the king for redress. By a narrow majority it had resolved on the third course, but the argument that had taken place in the committee was renewed in the House when Sir Edwin Sandys, one of the committee members,

[59] *C.J.* i, 496; Moir, 123; Williams, *James I*, i, 313. Spedding, v, 62 makes the point about the breach of the Lords' privileges. He considers that the Lords showed great restraint, but what were the Commons to do? They had been refused a conference, a very unusual development as Spedding himself points out: p. 57. The Lords had taken five days to reply to their message and reports of the bishop's words were not confined to parliament.

[60] *C.J.* i, 496-8.

spoke against the recommendation. He argued that it would create a dangerous breach with the Lords and might establish a precedent enabling the king to punish a member of one House on the complaint of the other. Digges supported him, suggesting that without the consent of the Lords, of whom there was no reason to despair, Neile would not be punished sufficiently. He added that if the Commons did not receive satisfaction from the Lords, then they should go to the king. These arguments, indicative of some procedural maturity, convinced the majority of members and eventually Hakewill changed his mind and agreed. Roe volunteered the encouraging, though inaccurate, information that the upper House had sent Latimer to the Commons for punishment, and the House then set up a small committee to frame the message to be sent to the Lords. It also resolved to transact no further business until an answer had been received from the Lords.[61] This last decision produced a protest from the king, but such was the mood of the House that his message was virtually ignored.[62]

The draft of the message to the Lords was presented for approval on the 27th and, after a dispute over part of its wording, a revised version was despatched next day. It reveals the accuracy of the Commons' information and makes no attempt to hide the weakness of their position. It expresses astonishment that anyone could have misconstrued their first message by putting a sinister interpretation on it. It goes on to record in some detail what 'by public and constant Fame' the bishop is reported to have said, and it concludes by asking the Lords to take notice of this scandal and to join with the Commons to determine how they may be given satisfaction. It adds that the Commons will undertake no further business until they receive a reply.[63] The Lords' first reaction seems to

---

[61] *C.J.* i, 498-9; *H.M.C. Report on the Manuscripts of His Grace the Duke of Portland* (London, 1891-1931), ix, 133; *C.D.* vii, 646. Notestein, *Winning of the Initiative*, 46, presumably referring to this episode, says that the Commons ignored Sandys' advice. This is clearly incorrect, though Sandys' earlier arguments seem to have been less convincing than his later ones: Moir, 125.

[62] Moir, 127-9.

[63] Moir, 126; *C.J.* i, 499-500; *L.J.* ii, 709. Petyt MS 537/18, ff. 49-49v appears to be a copy of the exact message which Sir Edward Hoby delivered to the Lords. It is similar to the message printed in the *Lords Journal* but has greater emphasis and numerous minor alterations in wording. It also suggests (f. 49v) that the

have been complete silence, but then, having told the Commons' messenger that they would reply as soon as possible, they began to debate their answer. Some of the privy councillors[64] who had previously opposed consultation with the Commons now came out against Neile, but Ellesmere, the Lord Chancellor, maintained that the Commons must either set down Neile's words or that some member of the Lords must charge the bishop with the words, if the House were to proceed against him. But, he told them, 'your Lordships are Judges, and theirfore cannot be his accusers, and by lawe their must be a partie accusinge.'[65] This was a point of some significance, and one of the advantages of impeachment, at least in its fully developed form, was that it avoided the difficulty by making the Commons accusers. Yet even as early as 1621 the problem had evidently ceased to be insuperable: the Lords asked their own committees to draw up the accusation against Bacon, and this was done.[66]

The Lords' reply to the Commons was framed by Ellesmere and the archbishop of Canterbury, and delivered to the Commons by their own messenger, Sir Edward Hoby, on the 30th. Predictably, it declared that the Commons' complaint was grounded upon insufficient proof, but it promised that if the lower House would state exactly what words were spoken and show how they were to be proved the Lords would give full justice. In delivering this message Hoby also reported that Neile had spoken to him privately, denying some of his

Commons claimed that, in them, the king, the Lords and the whole kingdom had been wronged. In the margin it contains instructions to the messenger: by the first paragraph: 'The Introduction Arbitrary att your Discretion—upon this ground'; by the second (main) paragraph: 'For this the body wee tye you precicely to the words and soe to the End of this direction without other conclusion.'

[64] Knollys, Worcester, and, to some extent, the archbishop of Canterbury. Knollys said that as Neile's words had been spoken in the Lords there was more evidence of the matter than that provided by common fame: *H.M.C. Hastings*, iv, 268-70.

[65] Ibid. iv, 271. This point may have been in Saville's mind on 25 May when he tried to persuade the Commons to go to the king rather than to the Lords: 'If we go to the Lords, this to make the Lords Accusers': *C.J.* i, 497.

[66] However, Selden confirms Ellesmere's point: 'the Lords who are only judges may neither accuse any to themselves . . .' In addition, Selden and Elsynge both make the somewhat different point that, when the Commons accuse, 'the Lords are not to ioyne therein . . .': Selden, *Of Judicature*, 11-12; Elsynge, 301.

remarks and saying that others had been misconstrued. Neither of these messages satisfied the Commons, but Edwin Sandys persuaded them to persevere with the Lords rather than turn to the king.[67] They therefore appointed another committee to frame their reply. This largely reiterated the previous message, but recognised that common fame would not have been acceptable as a basis for proof in any ordinary court of justice, though claiming that it was sufficient to induce the Lords to consider the matter. It virtually challenged the peers to say whether or not the words had been spoken.

The determination of the Commons led to another lengthy debate in the Lords, in which very few speakers still supported Neile. The result was that he solemnly protested that he had meant no harm to either House, but it was only with reluctance that he was later induced to add that he would accept any punishment the Lords might impose upon him. The Lords then told the Commons that Neile had stated that he meant no disrespect to the lower House and that he was deeply disturbed that his words had been strained further than he ever intended. This message concluded by saying that the Lords were satisfied with Neile's reply but that had they not been he would have received severe punishment; it warned the Commons, however, that in future common fame alone would not be a justifiable ground for accusation against a member of the Lords.[68]

Despite this warning, the Lords had made an important concession by accepting the accusation against Neile. The Commons had had to base their case upon common fame because they could obtain no definite proof that Neile had spoken as they alleged. But although their position was a weak one, as the Lords told them and as they doubtless recognised, this did not nullify their accusation. Perhaps the similarity between the concept of common fame and the medieval notion of an accusation based on notoriety helped them. At any rate, when in 1626 the Commons encountered similar difficulties in

[67] *H.M.C. Hastings*, iv, 272; *L.J.* ii, 710-11; *C.J.* i, 501-2; *C.D.* vii, 648. Sandys proposed that the Commons should send the Lords 'for Accusation, the Words in writing'.

[68] *H.M.C. Hastings*, iv, 274-7; *L.J.* ii, 712-13; *C.J.* i, 502.

accusing Buckingham, they again resorted to common fame, although the cool reception which they had encountered in 1614 was used by Buckingham's supporters as an argument against the course which the House adopted.

As for Neile's case, the Commons were deeply dissatisfied with the Lords' reply. In normal circumstances, this would almost certainly have provided the basis for an acceptable compromise, but the Commons were by now almost ungovernable. They held another debate in which they were bitterly critical of the Lords and ended by appointing the inevitable select committee. But this was to be their last act in the drama because the king, exasperated beyond measure by the character of the session, stepped in to threaten the dissolution which rapidly followed on 7 June.[69] Thus, proceedings against Neile were abruptly ended, but it is perhaps questionable whether the Commons would have achieved more if the session had lasted longer. Handicapped by the fact that Neile's offences were contained in his speeches, whereas those of Thornborough and Cowell were embalmed in their writings, the Commons received as much, if not more, satisfaction from Neile than from the other two men. They had sustained an insecurely based accusation and had compelled the Lords to listen to them, even though the power to punish remained firmly in the hands of others, as it had done previously.

The cases which have been discussed all exhibit some novel or unusual features, and several of them provide evidence of attempts by the Commons to extend the scope and nature of their judicature. All of them were conducted within parliament, and were not concerned with the judicature of other courts. But when Ellesmere wrote about the first session of 1610 and of the irregularities in the proceedings against Proctor and Spiller, he also complained that the Commons had interfered in the jurisdiction of the Courts of Admiralty and Chancery. They had passed a bill to allow an appeal from a

[69] *C.D.* vii, 649-50; *C.J.* i, 504; *H.M.C. Portland*, ix, 135; Moir, 136, 145. After the dissolution a number of the leaders of the Commons' opposition were punished: Hoskyns was among those imprisoned in the Tower, and Edwin Sandys, Digges, Owen, Crew, Hakewill and others had their notes burned: Williams, *James I*, i, 322, 325.

sentence given in the Admiralty Court, although the Privy Council had examined the case and decided that an appeal was not justified. They had examined 'in point of equity and conscience divers decrees made in the Chancery', and they had granted injunctions to stay suits being prosecuted there and in other courts. They had approved a bill attacking a point in law upon which a judgment had been based.[70]

Ellesmere illustrates some of his assertions by naming the cases in which the interference occurred. Unfortunately, in almost every instance, diaries and official records add only minor details to the account given by Ellesmere. However, they do provide factual confirmation of his accusations of trespass.[71] To what extent the Commons were successful in their poaching is difficult to say. Certainly the result was not always what they intended: for instance, the bill to permit the appeal against the Admiralty Court's sentence failed to pass the Lords.[72] But this is not the most important consideration. What is more significant is that the Commons' endeavours to extend their jurisdictional powers inside parliament were running parallel with similar attempts to expand their jurisdiction outside parliament. As a part of the story of the development of parliamentary judicature, the latter may be less important than the former, but as an indication of the assertiveness of the Commons on which the development of that judicature in part depended, such attempts are equally revealing.

In the parliaments of the 1620s, only occasional reference was made to the cases which have been discussed, although they were not totally ignored.[73] This was no doubt partly because the actions were not very successful. In addition, the

[70] Foster, *Parliament 1610*, i, 280-1.

[71] There is one exception. There is a full account in the *Lords Journal* of Lord Abergavenny's case, which settled a dispute with Lady le Despenser over the precedency of the two baronies and the sale of some lands. From the entries in the *Commons Journal* it appears that the Commons were only required to pass a bill sent to them by the Lords: *L.J.* ii, 613, 615, 618, 622-3, 625-8; *C.J.* i, 446-7, 449-51.

[72] Foster, *Parliament 1610*, i, 280 n. 11. It had its first reading by the peers only three days before the prorogation: *L.J.* ii, 653.

[73] Cowell: *C.D.* iii, 207; Proctor: *C.D.* iv, 77; vi, 353; Neile: *C.J.* i, 847.

types of judicature which were being exercised shortly before
1621 were not necessarily of great relevance to the parliamentary judicature re-introduced then. Coke and his associates
had to look back to the middle ages to find close parallels with
what they were trying to do. But this is not to say that nothing
could be learnt from more recent experience. The Commons
had discovered something of the reaction of the Lords and of
James to their more extravagant claims, and may have learnt,
in spite of disappointments, that they could skate on thin ice
with reasonable safety, provided that they advanced with
sufficient determination. They had compelled the Lords to get
used to the idea of collaborating with them in the realm of
judicature. They had had some indication of the weaknesses
of procedure by bill; and their experience with Proctor may
have reminded them that they lacked power to punish non-
members except when their privileges had been infringed.
They had also developed the use of committees to carry out
detailed work, to conduct examinations, and to advise on
procedure. In so far as these cases helped to define the opportunities and limitations of the existing judicature, they may
also have contributed to the noticeable smoothness and ease
with which parliamentary judicature was revived in 1621.

If the Commons in James's first two parliaments did gain
the type of experience suggested, the means for its transmission
to their successors was not lacking. Membership did not change
completely from one parliament to the next. Men like Robert
Phelips, Hakewill, Edwin Sandys and Digges, who were
among the leaders in 1621, had sat in either or both of these
earlier parliaments. Coke was in attendance on the Lords
before he entered the Commons in 1621. Sir Robert Cotton
was already searching for precedents in 1610 as he was so
often to do later.[74] There was to be no shortage of either
antiquarian knowledge or more recent experience in the
1620s.

[74] *C.J.* i, 422. In 1614, while ill at Cambridge, he sent the key of his study to
enable several of the Commons' critics of impositions to search for records 'for the
benefit of the Common wealthe'. The following day, 21 May, one of them, Sir
Roger Owen, challenged Wootton's suggestion that the king could impose by his
own authority: *C.D.* vii, 644.

CHAPTER IV

The Parliament of 1621: February and March

In the story of judicature in parliament, the trials and hearings before the Commons and Lords of 1621 have long held an important place. In the eighteenth century Francis Hargrave drew attention to the increase in parliament's judicial business, both civil and criminal, in that year.[1] Undoubtedly, part of the explanation of this activity lies in the political circumstances of the time, which gave rise to much dissatisfaction, though this is not to say that politics dictated these judicial developments. The presence in the Commons of Sir Edward Coke is another part of the answer, and much of the progress made in 1621 was due to his guidance. But whatever the explanation, pride of place in this development must go to the revival of parliamentary judicature—the procedure commonly named impeachment. Yet although this is the best known and probably the most important aspect of the development, it is not the only one, nor did it occur in isolation: there was also an expansion of the unicameral judicature of both Houses.

In the Commons this took various forms. First, the House evolved an efficient procedure for dealing with grievances. Petitions presented to the House led to enquiries conducted in accordance with a procedure evolved from that used for private bills. This procedure has been carefully examined by Mrs Foster, but it will be necessary at a later stage to summarise her findings because the first case of parliamentary judicature stemmed directly from the Commons' investigation into grievances.[2] Secondly, the Commons of 1621 attempted without success to establish a jurisdiction of their own over persons

---

[1] Hargrave's preface to Hale, pp. viii-ix.
[2] Foster, 'Patents and Monopolies', 59-85, especially p. 78.

who were neither members of the lower House nor guilty of violating its privileges. This endeavour appears most strongly in the case of Floyd, but it is perhaps not entirely absent in the early stages of the proceedings against Michell. Had the attempt prospered, the effects on the evolution of parliamentary judicature would almost certainly have been profound, and it must therefore be contrasted with that evolution. Thirdly, as in 1610, there are signs that the Commons were prepared to intervene in the jurisdiction of other courts.[3] However, the future of this type of judicature lay more with the Lords than with the Commons, and the activities of the latter in this respect in 1621 appear to have no connection with the development of parliamentary judicature.

This parliament also saw an extension of the unicameral judicature of the Lords.[4] In the course of the first session, the peers employed an original civil jurisdiction on petitions presented to them by private citizens, which, before the end of the parliament, seemed about to widen into an appellate jurisdiction—a development which did, in due course, take place. These private petitions, like those previously mentioned which complained of grievances, were often first addressed to the Commons, but as they normally asked for judicial remedy, the Commons did not regard them—as they did grievances—as falling within their special province, and through their committee of grievances, may have taken the initiative in redirecting the petitioners to the peers. The stages

---

[3] Two cases may be mentioned. In March 1621, the Commons adjudicated in a jurisdictional dispute between the Courts of Chancery and Wards. The case emerged from their enquiries into abuses in courts of justice. Lawyers pleaded at the Bar on behalf of each Court: the Commons decided that both had been at fault: Nicholas, *Proceedings*, i, 178-83. The second case, which has something of the flavour of an appeal, arose from a Chancery decree awarding Sir George Marshall 1,000 marks in conclusion of a long-standing dispute with Sir William Pope. Pope asked the Commons to reverse this decree and a committee pronounced it grievous. The two men were then ordered to plead their causes before the committee of grievances. After this hearing, members debated the next step. Some favoured an approach to the Lords in order to secure a reversal of the decree but this procedure was not followed, doubtless because the king intervened to give the Commons permission to judge the case themselves. The House concluded the case by ordering the removal of the decree from the Chancery files: *C.D.* iii, 2, 111, 116; iv, 270, 285; v, 106-7; vi, 467; Nicholas, *Proceedings*, i, 366.

[4] Relf, pp. ix-xxxii, especially pp. xviiiff.

by which the lords assumed responsibility for adjudicating on such petitions have been analysed by Miss Relf, who has found similarities in the origins of both this jurisdiction and parliamentary judicature. She has argued that the Lords undertook judicature on petition at the urging of a small group of members of both Houses, because the Commons possessed no means—apart from private bill procedure, which Coke disliked—of dealing with the large number of private petitions being received.[5] She has also pointed out that Coke gave much the same reason—the insufficient power of the Commons—for the recommendation to transmit Mompesson to the Lords, the decision which led to the revival of parliamentary judicature.[6] Miss Relf concludes that it was 'in keeping with the move made by Coke in Mompesson's case that . . . the commons should call upon the lords to answer petitions by judicial procedure': in order to increase the Lords' confidence in their ability to deal with Mompesson, Coke had stressed their power to judge alone.[7] It is therefore evident that parliamentary judicature and the Lords' judicature on petition shared a common origin, at any rate in one respect, in the Commons' realisation of the limitations upon their own power. But despite this the two procedures developed very differently. Although the first petitions may have been redirected by the Commons to the Lords, the upper House rapidly acquired the habit of receiving petitions direct from their sponsors.[8] The

[5] Relf, p. xix; Foster, 'Patents and Monopolies', 62, 78. For Coke's hostility to private bill procedure, see above, p. 72. Since the reign of Henry IV there had been a 'tendency to address petitions to the Commons to gain their mediation': Relf, pp. xix-xx.

[6] Relf, p. xiii. The Commons were ham-strung in dealing with both civil and criminal cases because they could not hear evidence on oath.

[7] Relf, p. xix. The power of the Lords to judge alone formed the second of the four types of judicature listed by Coke in his speech of 8 March 1621. Miss Relf comments that, in asserting that such a procedure existed, 'Coke had gone beyond anything justified by medieval precedent': p. xv. It will be remembered that when he discussed this judicature, Coke specifically stated that cases could originate before the Lords: above, see p. 46.

[8] Relf, pp. xi, xxff. The procedure embodied a committee for petitions. There is little doubt that this came to be 'recognised as performing the function which was once performed by the tryers' of petitions: ibid. p. xxvii and p. 55, above. The Lords' records of 1628 contain the first sign of conflict between the old procedure by private bill and the new procedure by petition: Relf, p. xxviii.

G

Commons took no part in this judicature, which remained firmly unicameral, and was, of course, fundamentally civil, while parliamentary judicature in the seventeenth century was basically criminal. It therefore seems that this extension of the Lords' judicature is procedurally separate from the development of parliamentary judicature. That development grew much more from the Commons' procedure for dealing with grievances, and from their unsuccessful attempt to punish men who were outside their customary jurisdiction.

A considerable part of the Commons' energies in the first, and main, session of the 1621 Parliament was absorbed in the investigation of grievances. Two months before the first meeting, the shrewder political observers had been urging the king to remove some of the more obvious grievances in order to forestall criticism, but little was done.[9] Moreover, the government's supporters faced an additional handicap. Investigations into grievances inevitably cast shadows over important people and were to lead on to several trials of major significance, but James was not a king who was easily persuaded to deny his subjects the opportunity to complete a serious enquiry into the alleged errors of individuals, however eminent these men might be. The very fair-mindedness of the king prevented him from seriously interfering with investigations which were, ultimately, to weaken the whole monarchical position.

Although the Commons seem to have been determined to leave no complaint uninvestigated, regardless of how trivial it might appear to be, they concentrated on patents, monopolies, and grants of dispensation from the penal laws, as the major grievances. Such abuses were widespread, and it was the Commons' work on the first two which provided the basis for the revival of parliamentary judicature in 1621. To deal with patents and monopolies the Commons evolved a fairly stereotyped procedure. The complaint might originate from any source, from privy councillor to private citizen. The committee or sub-committee charged with the task of detailed investigation summoned before it the patentee and his opponents, together with witnesses and documents on both sides. Either party might seek permission to appear with or by counsel,

[9] *C.S.P. Ven. 1619-21*, 479.

while refusal to obey a summons was treated as contempt. Both sides were entitled to a hearing, though defendants were not allowed written copies of the charges. The chairman of the committee probably led the questioning but members were free to intervene; evidence was not given on oath—though this possibility caused a good deal of discussion in both 1621 and 1624—but the House compensated for its impotence in this respect by being prepared to punish witnesses who lied. The committee acted as a fact-finding body, but it also heard discussion of these facts and considered the effects of the grant's existence. When it had completed its investigations, it pronounced judgment on the patent or monopoly and reported this to the House. In every case of which records remain the Commons confirmed the report of their committee. After the patent had been formally condemned, the House might proceed either by passing a special bill to deal with it, or by including it in a general petition to the king at the end of the session; and in 1624 an attempt was made to deal with the whole problem of such grants by passing the Statute of Monopolies.[10]

Mrs Foster has emphasised the essentially legal nature of these enquiries into patents and monopolies. 'The Commons had, in fact, evolved out of the old private Bill procedure a method of investigation and of passing judgment very like a court procedure.'[11] But although the judicial or semi-judicial processes employed to deal with private bills might lend an air of respectability to these investigations, the House had effectively extended its jurisdiction. 'Patents and monopolies could not be construed as offences against the House. For their jurisdiction in this field the Commons relied on the idea that grievances were the special province of the representatives of the realm.'[12] It may be noted in passing that this concept was to prove useful to the Commons in the slightly different context of parliamentary judicature.

The procedure which has been described was no doubt effective in dealing with the patents and monopolies themselves: often enough the grant was cancelled. But, although the voiding of a grant might damage the livelihood of its holder,

---

[10] Foster, 'Patents and Monopolies', 66, 67, 69, 72, 76-8, 81 n. 44.
[11] Ibid. 74-5.   [12] Ibid. 75.

the machinery did not extend to the punishment of the patentee or monopolist. The Commons did have some debate on how to punish patentees, but only those who happened also to be members of the House were actually punished.[13] Moreover, even if a patentee came within this category, the House might decide that the punishments which it could inflict were inadequate. It was to cope with precisely this situation in its proceedings against Mompesson that the Commons of 1621 turned to the Lords, and thereby revived parliamentary judicature. It is now necessary to consider the development of that judicature as revealed by this case and its successors.

On 6 February, 1621, the Commons, on a motion of Alford and Sackville, arranged for the reference of grievances to a committee appointed for the purpose of considering them. This was one of four committees of the whole House which were set up with various functions at different times in 1621. These and their sub-committees were to carry out much of the detailed work connected with the cases of parliamentary judicature, using powers already largely established in previous parliaments.[14] There were two levels at which the committee of grievances and those with the narrower purpose of investigating trade and courts of justice could operate. In the first place, they could concern themselves with the more superficial aspects of the allegations brought before them, earnestly calling to account the rather unimportant men who had been responsible for the day-to-day enforcement of the patents which were alleged to be grievous. This level of activity was unlikely to bring down upon their heads any significant anger from the king, but equally it was unlikely to be of any lasting benefit to the community. The alternative course open to the committees was to strike at the real heart of the matter in the hope of producing a lasting cure; but this would involve identifying and examining the referees—the men, often the most prominent in the kingdom, responsible for advising the king on the legality and suitability of the patent under consideration. To

---

[13] Foster, 'Patents and Monopolies', 84 n. 98. They were sequestered or expelled from the House.

[14] *C.D.* iv, 19; Notestein, *Winning of the Initiative,* 37.

avoid impairing the deeply held doctrine that the king could do no wrong[15] involved fixing responsibility for the poor state of affairs upon these advisers, but as the king had appointed them he was likely to disapprove strongly of suggestions that they were really inadequate.[16] Nevertheless, certain members of the Commons were prepared to take this risk and Sackville suggested that while the committee was examining the patent for the sole manufacture of gold and silver thread it should try to find out who had acted as referees in granting the patent 'that so his Majesty may be cleared, and the Saddle set on the right Horse'. Nine days later the Master of the Wards, Lionel Cranfield, urged the Commons, meeting as a committee of the whole House, to a course of action which would clearly identify the source of the errors in the patents. He said that as the king always referred projected patents it would not dishonour him to call to account those that had abused him.[17] How strong was the wish to deal directly with the referees it is difficult to say[18] but the investigating committees and the Commons adopted a compromise position between the two extremes of behaviour open to them.

During the last two weeks of February the committee for grievances met very frequently and on the 19th Mompesson's patent for the licensing of inns was first discussed. The declared

---

[15] Just how deep was the belief in this doctrine is one of the greatest problems of the 1620s. Adherence to it undoubtedly had its uses in dealing with unpopular ministers. Raleigh had discussed some of its implications in *The Prerogative of Parliaments in England*, (London, 1657), 99. See also Roberts, 4-7, 35, 41, 59, 69, 74, 75.

[16] Although James was quick to shift responsibility from himself to the referees, an attack on them was fundamentally an attack on the legality of the king's grants: Foster, 'Patents and Monopolies', 71-2.

[17] *C.D.* iv, 20, 58-9; *C.J.* i, 511. It is interesting to note that this speech gained the approval of John Chamberlain: *The Letters of John Chamberlain*, ed. N. E. McClure (Philadelphia, 1939), ii, 345. At the end of February, Chamberlain was taking a pessimistic view of the Commons' chances of success against the referees whom he considered 'such as are like to be out of their reach'. He also observed that the House had 'so many hares on foote at once that they hinder one another': Chamberlain, ii, 347.

[18] Unrestrained comments were certainly made, as, for example, in the hostile diary, Rawlinson MS B. 151. This states categorically that many great men were doers in the patents and should be questioned for such an abuse of the commonwealth for if they had not certified the fitness of the patents the king would not have granted them: *C.D.* vi, 377.

intention of this patent was to regulate the management of
inns by granting licences so that good behaviour might be
assured in those licensed, and that unlicensed inns might be
closed down. Fees were charged for licences and punishments
inflicted upon offenders. Mompesson had made use of his
patent to enrich himself, causing much hardship.[19] The
committee, with Sir Edward Coke as its chairman, ordered
Mompesson and his fellow patentees to produce the documents
connected with the patent, and on the 20th the patent was read
to the committee.[20] Coke stated clearly that as the king had
granted it only after taking advice he was free of all blame. In
the ensuing debate strong criticisms of the patent were made
and Mompesson declared that if it were shown to be evil he
was ready to be the first to suppress it. After hearing Coke's
report on the 21st the Commons ordered the sequestration of
Mompesson from his place in the House while the case was
being dealt with, though he was commanded to be available
every day—a jurisdiction which it was, of course, entitled to
exercise over its own members. At the same time an attempt
was made by Seymour to have the House consider the possible
fault of the referees in this patent and Sir Thomas Wentworth,
looking ahead one stage, proposed that enquiries be made to
discover what laws existed by which patentees could be
punished.[21]

   While witnesses were being examined and evidence collected
in Mompesson's case, the Commons and their committee for

---

[19] D. C. Spielman, 'Impeachments and the Parliamentary Opposition in
England 1621-1641' (unpublished Ph.D. thesis of the University of Wisconsin,
1959), p. 23 and n. 8. For example, Bath had had six inns, apparently sufficient to
satisfy the needs of the populace, but Mompesson had gradually increased the
number to twenty: Nicholas, *Proceedings*, i, 66. Among the later evidence against
Mompesson was an allegation that he had issued more than 3,500 writs of *quo
warranto* against inn-keepers, bringing only two of them to issue. He had also
declared at least 100 outlawries: *C.D.* v, 488-9.

[20] The patent had been granted to Mompesson, Gyles Bridges and James
Thurborne: *C.D.* iv, 84. According to Wentworth's account the committee had
first to obtain the approval of the House before making this order, but this is not
confirmed by the other diarists: *C.D.* ii, 106, v, 476.

[21] *C.D.* ii, 109. The referees were Bacon, Crooke, Nicolls, Winch, and Finch for
law; Bacon, Suffolk, Winwood, Lake, and Finch for conveniency: Nicholas,
Proceedings, i, 103-4. Mompesson was a member for the borough of Great Bedwyn,
Wiltshire.

grievances dealt with another patent, that concerning recognisances for alehouses. This patent operated on similar lines to that for inns and infringed one of the powers of the justices of the peace. The chief target for the Commons' attack was Sir Francis Michell, who was not an M.P. As commissioner for enforcement of the patent, he had not only profited directly from it but received a steady income of £40 a year from Newgate prison on condition that he made use of its services for his prisoners. On 21 February Michell admitted to being a dealer in the patent and the committee extended its authority by judging the patent to be a grievance both in grant and execution, a sentence confirmed by the House next day. Its appetite whetted, the committee continued its investigations and Michell, apparently thoroughly alarmed and privately advised by some of his inquisitors, resolved to petition the House.[22] The petition was read on the 23rd, just before Coke was due to make a further report from the committee. In it Michell denied having had any part in the creation of the patent, which he said had been approved by some of the most learned men in the kingdom, and claimed that he had merely endeavoured to execute the king's grant to the best of his ability. Angered by what it regarded as the offensive wording of this petition and its author's attempt to take refuge in the prerogative, the House held a debate which was far from being coolly judicial. It did, however, heed the warnings of Glanville not to overreach itself and it ignored the irrelevant precedents for punishment produced by Hakewill.[23] Without giving any specific reason, it declared Michell unworthy to be a J.P. or to hold any future commission and sentenced him to imprisonment in the Tower during pleasure. Michell's attempt to reply at once was refused and Coke told him that he could say what he had to say when he made his expected submission.[24]

[22] *C.S.P. Dom. 1619-23*, 225; *C.D.* iv, 89; vii, 499-502.
[23] Hakewill gave two precedents: a mayor of Westminster who, in 13 Elizabeth, accepted a bribe from a burgess to return him to parliament; and an M.P., Arthur Hall, who wrote an attack on the House and its proceedings: *C.D.* ii, 131. For Hall, see J. E. Neale, *Elizabeth I and her Parliaments 1559-1581* (London, 1958), 407ff.
[24] *C.D.* ii, 132. Michell's sentence perhaps bears some similarity to the medieval notion of conviction by notoriety.

It is not easy to be sure whether the Commons were justified in punishing Michell in this way. Within a few weeks the Lords were hearing that the Commons had committed him for contempt, and Michell's action could certainly be construed in this way. But this does not seem to be the only reason for the Commons' sentence. The entry in their Book of Orders for 23 February says that he was imprisoned 'for his many misdemeanours in and aboute the procureing and execucion of the pattent concerning the forfeitures of the Recognizances of Ale howses Keepers . . .'[25] Moreover, in rejecting Hakewill's precedents, Phelips pointed out that they were concerned with offences against the House whereas Michell had offended against the country.[26] Perhaps the Commons had extended their existing jurisdiction in a direction difficult to justify, but for the moment the case rested.

Within a few days the Commons were possibly regretting the hastiness of their action over Michell as the need emerged to justify a rather different course of procedure in dealing with Mompesson. But their quick success had the effect of increasing their boldness so that when, on the 24th, Mompesson hoped to curry favour by a submission which promised the discovery of 'some things which shalbe for the publick good', his petition was rejected and he was ordered to appear before the committee on the following Monday. At the same time further attempts were made by Seymour and Cranfield to have enquiries widened to include examination of referees, and Coke suggested that this become standard practice.[27] Cranfield's suggestion, which related specifically to the Mompesson case, was agreed to and it can hardly have passed unnoticed that a small encroachment had been made upon the entrenched position of the Villiers family: Mompesson was a relation by marriage of Buckingham; Christopher Villiers was involved in the alehouse patent; and within the next few weeks Buckingham himself was to protest his innocence to the Lords and to declare

---

[25] *L.J.* iii, 63; *C.D.* vi, 453; J. P. Kenyon, ed. *The Stuart Constitution* (Cambridge, 1966), 93; Harl. 158, f. 239.

[26] *C.D.* ii, 131. See also the full debate on the report from the committee of grievances: *C.D.* ii, 127–33.

[27] *C.D.* ii, 134; iv, 99.

that he would not protect his brothers against legitimate censure.[28]

When Mompesson was questioned by the committee for grievances on 26 February he was asked about a number of other patents he was thought to have held. Of these, the two most important were the patent for the manufacture of gold and silver thread[29] and the patent for the investigation of the concealment of wards' lands. He did his best to minimise his share, both administrative and financial, in both, but when the following day the committee reported to the whole House Pym made much of the patent for the investigation of the concealment of lands and Coke compared Mompesson to Empson, whose fate he mentioned.[30] Up to this point the method of dealing with Mompesson had closely resembled that employed against Michell, but a new pattern now emerges.[31] Instead of condemning him and passing sentence the Commons this time proceed much more circumspectly, despite the fact that, unlike Michell, Mompesson was a member of the House. There are several possible reasons for this. First, Mompesson had not enraged the Commons with excuses to the same extent as Michell so that there was little justification for proceeding against him summarily. Secondly, there was

---

[28] Arthur Wilson, who was strongly anti-Stuart, said that 'All the world knew that Montpesson was Buckingham's creature': J. Nichols, ed. *Progresses, Processions and Magnificent Festivities of King James the First* ... (London, 1828), iv, 660, n. 3. Mompesson and the Villiers family were related by marriage: D. Mathew, *James I* (London, 1967), 291n. There is a letter of January 1618 in which Buckingham asks for Bacon's help in furthering the alehouse patent referred to him, because it concerns Patrick Maull and Christopher Villiers. Bacon agreed provided that the grant was not one of the grievances put down in parliament: *C.D.* vii, 312.

[29] Sir Edward Villiers had invested money in this patent. No separate charge was preferred against him to the Lords, but he was eventually cleared by them in the aftermath of their investigations into Mompesson's offences: *C.D.* ii, 412, 426; iii, 131-4.

[30] *C.D.* iv, 107. It is interesting that Pym's careful determination appears even at this early stage in this, the first parliament in which he sat. In the course of his speech he outlined the three stages of justice to which a guilty man was liable— inquisition of the fact, judgment, execution of judgment—and said that only in the third was there room for mercy: *C.D.* iv, 110. Speakers subsequently made much of the similarity of the names of Mompesson and Empson.

[31] His patent, like Michell's, had been condemned by the committee: *C.J.* i, 530; *C.D.* ii, 145.

doubt as to the degree of punishment that the Commons could inflict upon him. Coke pointed out that they could do no more than punish him for an indignity to the House and send him to the Tower, but the suggestion implicit in the mention of Empson was that imprisonment was too good for him.[32] Again, doubts had been raised about the legality of the Commons' action against Michell;[33] and finally, the House might understandably have been worried about the nature of the king's reaction to a repetition of its earlier proceedings but on this occasion with a more important victim. Some of those considerations may have lain behind Sackville's suggestion, made before Coke spoke again, that the Commons should collaborate with the Lords in Mompesson's punishment. This proposal met some opposition, but the House did agree to a suggestion of Sir Edwin Sandys that a search be made of the records in the Tower to determine the extent of the Commons' powers.[34] By the time, later in the day, when Coke rose to speak again, there were therefore several reasons to persuade him to leave the choice of action as open as possible. His speech made a deliberate distinction between the cases of Michell and Mompesson. He defended the Commons' punishment of Michell on the grounds that Michell, although having committed his offence while parliament was not in session, had defended his action before the Commons after this had been condemned. He had thus offended the House and had been punished for so doing.[35] Mompesson had not done this and the Commons must therefore consider what power they possessed

[32] Relf, p. xiii.
[33] C.D. vi, 431. Michell, writing afterwards to vindicate himself, discussed it in terms which Floyd's case later made familiar: 'I conceived that howse had no power of Judicature, and I being no member of the howse that they could not comitt me.' He also drew attention to what he obviously believed to be procedural innovations: as he had not made a confession, he had expected the Commons, before censuring him, to require evidence from at least two witnesses. He had also assumed that he would be given an opportunity to speak before judgment was pronounced against him: Harl. 158, f. 229.
[34] C.D. ii, 146; iv, 111.
[35] C.D. vi, 14-15. If, as suggested above (p. 92), this was not the whole reason for Michell's punishment, it may be that it was at this moment that the Commons began their withdrawal to a more defensible position: S. R. Gardiner, *The History of England from the Accession of James I to the Outbreak of the Civil War 1603-42* (London, 1896-1901), iv, 43-4. See also Kenyon, 93.

independently of the Lords. He accordingly proposed a search for precedents.[36] When Coke had finished speaking a committee of twelve was appointed, on Pym's suggestion, to examine the particulars of Mompesson's offences, and two of its members, Noy and Hakewill, were sent to the Tower to carry out the search, 'to show how far, and for what offences, the power of this House doth extend to punish delinquents against the State as well as those who offend against this House'.[37] Seymour once again raised the question of examining the referees and received the support of Cranfield. Mompesson then made a confession in which he named the referees and was, apparently, placed on his honour to remain at home until required again.

The following day Noy and Hakewill reported to the committee about their search in the Tower. We do not know exactly what they said, but it seems probable that they stated that the House lacked power to punish any except those who offended it. The present grievance was, of course, harmful to the interests of the community, not merely to those of the House; and the committee concluded that Mompesson had been the author of 'no Offence against our particular House, or any Member of it, but a general Grievance'. Coke then addressed the committee on the subject of the Commons' power. In this speech, already analysed in some detail,[38] he drew a distinction between the matters of fact, which were tried in the Commons, and the judicature for which the House had 'often resorted to the Lords'. He said that sometimes the Commons had merely presented the case to the Lords, sometimes they had been made a party to it, and sometimes they had had sole cognisance of it.[39] As a result of the committee's work Coke proposed to the House that the Commons, in accordance with the precedents, should address themselves to the Lords.[40] The House

[36] The suggestion appears to have originated with Sir Robert Phelips but Coke gave it firmer support than Gardiner suggested: *C.D.* iv, 111; v, 260; vi, 14-15. Cf. Gardiner, *History*, iv, 43-4.

[37] *C.D.* ii, 146; Nicholas, *Proceedings*, i, 103. It will be remembered (above, p. 92) that Phelips had asserted that Michell's offence was against the country, not merely the House.

[38] See above, pp. 44-5. This was the first of Coke's two speeches on the subject of judicature.

[39] *C.D.* iv, 115-6; Nicholas, *Proceedings*, i, 109.

[40] *C.D.* ii, 148-9; iv, 116.

agreed to this and handed Mompesson over to the serjeant for safe keeping.

The decision to go to the Lords was obviously of crucial importance: without it, Mompesson and those who came after him would probably have emerged virtually unscathed from the enquiries of 1621. A number of considerations brought about this decision. First of all, as the committee had concluded, the House alone simply did not have jurisdiction in this type of case. There existed neither recent experience, historical fact, nor pious legend to disprove this finding. Secondly, Coke said that the records indicated that 'on a great and general Grievance we are to join with the Lords for the punishing of the Offenders', while a few days later he told the Lords that the case concerned them as well as the Commons.[41] Coke, of course, produced precedents to support the proposal to join with the Lords, but the accounts of his speech give only the briefest indication of what he said on this aspect of the matter. Indeed, it is possible that he said very little: perhaps the power to go to the Lords was sufficiently well known and needed little proof. However, he did claim that relevant evidence survived from the time of Edward I to that of Henry VI, but the *Commons Journal* suggests that he made only a passing reference to what might, presumably, have been his richest quarry: 'In Ed. III time (a most happy Time) *adjudicata Parliament*.'[42] Another probable reason for the Commons' decision to approach the Lords was that they believed that the peers were willing and able to act in the matter. Yet it is difficult to be certain of this. Contacts between a few members in both Houses certainly seem to have developed as the session pro-

[41] Nicholas, *Proceedings*, i, 108; *C.D.* ii, 158. On 1 March, Hakewill reported that, in the committee's view, the case should have a full hearing by both Houses: Nicholas, *Proceedings*, i, 112.

[42] *C.J.* i, 531; Nicholas, *Proceedings*, i, 108-9. Curiously, if the accounts summarise fairly, Coke gave most attention to the case of Speaker Thorpe in 32 Henry VI. Thorpe had apparently been imprisoned at the instance of the duke of York, and the Lords had confirmed the sentence. The Commons complained to the Lords that they had been deprived of their Speaker, but the judges, whom the Lords consulted, said that his offence was too great for parliamentary privilege to protect him. The Commons therefore had to choose another Speaker. Coke's comment on the case is '. . . this was done by our joining with the Lords': Nicholas, *Proceedings*, i, 109; *Rot. Parl.* v, 239-40.

gressed, but it is hardly possible to say at what stage they became really useful.[43] On the other hand, on 3 March Coke did tell the Lords that they had power to punish Mompesson and he was to dwell on the same theme in his speech on the four types of judicature less than a week later.[44] It is therefore reasonable to conclude that the Commons resolved to join with the Lords because they believed that the peers possessed the power which they realised they themselves lacked.

The vital decision to go to the Lords was taken on 28 February, but the first fruitful contact between the Houses, at which the Commons asked for a conference, did not take place until 3 March. There is some evidence that this delay was, at least in part, the result of an intrigue involving the Court. On 1 March Bacon wrote to the king in reply to a letter which he had received from James on the previous day. Bacon's reply makes it clear that the king had warned him of the Commons' intention to go to the Lords about Mompesson. Because of this warning Bacon had met the Prince and the Lord Treasurer shortly after 7 a.m. that morning, such an hour being chosen to avoid notice. The meeting had decided that the Commons should be told that time would be required to prepare an answer so that the proposed conference might be more fruitful. According to Bacon's letter messengers appeared from the Commons on 1 March (presumably to ask for the preliminary meeting) but 'as good luck was' Bacon had just adjourned the Lords to 3 March. The motion of adjournment had been proposed, in all innocence, by the archbishop of Canterbury, but Bacon had done nothing to hinder its adoption. Bacon adds gleefully that many lords would have liked an immediate recall but that this was not possible. If

---

[43] Relf, p. xx. When Coke told the Commons that they must address themselves to the Lords, he also said that he was glad that relations within the House, with the Lords, and with the king were happy. One wonders how far this was wishful thinking or whether he already had reason to believe that the Lords would give the Commons a fair hearing. If he had, this confidence was not shared by Rich who, to preserve the liberty of the Commons, proposed that if the Lords would not join with them the Commons should punish Mompesson themselves: *C.D.* ii, 148; iv, 116. (Mr Conrad Russell has pointed out to me that Rich's attitude may be explained by the fact that he was acting as spokesman for Warwick and Holland, whom the monopolies investigations might have touched.)

[44] *C.D.* ii, 158.

therefore it was the government's intention to manufacture a delay this had come about quite legitimately, without the need to resort to the rather transparent excuse devised at the early morning meeting.[45]

However, no hint of discomfiture appears in the arrangements made by the Commons during the three days after 28 February. On 1 March the House agreed that Coke, the privy councillors, the committee responsible for collecting the evidence and anyone else who so wished, should be sent to the Lords on 3 March to request them to join 'with us after the fashion of former tymes' to punish Mompesson. The following day instructions were given to the delegation: care was to be exercised over the presentation and content of the message; subservient language—'words of dutie'—was not to be used because both Houses were counsellors in parliament; Coke was to deliver the message orally although he had it written down; Mompesson was to be described as having dishonoured the king and state. At the same time evidence against Mompesson was still being collected and the committee was examining the patent of gold and silver thread.[46]

This steady development was interrupted by the news of Mompesson's escape from the serjeant's supervision.[47] When, therefore, the Commons' representatives met the Lords to request a conference Coke also asked for their help in appre-

---

[45] Spedding, vii, 189-90. One is still left wondering what the government hoped to gain. Such a delay would certainly not stop the Commons in their tracks but it may not be without significance that Mompesson escaped on 3 March, only minutes before he was due to appear before the House again. If the delay was to enable him to make preparations for his escape he left matters dangerously late. Perhaps, like Strafford in 1641, he could not believe that his protectors would permit the situation to deteriorate so disastrously. He certainly hoped that Buckingham would be able to obtain details in writing of the charges against him: *C.D.* v, 22; vi, 28; S. R. Gardiner, ed. *Notes of the Debates in the House of Lords, officially taken by Henry Elsing, Clerk of the Parliaments, A.D. 1621* (Camden Society, ciii: London, 1870), 150. It has been suggested that Bacon was also behind the disruption of the Commons' proceedings on 8 March: D. H. Willson, *The Privy Councillors in the House of Commons 1604-29* (Minneapolis, 1940), 151n.

[46] *C.D.* v, 17, 19, 266, 268; vi, 25-6.

[47] Arthur Wilson says that this was with Buckingham's connivance. Camden says that Buckingham forsook him at this time: Nichols, iv, 660 n. 3; *The Annals of Mr William Camden in the Reign of King James I*, in J. Hughes and W. Kennett, eds. *A Complete History of England; with the Lives of all the Kings and Queens thereof* (London, 1706), ii, 656.

hending Mompesson. Coke gained the Lords' assent to both requests, telling them that the conference was a method hallowed by precedent and that they had an interest and power in the redress. The conference was arranged for the following Monday, the Lords exhibiting considerable pleasure at the notion.[48] Coke undertook to arrange matters to cause least trouble to the Lords and returned, with his associates, to report to the lower House. The Commons then expelled Mompesson from his seat in the House and arranged for the examination of two further sources of evidence, Michell and the ex-Attorney General Yelverton, both of whom were imprisoned in the Tower.[49]

The examination of Yelverton bore interesting fruit. He was in the Tower as a result of revelations by Buckingham of illegalities in his conduct as Attorney General.[50] He had been one of the referees when the patent of gold and silver thread was established and he was now to be questioned about his part in imprisoning people whose attitude to that patent had offended Mompesson. Yelverton provided evidence of unjust imprisonment, implicating Buckingham's brother, Edward, but excluding the favourite himself, and claimed that he had passed the patent against his better judgment because of fear and threats.[51] The report of these revelations to the Commons led Sir Henry Vane to renew the proposal to examine the referees. He made it clear that he did not believe that the Commons could punish the great but that his suggestion would enable the Commons to examine matters so that 'the King may have his dew honor'. The House referred his motion for consideration by the committee examining Yelverton.[52]

On the same day, 5 March, Hakewill reported the advice

---

[48] Prince Charles was 'verie forward' against Mompesson. Buckingham also protested his innocence in dealings with Mompesson, blaming the referees who misled him: *C.D.* v, 22, 270. Although Monday was 5 March, the conference did not take place until the 8th.

[49] The examination was to be conducted by Coke, Cranfield, Phelips, and Sackville: Williams, *James I*, ii, 235.

[50] Nichols, ii, 703.

[51] He claimed that at the insistence of Edward Villiers, who had invested £4,000 in the venture, Bacon had imposed sentences of imprisonment. This situation encouraged Mompesson and Michell to break into men's houses and seize their property: Nicholas, *Proceedings*, i, 138-9; *C.D.* vi, 311.

[52] *C.D.* vi, 31; *C.J.* i, 539.

given by the committee on the procedure to be followed in the forthcoming conference with the Lords. The matter was to be discussed under six heads and each of these was to be the responsibility of one man. After debate the House accepted this advice and the speakers were agreed to.[53] Cranfield warned the House that the conference should be asked to consider only what was both important and proved.[54]

By this time the peers had begun to take an active interest in the case and both Houses were concerned with the accumulation of yet more evidence. Bacon reported to the Lords on 5 March the search and seizure of papers concerned with the thread patent found in the office used by the patentees and in the houses of Mompesson and Michell,[55] and shortly afterwards the House granted a Commons' request to hand over this or similar evidence to them. On the 7th the Commons had a full debate on the patents and eventually pronounced them illegal in inception, grant, progress and execution.[56]

The House had now reached the eve of the conference which represented its real hope of scoring a decisive victory over the monopolists and even of reducing some of the arrogant self-assurance of the men who lurked in the shadows behind them. Nevertheless, the prospect did not look too unhealthy to one of these very men. Writing to Buckingham on the day before the conference Bacon said that he did not expect it to be troublesome over the matter of referees. Cranfield was not intending to meddle in this and most members of the Commons seemed

[53] The heads were: introduction, abuses of inns and hostelries, gold and silver thread, concealments, aggravation of these, precedents for the course taken: *C.D.* ii, 163-4. Those chosen were, respectively, Digges, Crew, Heneage Finch, Hakewill, Edwin Sandys, Coke. Pym was to assist with concealments: *C.D.* ii, 170-1.

[54] Foster points out that by insisting that charges sent to the Lords be fully proved and that judgment be based on the charges presented, the Commons 'were raising their role from mere informers to partakers in the act of judicature itself': 'Patents and Monopolies', 75, 85 n. 102.

[55] The *Lords Journal* has a blank in place of the name of another whose house was searched: *L.J.* iii, 36. No one seems to have suggested that these activities of the Lords might compromise their position as judges.

[56] *C.D.* ii, 174-6. The way was therefore clear for naming the referees. The debate was perhaps fuller than the government's critics intended. Mrs Spielman believes that the courtiers' resistance successfully prevented a full rehearsal of the following day's conference. If so, this may help to explain the confusion on the 8th: Spielman, 31.

to agree with him. Bacon's only source of anxiety was Coke and he told Buckingham that he believed that a warning would silence him, though it would have to come from no one but the king.[57] One wonders whether Cranfield, previously one of the most determined advocates of boldness in dealing with the referees, had already received a warning.[58]

Bacon's optimism was, at first at least, justified. The Commons met the Lords on 8 March in the Painted Chamber and the presentation of the evidence took place as planned. Coke closed the conference with his long speech on the four types of judicature exercised in parliament. He stressed the right of the Lords to judge without the king, undoubtedly to convince them that they were justified in trying Mompesson.[59] But not one of the speeches mentioned the referees. When, on the following day, the Commons held a post-mortem on the conference, great anger was exhibited at this omission and the speakers did their best to excuse themselves.[60] Cranfield returned to his normal theme, maintaining that if the referees were not involved all the blame for the grant would fall upon

[57] Spedding, vii, 191-2.

[58] On 2 March he had addressed the House on the limits of its power. He said that it had no power to determine the jurisdiction of the courts: this belonged to the king. The Commons could enquire and complain, but only the king could reform. Alford disagreed with him, saying that the jurisdiction of courts was to be limited by parliament: *C.D.* v, 20. Cranfield's attacking methods were also used against him. Locke wrote to Carleton on 3 March that he had admitted to abuses in his court—but had claimed that these were much more numerous in Chancery: *C.S.P. Dom. 1619-23*, 231. If he did receive such a warning its effect quickly wore off, as will be seen, but Cranfield harboured a deep resentment towards Bacon and took pride in the part he played in his ruin: C. D. Bowen, *Francis Bacon* (London, 1963), 146; Prestwich, 287. Such warnings were not unknown in 1621: both Sandyses were threatened by Cranfield and Sir Dudley Digges was probably warned by the Court: Willson, *Privy Councillors*, 158.

[59] Relf, pp. xiv-xv. For an analysis of Coke's speech, see above, pp. 45-7. Miss Relf considers that Coke's advocacy of the Lords' power to judge alone exceeded 'anything justified by medieval precedent'. However, he may not have exaggerated as greatly as she suggests: most (but not all) of his precedents in support of this judicature are taken from the Good Parliament of 1376 when, with Edward III senile and the Black Prince dying, the judicature was, for all practical purposes, vested in the Lords alone.

[60] It seems impossible to know exactly why this omission occurred. The committee dealing with Mompesson's case may or may not have recommended that the referees be mentioned, though if it did Bacon's optimism is surprising (but it may not have reached its decision until after Bacon's letter to Buckingham was written). In the feverish and incomplete preparations in the Commons on the 8th,

H

the king, and the House agreed to request another conference
with the Lords at which the omission might be repaired.[61]

Coke carried this request to the Lords who consented to a
further conference to be held on 10 March and the Commons
arranged for their speakers to be sent back to the Lords then
'with theyre lesson punctually set downe to them what to say'.
James at this point made two further attempts apparently to
divert the danger implicit in this decision. He asked the
Commons to postpone the conference because it would delay
discussion of the subsidy, and received an assurance that this
would not happen.[62] He also addressed the Lords before the
conference on 10 March, in an attempt to impose his guidance
upon the forthcoming developments. He spoke of the procedure in cases of the Mompesson type, stating that the
Commons should act as accusers and the Lords as judges.
'The accusers are to lead, but it must either be confessed or
proved by witnesses. Accusers are good informers but bad
judges. The clamor must be well proved otherwise it is a
Calumie.'[63] James also commented upon the use of precedents.
These were valuable but he had warned Coke to use only
those arising in the reigns of good kings, not weak ones. He
tried to draw the sting from Yelverton's accusations by de-

just before the conference, Mallory proposed that the referees be named, but the
Speaker either did not hear or did not want to hear, and, according to all but
one account, he adjourned the House without putting the question. Because of
this the Commons' speakers could justly claim that they had received no authority
to mention the referees, whose names they did not officially know. It is, however,
clear from the indignation aroused that many members had expected the subject
to be raised and in a letter to Mead, on 9 March, his anonymous correspondent
actually said that the Lords and Commons had met on the previous day to consider
the punishment of monopolists and referees. Camden said that the Commons
complained that the members sent to the Lords 'acted deceitfully, and prevari-
cated': Camden, ii, 656; *C.D.* ii, 171; v, 282; Williams, *James I*, ii, 235.

[61] *C.D.* ii, 202; *C.J.* i, 547; Nicholas, *Proceedings*, i, 137. On 10 March Chamberlain wrote to Carleton that the Commons were not willing to spare the referees
'be they never so great'. A comparison with his opinion only eleven days previously
(see above, p. 89 n. 17) provides an interesting yardstick of the Commons'
achievement in this vital matter: Chamberlain, ii, 350.

[62] Chamberlain, ii, 350-2; *C.D.* ii, 205.

[63] Relf, 14. Attention must be drawn to James's reference to 'clamor'. Is he
thinking in the same terms as Hakewill who, a few weeks later, was to remark:
'I have observed when we have gone to the Lords it hath been by impeachment,
clamor or accusation'? (See above, p. 48).

scribing him as a rash attorney whom he had been compelled to dismiss, and, as a logical extension, he defended Buckingham. However, he encouraged the Lords to proceed with the matter of Mompesson—giving him a fair trial and not accepting the Commons' legal opinions too uncritically—but not to spend too much time on him.[64] The king also showed that he was not prepared to protect Bacon or Mandeville, whom the Commons were shortly afterwards to name as referees; but he did distinguish between punishment of persons and examination of the legality of patents, saying that the latter must be left to the judges.[65] If the speech was an attempt to seize control of the situation and divide the Lords from the Commons it was not very successful: it contained too many subtle changes of emphasis and revealed weaknesses of attitude that were to make the concessions derived from it lasting. The king had made a speech which he would not have chosen to make had not the pressures upon him and his favourite, Buckingham, been mounting.[66]

The first consequence of the king's speech was that Bacon and Mandeville, clearly thoroughly alarmed by the king's lack of support for them, made grovelling and submissive speeches at the conference of the two Houses. To speak in this way in their own defence was against the orders of the House and the Lords later expressed their irritation by censuring both men.[67]

[64] He said that the Lords, unlike the Commons, were a court of record and could act as such. There was no need to search precedents to prove this.

[65] Relf, 14; E. de Villiers, ed. 'The Hastings Journal of the Parliament of 1621', *Camden Miscellany*, xx (Camden 3rd series, lxxxiii: London, 1953), pp. viii-ix. In a letter to Carleton on 12 March, Locke said that the king had thrown all blame on the referees: *C.S.P. Dom. 1619-23*, 234.

[66] Miss Relf believes (p. xv) that James's speech shows that he disliked the whole proceeding on which the two Houses were engaged, but that he could find no grounds for objection although, as one of the diarists points out, Mompesson was a servant of the king: *C.D.* v, 35. Lady de Villiers, however, sees (p. ix) the speech as winning for the king a tactical victory, and says that James believed that, if the trials were conducted on the lines he had laid down, the crown had nothing to fear from the revived judicial power.

[67] De Villiers, 29-30; *L.J.* iii, 42. Southampton and Wallden led the attack on Bacon and Mandeville: ff. 7-8 of H. L. R. O. Braye MS 11 which is Elsynge's first draft of the *Lords Journal* for the period 12-27 March, 1621. Mandeville tried to clear himself on the patent for alehouses 'which was not by us [the Commons] spoken of'. As a result the Commons resolved to examine it and Noy was put in charge of reporting on it: *C.D.* iv, 146; vi, 54.

The Houses then made arrangements for another conference, the Lords choosing twenty-four of their number who, with the prince, were to meet fifty members of the Commons.[68]

From 13 March until the Lords' sentencing of Mompesson on the 26th the two Houses met in frequent conference. Assured of the king's encouragement the meetings made solid progress. The Commons acceded to the Lords' request to present their evidence in writing provided that this did not become a precedent.[69] Buckingham acknowledged his mistakes but asked that these be excused on the ground of his youth and inexperience. He declared that if his brothers were found guilty he would be the first to condemn them.[70] But the Villiers family was still too entrenched and the Commons were not prepared to jeopardise their chances of success against Mompesson by a reckless chase after Buckingham's brothers. Perhaps for the same reason, when Coke handed the Commons' written evidence to the Lords on 15 March he made little mention of the referees.[71] He compared Mompesson with Empson and Dudley, to the detriment of Mompesson, and asked the Lords for condign punishment. His report ended, he received the congratulations of both Prince Charles and the

[68] *C.D.* ii, 209. Curiously, the *Lords Journal* lists twenty-five members of this committee, apart from Charles: *L.J.* iii, 42. Elsynge's first draft journal for 12 March records a proposal that a committee of the Lords should be appointed to examine the Commons' evidence so that 'the worlde [might know] whether the blame therof [i.e. for the grievances] ought to be layed on the Referees of the sayd graunts, or uppon them whoe unduly (as yt is reported) executed the same'. This account, written by Elsynge on the first day he presided at the Table, was rejected by the Lords' sub-committee, and in his next draft—which he calls his first draft—this proposal is omitted, as it is in the final *Journal*: H. L. R. O. Braye MS 11, ff. 1-13; H. L. R. O. Braye MS 69, ff. 2-2v (the rejected draft); *L.J.* iii, 42.

[69] Coke said that in all conferences between the Lords and the Commons, business had always been transacted orally: Nicholas, *Proceedings*, i, 167.

[70] *C.D.* ii, 212, 227.

[71] *C.D.* ii, 227ff; vi, 66. But their names were handed to the Lords, contrary to what Gardiner said: *C.D.* ii, 230; vi, 66; Gardiner, *History*, iv, 53-5. Gardiner believed that the Commons' change of attitude was due to the king's conversion to support for their proceedings under the influence of Williams, dean of Westminster. But was this the main reason for the change? The referees, as referees, had always looked fairly secure and since the uncovering, on the previous day, of another type of evidence—of corruption—against Bacon there was less reason for the continuation of the rather forlorn hunt (see p. 110, below). Furthermore, if the bill against monopolies, which was then under discussion in the Commons, went through, there was less cause to worry about referees as such.

Commons.[72] The Lords then appointed three committees to examine Mompesson's patents, one each for inns, gold and silver thread, and concealments, and arranged that these should examine witnesses on oath because their evidence before the Commons had not been sworn. As some of these witnesses were members of the Commons, and others its prisoners, the lower House at first found the Lords' intention unpalatable: if the evidence they had collected required confirmation on oath this reduced their status.[73] Brooke maintained that the Commons acted as a grand jury for the whole commonwealth, and that it was therefore improper to require oaths of members. Coke objected to the Lords' request on the ground that, as judges of fact, members should not be sworn as witnesses. Hakewill suggested unsuccessfully that precedents be examined; and the debate meandered along in a fashion which revealed how uncertain the House was of its position.[74] Eventually, it was persuaded to consent to the attendance of witnesses at the Lords by a calmly practical speech from Sir Edwin Sandys:

The Question before us was of the Pattents and the Projects, which we have adjudged to be greivances both in the originall and in the execution. The Question before the Lords is of the punishment, which may reache to life, and God forbid they showld proceede upon an implicite faith of the examinacions taken by us without oathe.[75]

Sandys also challenged Brooke's point about the grand jury, pointing out that it was well known that a grand jury's verdict did not lead to condemnation without further trial. Eventually, a compromise was reached: witnesses who were members said that they were prepared to take the oath as private

[72] Two days earlier Buckingham had ridiculed those who doubted Coke: *C.D.* vi, 381.

[73] *L.J.* iii, 46-7; *C.D.* vi, 70. That this might lead to an awkward situation was shown later when Davenport made accusations against Field which he was unprepared to repeat, on oath, before the Lords. Chamberlain said that there was a suspicion that the matter of witnesses was being used to break the amity between the Houses: Chamberlain, ii, 355.

[74] *L.J.* iii, 48; *C.D.* iv, 162; v, 303; vi, 70; *C.J.* i, 557-8.

[75] *C.D.* iv, 163.

individuals so that no order of the Commons was required on this issue. In consequence, the argument about the Commons' jurisdiction died down for the time being, and a few days later in a message of appreciation to the Lords for their concern in examining grievances the lower House specifically thanked them for 'giving the Oath unto the Examinants, which they cannot do'.[76]

However, this was neither the first nor the last time that this issue was debated. Bound up as it was with the question whether or not the Commons were a court of record, the power to administer an oath was central to any discussion of the jurisdiction of the House. The right was vigorously claimed and as vigorously denied. In 1610 a committee had been appointed to consider whether the Commons possessed the right. In the middle of February 1621 Coke had explained why the House could not administer an oath—'because Nothing should be brought before them but that which is Notorious and knowne'; and in the debate just discussed Glanville gave another explanation: as the House was the representative body of the realm it was 'not to be presumed to be ignorant of the affaires of the countrie'. Later in the session, after the Floyd affair, Samuel Sandys claimed that the House might administer an oath in examining matters which were within its cognisance; and in 1624 Edwin Sandys repeated this but acknowledged that there was an unresolved doubt about the existence of such power in areas where the Commons lacked the right to give a final judgment.[77] That the right to use an oath was for so long a matter of debate is a measure both of the Commons' growing judicial authority and of their frustration.

To return to Mompesson: once the question of re-examination of witnesses had been settled the Lords' committees were able to proceed with their work and by 22 March the Commons' accusations against Mompesson were declared sufficiently proved for the peers to sentence him. They reserved the right to deal, after the Easter recess, with Michell and the patentees for gold and silver thread, but hurried on arrangements for

---

[76] *L.J.* iii, 61.

[77] Foster, 'Patents and Monopolies', 82-3 n. 63; *C.D.* v, 46; vi, 430; Nicholas, *Proceedings*, ii, 49; Foster, *Parliament 1610*, ii, 361.

completing the Mompesson case so that the extent of parliament's justice might become known.[78] The Lords appointed a committee to survey the precedents of 'Judicature, Accusations, and Judgments', and this almost certainly took the expert opinion of John Selden who was employed by the House at this time.[79] On 26 March the king addressed the Lords, giving his consent to the sentencing of Mompesson. The House then debated the punishment and considered the precedents now presented to it. Empson's indictment was read but Charles carried the peers with him when he said that the precedent was irrelevant: Empson had been indicted for treason and his trial had been before commissioners in the country, not the Lords. Mandeville, the Lord Treasurer, then proved that none of the actions of which Mompesson stood accused was more than a misdemeanour and he proposed a punishment which the House debated and then adopted.[80]

Meanwhile the Commons had been discussing their own part in the punishment of Mompesson, citing precedents to show whether they merely had a right to be present, or to be present and to demand judgment, or even to insist on an increase in a sentence which they found inadequate.[81] When

[78] *L.J.* iii, 63. Michell was associated with Mompesson in the thread patent, as well as being commissioner for enforcing the patent for recognisances of alehouses, so that if the case against him were to be kept alive the examination of the thread patent had to remain open. In fact, all these investigations continued after the recess, bringing under scrutiny the activities of men like Fowle and Geldard, agents and associates of Michell and Mompesson. Fowle was examined by the Lords on a complaint which the peers said had been transmitted to them by the Commons; but there is no surviving evidence that the Commons had resolved on this, or that they had sent Fowle himself to the Lords—as the peers also claimed: *L.J.* iii, 63, 65, 91, 92, 123; Gardiner, *Debates 1621*, 24.

[79] *L.J.* iii, 65. The committee reported on the day it was appointed, presenting the Lords with a list of precedents. This named Sir John Maltravers, Borges de Bayons, John Deverill, Thomas Gurney and William Ogle (from 1330), Sir John Lee (1368), and William Latimer and Richard Lyons (1376); and a note in the manuscript indicates that other cases were also reported: H. L. R. O. Braye MS 11, f. 105. The cases from 1330 illustrate action by the Lords on capital offences. The Commons evidently took no part in these cases, which, interestingly, appear here in exactly the same order as they do in Selden's work, *The Priviledges of the Baronage of England*, which was composed at this time.

[80] Relf, 42ff.

[81] The precedents were all drawn from 1376: Neville, Peach, Latimer. According to Hakewill the Commons had demanded an increase in Latimer's punishment: *C.D.* ii, 268; iv, 200, v, 323; Nicholas, *Proceedings*, i, 228. I have found no

the summons came to them to attend in the house of lords they demanded judgment through the Speaker.[82] Mompesson was sentenced by the peers to fine and outlawry. He was excluded from office, banished from the king's presence, his Court and the law courts, and exempted from any general pardon. He was degraded from knighthood and was to suffer life imprisonment when found.[83] To mark the day it was proposed not only that sermons should be preached at each anniversary, but that brass statues should be raised to the king and prince. Part of the following day was spent in mutual congratulation and thanks.[84] The king approved the sentence and used the opportunity provided by an address from the Commons to ask for an increased subsidy. Earlier Coke had grumbled that the patent of concealments had not been judged, but in the goodwill and satisfaction of the royal audience the House made no mention of this and members adjourned happily for the Easter recess. Three days later the king, by proclamation, cancelled the patents of thread, inns and alehouses.[85]

The trial of Mompesson marked the revival of parliamentary judicature. Although this process had lain unused for so many

evidence that the Commons formally demanded judgment or that they asked for an increase in Latimer's sentence, although they were, of course, active in all three cases.

[82] Chamberlain felt that the Commons were present merely to give their assent and were summoned purely out of courtesy: Chamberlain, ii, 357.

[83] Selden claimed that, by the precedents, the procedure adopted was faulty. As Mompesson had fled, proclamations should have been sent out that he must appear on a certain day, or a (specified) judgment would be given against him. He gave precedents for this and suggested that the failure in procedure stemmed from the long disuse of the judicature of parliament: *Of Judicature*, 90-1, 95. The procedure of issuing a proclamation was followed during the impeachment of Sir Thomas Mortimer in 1397.

An interesting sidelight on the novelty of the proceedings against Mompesson is provided by Elsynge who was clearly worried about how these should be entered in the *Lords Journal*. He had, of course, only recently become Clerk of the Parliaments: H. L. R. O. House of Lords Main Papers, 4-27 April, 1621, f. 22.

Gardiner saw the sentence on Mompesson as an indirect censure on James. Buckingham's action in excusing himself from attendance at the sentencing perhaps lends support to this view: Gardiner, *History*, iv, 84; *L.J.* iii, 71. Charles had protested against degrading Mompesson, maintaining that only the king might impose this punishment: Relf, 45.

[84] Relf, 49; *C.J.* i, 576. Brooke and Montague in the Commons thought that the Lords had been thanked sufficiently.

[85] *C.D.* iv, 207; *C.S.P. Dom. 1619-23*, 241.

years, its resurrection was achieved with remarkably little difficulty. Mompesson was probably a very suitable victim—neither so important that the proceedings would suffer from undue interference, nor so unimportant that they would pass unnoticed. Subsequent trials both in 1621 and later, would exhibit significant procedural changes, but the trial of Mompesson had established a precedent which did not have the disadvantage of being two and half centuries old.

When Selden wrote about this case in his treatise *Of the Judicature in Parliaments* he said 'The Commons accused and impeached by word of Mouth Sir Giles Mompesson . . .', but later he indicates that the proceedings were conducted *ex parte regis*.[86] Now it will be remembered that, when both Selden and Elsynge drew a distinction between impeachment and complaint, they said that in cases of the first the suit belonged to the Commons and in the second to the king.[87] Selden therefore seems to have had some difficulty in classifying Mompesson's case, which does not fit easily into either of his categories, and as will be seen he faced similar problems with Middlesex. Unfortunately, the records of 1621 are of no help in classifying the first case of parliamentary judicature—or indeed any other. Coke's two speeches on judicature testify to the existence of more than one method of association between the Commons and Lords, but there is no evidence that he ever stated which method was used to deal with the cases in which he played such an important part. The very full records of this parliament contain no indication that any member ever said that Mompesson was being impeached; Coke and Hakewill both refer to the Commons' complaints against him, but whether they were using the word in its general or technical sense seems impossible to say.[88] For the moment, therefore, it will probably be as well to resist the temptation to classify this

[86] Selden, *Of Judicature*, 30, 63.

[87] See pp. 38-1, above. According to Selden, the suit also belonged to the king in cases where the Commons presented information.

[88] *C.J.* i, 576; *C.D.* ii, 188. Hakewill began his speech to the Lords at the conference on 8 March with the words: 'There is another complaint against Sir Giles Mompesson . . .': *C.D.* ii, 188. On 26 March, Coke supported the view that the Commons were entitled to demand judgment from the Lords and said '. . . where the Commons complain to the Lords, they judge it; and the Commons present': *C.J.* i, 576; Nicholas, *Proceedings*, i, 229.

case, especially as it is at least possible that members, concerned with results rather than careful distinctions, would have been unable or unwilling to do so themselves.[89] Nevertheless, we can at least think twice before assuming that this case marked the revival of impeachment.

By the time that Mompesson's punishment was pronounced the Commons had become deeply involved in the pursuit of a very important victim. Francis Bacon was not only Lord Chancellor and, as such, identified with the enemies of the common law; he was also one of the king's close advisers, a friend of Buckingham, and the owner of an intellect which repelled as many as it attracted. When the parliament of 1621 opened he seemed completely out of the reach of his enemies and the sniping at the referees had brought him little nearer their grasp. The means which led to Bacon's ruin was the Commons' committee appointed to investigate abuses in courts of justice. On 8 February Cranfield had proposed the creation of such a committee but although this was done it speedily lapsed until he proposed its revival on 12 March.[90] On this occasion his brainchild proved to be tougher and the world into which it was born better equipped to sustain it. Animosity towards Bacon had been growing, and on 14 March the answer to the prayers of those who wanted to destroy the referee appeared in the form of evidence of corruption in the judge.[91] This very soon showed itself to be a more hopeful line

[89] A statement of Cotton's provides another type of warning: 'To infer, that because the Lords pronounced the sentence, the point of Judgment should be only theirs, were as absurd, as to conclude that no authority was left in any other Commissioner of Oyer and Terminer, than in the person of that man solely that speaketh the Sentence': R. Cotton, *Cottoni Posthuma; Divers Choice Pieces of that Renowned Antiquary Sir Robert Cotton* (London, 1651), 352.

[90] *C.D.* ii, 22, 44; vi, 55. He had suggested investigations into the administering of justice on 5 February.

[91] On 25 February Mead had written: 'It is said, that there are many bills ready to be put up against my lord chancellor', and there is a hint that the real reason for Sackville's removal from reporting the proceedings in the committee for courts of justice was his refusal to report complaints received against Bacon: Williams, *James I*, ii, 232; *C.D.* v, 258. But for Sackville, see Prestwich, 292-4. Mrs Prestwich states that Bacon and Sackville were relentless enemies throughout 1621 but she also points out Sackville's ability to change sides rapidly.

If Cranfield did not foresee what the committee might uncover, his motions were remarkably well favoured.

of attack. The first evidence came from Christopher Aubrey and Edward Egerton who claimed that, in the hope of speeding up Chancery suits in which they were involved, they had given Sir George Hastings and Sir Robert Yonge, two of Bacon's servants and both members of the Commons, sums of money intended for Bacon.[92] Egerton had also entered into an arrangement with Dr Theophilus Field, once Bacon's chaplain, now bishop of Llandaff and a friend of Buckingham, and with Randolph Davenport, one of Bacon's Chancery officials. The plan was that Field was to persuade Buckingham to write a letter to Bacon to ask him to hurry along Egerton's suit. Field was to receive £6,000 when Egerton received his decree. This sum was to be divided but Egerton did not know the names of the other participants. As a guarantee of his good faith Egerton immediately entered into a recognisance for £10,000 with Field. Both of Egerton's schemes failed because Bacon gave an adverse decision and because Davenport, acting for Field, was unable to persuade either Buckingham or the king to intervene with Bacon. The committee arranged to collect further evidence and refused the request of Meautys, Bacon's secretary, for copies of the petitions against his master and of the letter, written by Field, which had been read to the committee.[93] When Phelips reported to the House on 15 March he suggested that the evidence should eventually be sent to the Lords.

On the 16th the committee gathered further information from Hastings and Yonge. They described how they had told Bacon that they had admitted to handing him presents, and how he had replied that he would have to deny this. Hastings also maintained that Bacon had tried to divert Aubrey from presenting his petition by promising him a favourable decision which he had subsequently not delivered. When this evidence was reported, some members found it too good to be true and

---

[92] *C.D.* ii, 224-5; iv, 155. Edward Egerton's dispute was with a distant relative, Roland Egerton, over land left by the will of Sir John Egerton, Roland's father. Roland had obtained letters of administration from Sir John Bennet, another of the men presented by the Commons to the Lords in 1621: *L.J.* iii, 56-7.

[93] *C.D.* ii, 225-6; iv, 156, 161; vii, 578-9; *L.J.* iii, 53-7. Field's letter was described as most 'dishonest in corruption': *C.D.* v, 298.

questioned the reliability of the witnesses.[94] In attempting to restore their confidence Coke argued that 'you will make bribery to be unpunished, if he that carrieth the bribe shall not be a witness'. The use—for the first time in this case—of the word bribery perhaps had its influence in persuading the Commons to accept their committee's recommendation that all the evidence be sent to the Lords.[95]

The committee gave three reasons for its suggestion: there were precedents to support it, from the time of their ancestors; as a peer Bacon could not be dealt with by the Commons; and the lower House, lacking the power to administer an oath, had no way of discovering the truth. In the ensuing debate the Secretary, Calvert, suggested that the evidence should be shown to the king as well as to the peers, but most members were more concerned to discuss the manner of the reference to the Lords. Should the Commons simply refer petitioners to the upper House, or should they present the evidence themselves? How far should they repeat their actions in Mompesson's case? Mr Recorder Finch objected to the presentation of evidence on the ground that this would resemble an accusation, while Noy believed that the Commons were obliged to take the matter to the Lords but advised his fellow members 'not to deliver it as a thing certayne, as wee did in Sir Gyles Mompessons case But as an Informacion . . .'[96] Eventually, as so often, it was Coke's proposal which was adopted. He urged the House to lay the evidence before the Lords and to search for the precedents which he believed to exist. He received the support of Calvert on the grounds that this would

---

[94] *C.D.* ii, 237ff; v, 40, 44. Hastings had at first stated that he had hidden the purpose of the gift from Bacon. His subsequent evidence suggested the reverse.

[95] *C.D.* ii, 242. For a discussion of Coke's apparently unwarranted use of this word, see Spielman, 29-40. Was its use quite unwarranted in view of Hastings' testimony about Bacon's reaction to Aubrey's petition?

[96] *C.D.* iv, 167. It may be recalled that Selden lists three ways in which the Commons might be associated in a case: by impeachment, by complaint, or by information. In the last two, according to Selden, proceedings were conducted *ex parte regis*: see above, pp 38-9. According to Nicholas's account, Noy said that the Commons could not claim to have 'found this [the evidence against Bacon] as a Truth, but that there is such a Clamour amongst us; and that we should desire their Lordships so to take this unto them, as that they will not exclude us': Nicholas, *Proceedings*, i, 185.

be the fairest course for Bacon's sake and the House resolved to present the evidence orally but without attaching to it any accusation. The temperature of the debate had been a good deal lower than when the House had dealt with Mompesson, and the decision on procedure significantly different.[97] Bacon's peerage as well as the Commons' lack of jurisdiction had persuaded them to go to the Lords.

On the 19th the Commons requested a conference with the Lords and replied to a message from the king about procedure. James suggested that a commission of six lords and twelve members of the Commons, chosen by the Houses, should examine the evidence against Bacon and then hand it to him for judgment. The Commons, disliking the proposed interference and its inherent dangers to parliamentary jurisdiction, returned a cautious answer that they could make no reply until the Lords had received the proposal, and resolved to continue as already planned.[98] The king never sent his message to the Lords:[99] another attempt at royal adjudication had failed. The conference took place and Phelips spoke on behalf of the Commons.[100] The Lords agreed to examine witnesses and during the next few days, while the Commons' committees continued to collect evidence against Bacon to present to the Lords, the peers obtained the lower House's consent to the appearance before them and examination on oath of Yonge and Hastings. The Commons handed over the bishop of Llandaff's correspondence, and the Lords, to cope with the volume of evidence, appointed three small committees for which they drew up a list of questions to be asked of the witnesses.[101]

[97] *C.D.* ii, 237ff; iv, 166ff; *C.J.* i, 560-1. The Commons ignored the embittered speech of Neville, who suggested that Bacon should have to give evidence on oath because he had denied to the Lords their privilege of answering in the Chancery on their honour: *C.D.* ii, 240.

[98] *C.D.* ii, 244-5.

[99] But the feeling of the Lords seems to have been against the proposal: *C.D.* vi, 385.

[100] He 'made a Declaration of the Complaints against my Lord Chancellor and the bishop of Llandaff'. He had earlier been sent to ask for the conference 'touching the Informacions against' Bacon and the bishop: *C.D.* iv, 171.

[101] *C.D.* ii, 246; iv, 174; *L.J.* iii, 60; de Villiers, 31-2. The committees were headed by Arundel, Huntingdon and Southampton. A similar number of committees had been used in Mompesson's case.

As the evidence against him accumulated, Bacon himself attempted to ward off at least the worst of the blow. He wrote submissively to the Lords, and though this had no effect the House did consent to give him notes of the general objections against him. However, he suffered from the absence of genuine support in the Lords and even the illness—real enough—to which he succumbed at this time caused suspicion.[102] He also made attempts to find out where the Court stood, using Buckingham as his intermediary, but the only favour the king was prepared at this moment to show his Lord Chancellor was to ask the Lords to ensure that 'the witnesses against him were sufficient'. Perhaps by now the king considered the issue lost in the face of the Lords' determination: they had recently arranged for the protection of their witnesses and for the continuation of the examination during the Easter recess; and as parliament adjourned on 27 March political observers reported little of comfort to James or Bacon.[103]

[102] Relf, 52. But Chamberlain, on 24 March, reported that many lords visited him each day, Buckingham being the most frequent visitor. However, he also said that his letter was meant only to gain time until the heat of the prosecution had passed: Chamberlain, ii, 356; *C.S.P. Dom. 1619-23*, 240.

[103] *Cabala, Mysteries of State, in Letters of the great Ministers of K. James and K. Charles* (London, 1654), 10-11; D'Ewes, *Autobiography*, i, 179; Williams, *James I*, ii, 243; *L.J.* iii, 67, 74. Lando reported that many of those nearest to the king wished that parliament had never been summoned. The only sign—and this proved abortive—of any change in parliamentary sympathies is Chamberlain's remark that Coke's popularity had declined and that his choice of precedents had become careless: *C.S.P. Ven. 1619-21*, 618; Chamberlain, ii, 358. In fact, James seems to have encouraged the Lords in their proceedings against Bacon: Williams, *James I*, ii, 243; *C.D.* vii, 590-1.

CHAPTER V

The Parliament of 1621: April to June

The Easter recess marked no improvement in the Lord Chancellor's fortunes. When the Houses reassembled on 17 April, 1621, the question was not so much whether the Lords would pass judgment upon Bacon as how the last stages were to be dealt with. A mass of evidence had been heard by the Lords' committees during the recess: this was now reported by the three chairmen and on 19 April they were asked to draw up a charge—work which in the previous case had been undertaken by the Commons. To accomplish it the committees amalgamated. These developments caused a breakdown in the defence which Bacon seems to have been preparing. He had drawn up a list of precedents which might have helped him and he could almost certainly have used at least one of these—that of Chief Justice Thorpe in 1351—with effect.[1] He had also seen the king and worked out a plan which would have involved an admission of guilt where this was unavoidable but a protestation of innocence whenever he could make a clear answer. He had asked the king for help in obtaining a copy of the charges, which though not yet drawn up were clearly about to be made. The king, however, had merely referred his request to the Lords. Now, faced by a growing volume of evidence and burdened with continuing ill-health, he submitted to the Lords and threw himself on their mercy.[2] He admitted the correctness of the accusations—which he had not seen—and hoped that loss of office would be sufficient punishment.

---

[1] Thorpe had been found guilty of taking bribes and the prosecution had been based partly on his oath of office which placed heavy restrictions on receiving presents. Bacon's oath of office was less rigid in this respect: Spedding, vii, 232-4.

[2] *L.J.* iii, 75, 80; Spedding, vii, 232-4, 240, 242-5; de Villiers, 32; Gardiner, *History*, iv, 87-8; J. Rushworth, *Historical Collections* (London, 1659-1701), i, 29-30. In his plan he had intended to do this only where he was forced to admit guilt: de Villiers, 32.

Doubtless astonished at the totality of Bacon's submission, the Lords sat in silence for some time after the reading of his letter. They then debated two issues. They first decided that the submission was not a sufficient basis for a censure and that an examination of Bacon himself was required. This gave rise to a debate upon the conduct of the examination. The Lord Chamberlain suggested that the charges be sent to Bacon as a mark of his importance; Lord Saye argued that both de la Pole and Yelverton had attended the Lords to answer in person and that Bacon should do so. But eventually the House decided that the charges, though not the proofs, should be sent. This was done and on the following day the Lords asked Bacon whether he would be making a confession or a defence. He replied that he would be confessing and was given five days in which to do so.[3] He made his confession in writing on 30 April, by which time he had recovered his previous poise. He admitted most of the charges but denied a few and explained his actions in some cases.[4] The House next required the document to be acknowledged as his own by Bacon and sent a delegation to him for this purpose. They also asked the king to sequester the Great Seal, which was done, and on 3 May sentenced Bacon in his absence. The sentence was debated in committee, precedents were quoted but little used, and the only real disagreement was over the question of degrading him from his peerage. When the House resumed and the questions were put by the Lord Chief Justice this proposal was defeated, but Bacon was sentenced to fine and imprisonment, exclusion from parliament, Court and office. Only Buckingham voted against the punishments. The peers then sent a message to the Commons inviting them to come to demand judgment. That afternoon, 'at the prayer and demand of the Commons by their Speaker', this was pronounced by the Lord Chief Justice. He said that 'the Lords had duly considered of the complaints presented by the Commons against the . . . late Lord Chancellor, and

[3] Gardiner, *Debates 1621*, 13, 20-1; Spedding, vii, 248, 250.

[4] The Lords did not examine Bacon's replies in detail and, in pronouncing him guilty, made no distinction between the charges to which he had confessed and those which he had denied. Mompesson's offences received rather more detailed examination before the Lords decided on his punishment: Relf, 40ff; Spedding, vii, 263ff.

have found him guilty. . .' He then read out the Lords' sentence.[5]

Bacon was convicted as a taker of bribes, whatever the force of the deeper political reasons which spurred on the attack. Of corruption he was, in parliament's view, just as guilty as was Mompesson of creating grievances. But, unlike Mompesson, he had broken the law: the Commons had to vote Mompesson's activities grievous, thus in effect creating an offence; but Bacon confessed to an offence. The two trials also differed in that in the case of Mompesson the Commons, by framing an accusation, brought it closer to completion than in that of Bacon where the drawing up of the accusation and the collection of much of the evidence was the work of the Lords. If the Commons' approach to Bacon's case was more diffident than its bitter attack on Mompesson this can be explained by the difference in status of the two men and the early difficulty over the matter of the referees. But once the means for an attack on Bacon had been discovered this was pressed forward with determination equal to that shown in the earlier trial.

For Coke, the condemnation of Bacon must have represented a considerable personal triumph, yet the case receives no more than a passing mention in his writings. To which of his categories of judicature he would have assigned it is unknown. The Commons had recognised that Bacon's peerage compelled them to approach the Lords; and, although the position changes after 1621, the Commons' part, at this time, in proceedings against members of the Lords was not very substantial. Noy's speech in March, when he recommended that the Commons should merely lay information before the Lords, epitomised the tentative approach of the lower House. Furthermore, Noy was evidently anxious to avoid a danger that this course might terminate the Commons' connection with the case, because he adds that, notwithstanding his proposal, 'we will not desert [the case], but desire that we may repaire to their Lordshipps againe for Judgment.'[6] If a choice must be made between the

[5] *L.J.* iii, 101, 102, 106; Gardiner, *Debates 1621*, 61-4; *C.D.* ii, 341-2; v, 138; *C.J.* i, 606. The proposal, by Saye, to degrade Bacon was lost by only two votes, according to Chamberlain. The margin seems surprisingly small: Chamberlain, ii, 371. The fine of £40,000 was remitted; the imprisonment very short.

[6] *C.D.* iv, 167.

various categories of judicature described by Coke in 1621 and, probably rather later, by Selden and Elsynge, it can hardly be suggested that Bacon's case fits into one which lays much emphasis on the Commons' share in the procedure.[7]

The condemnation of Sir Henry Yelverton which followed shortly after Bacon's fall bears more similarity to the fate of Cranfield in 1624 than to the trial of the Lord Chancellor. Yelverton was the victim of his own stupidity and of the hatred of the king and Buckingham. James openly told the Lords that he expected a judgment against Yelverton, and his part in obtaining this was plain. If further evidence is needed of the lack of a Court plot against Bacon it is provided by the sight of the royal activity against Yelverton. Unlike the attitudes of Bacon, those of Yelverton elicited sympathy from the more independent members of the Lords and yet the king did not hesitate to enter the lists against him. If James had been anxious to destroy Bacon an open attack would have been quite in order.[8]

Yelverton had already fallen foul of the Court before the parliament of 1621 opened. Early in the reign he had opposed the king's Scottish policies, but in January 1610 he had expiated this offence and in 1616 had been made Attorney General. Causing further offence he had been accused in the Star Chamber by Buckingham of illegal practices. He lost his job and was imprisoned in the Tower where in 1621 he was awaiting his opportunity for revenge against the favourite.[9] This came early in March, during the Commons' investigation

[7] Selden merely describes Bacon as having been 'accused' by the Commons: *Of Judicature*, 31.

[8] It is possible that, unknown to James, Buckingham was intriguing against Bacon and Mrs Bowen leans towards the view that the duke 'had consented to this impeachment from the first'. Her source is a hint by Clarendon. Against this opinion must be set Buckingham's solitary vote against Bacon's punishment. He may have been protecting himself but, as James had hardly rushed to Bacon's defence, there seems little reason for Buckingham to have gone to such lengths to disguise his hostility to the Chancellor, if such existed: Bowen, *Bacon*, 152. See also Spielman, 55-6 and n. 60; Roberts, 23-4. A line in a probably contemporary poem on Bacon's fall should, however, be noted: 'Perhaps the game of Buck, (no name), hath vilified the Bore': Bodl. Rawlinson MS B. 151, f. 102v.

[9] Chamberlain, ii, 335; Nichols, ii, 703.

of patents, when the committee sent to the Tower heard from Yelverton that his consent to what he maintained were bad patents had been extracted from him by threats.[10] On 9 March members were told that Yelverton, among others, had signed a warrant dormant to permit search, arrest and seizure of goods in connection with the thread patent. The House agreed, without giving a reason, to send this piece of evidence to the Lords, telling them that, in the Commons' opinion, it was against the law. There does not seem to have been any vote to send Yelverton himself to the Lords, but on 18 April he was summoned before the peers to answer the Commons' charge that he was responsible for imprisoning merchants who had offended against the patent. The Lords appear to have been responsible for adding another charge—that Yelverton had perpetrated abuses in issuing writs of *quo warranto* in connection with the inns' patent. Well before this the king had weakened his position in the case by formally handing Yelverton over to the Lords to deal with,[11] but now, angered by Yelverton's defence that he had actually tried to safeguard the king's profit (and had suffered imprisonment for doing so) by attempting to control the number and the evils of patents, he announced to the Lords that he regarded such a defence as a personal insult. Furthermore, he strongly objected to Yelverton's being put to answer the second charge which he regarded as outside the scope of the investigations which he had authorised the Lords to conduct. For the moment, however, he made no attempt to take control of the prosecution and simply asked the Lords to punish Yelverton.[12]

[10] See above, p. 99. Yelverton was being questioned about the patent for gold and silver thread for which he had been one of the referees: *C.D.* ii, 164-6.

[11] As Yelverton had been sentenced to imprisonment by the Star Chamber, the king's action was presumably necessary if the Lords were to avoid the difficulties which had faced the Commons over Proctor. It will be remembered that James protested when Proctor, who was his prisoner, was committed to the custody of the Commons' serjeant for an offence against their privileges: above, see p. 67.

[12] *C.D.* iv, 139-140; v, 71; *L.J.* iii, 77, 82; Rushworth, i, 31ff. James was shown evidence that few of the writs of *quo warranto* issued by Yelverton had been completed according to due process of law: *L.J.* iii, 96. It appears to have been the inclusion of this second charge and the nature of Yelverton's defence, rather than, as Gardiner suggested, the Lords' readiness to allow his remarks to pass unchecked, which annoyed the king: *L.J.* iii, 81-2; Gardiner, *History*, iv, 111.

The storm broke in earnest on 30 April. Yelverton was required to explain his defence. He described the threats he had received of loss of office if he did not support the patents and, in a dramatic outburst identifying the author of the menaces as Buckingham, warned the favourite: 'If my Lord of Buckingham had but read the Articles exhibited in this place against Hugh Spencer and had known the danger of placing and displacing officers about a King he would not have pursued me with such bitterness.' After considerable interruption Yelverton was permitted to continue and finished by asserting that he was ready to prove all that he had said.[13]

A critical moment had arrived in the development of parliamentary judicature. Yelverton was making a much wider defence than the charge brought by the Commons required, yet he was before the house of lords as a result of that charge. What happened next might well be vital to the continuance of this judicature. For the first time in the investigation of monopolies Buckingham's name, so long hinted at, had been explicitly mentioned. Hints could be ignored by the Court; this could not. Furthermore, if Buckingham could be likened to Despenser, James could be compared with Edward II, so that by extension Yelverton's attack on the favourite cast a shadow across the monarch.[14] The government was faced with tragedy: it could not win. If the king took the examination into his own hands he would raise a storm of protest and would be confronted with his own abandonment of jurisdiction on 17 March; if he allowed the Lords to proceed with the full investigation which was essential to disprove Yelverton's charges, this would involve the questioning of Buckingham and an uncomfortably close and perhaps unprecedented examination of the government's activities.[15]

In the event, the king's only success was against Yelverton himself, but this was sufficiently conspicuous to hide, to some extent, the gain to the Lords. Moreover, the Lords had to proceed cautiously for fear of losing their advantage in an outburst of royal anger. When, therefore, on 2 May the king told the Lords that, while they might deal with Yelverton's

[13] *L.J.* iii, 121; Gardiner, *Debates 1621*, 43-9.
[14] De Villiers, p. x.   [15] D'Ewes, *Autobiography*, i, 186.

onslaught on Buckingham, he alone must judge the attack on his honour, the House debated how far the royal honour had been impugned but decided on a tactful procedure. On 6 May, with the archbishop of Canterbury as spokesman, the whole House presented itself before the king at Whitehall. Begging to be allowed to continue with the case, the Lords assured him that he would thereby show his trust in their readiness to do him justice. Their remarks upon the infringement their liberties were suffering as a result of the king's intentions caused James to comment upon the consequences of an acquittal of Yelverton and on the stand they were taking upon reason and precedent, a stand which he disliked.[16] However he promised them an answer the following afternoon and when this came it returned the case entirely to the Lords.

Despite their procedural victory the Lords were virtually obliged, because of the king's attitude to the case, to find Yelverton guilty. Even so, some days elapsed before the matter was finally settled. Yelverton's account was shown to be partly false, yet on the 12th, although the peers were prepared to vote that he had offended against the king's honour, they declared that they might reverse their decision if he were able to defend himself successfully. In fact, Yelverton's defence two days later was very disappointing. He retracted his charges against Buckingham and was censured unanimously. A sentence of fine, imprisonment and public submission was fixed and, on the 16th, formally pronounced. The Commons were not called to hear it, although their complaint was one of the reasons given for the punishment.[17] Perhaps earlier procedure was not followed because the Commons had apparently never formally transmitted Yelverton to the Lords.

Yelverton was sentenced by the Lords partly to preserve the privileges which had so nearly been snatched from them. There is considerable evidence to show that they acted reluctantly; they do not appear to have been unanimous over the

---

[16] Gardiner, *Debates 1621*, 54-60; de Villiers, 32-3. James said that they would be judging the king, adding that those who did this might depose him. He would never give them this right: de Villiers, 33.

[17] *L.J.* iii, 114-5, 119, 121-5. The Commons heard of the sentence on the same day: *C.D.* ii, 373.

size of the fine, and the Lord Treasurer proposed that the share
of it due to Buckingham be remitted; throughout there seems
to have been general sympathy for Yelverton and probably a
belief that, although he had failed to prove it, there was something in what he had originally said against Buckingham.[18]
The case had tested to a greater extent than previously the
relative strengths of Court and Lords, and although the king
had, on this occasion, successfully averted an attack on Buckingham, this had been achieved more by luck than judgment.[19]
Parliamentary judicature had been strengthened and parliament's control over it confirmed. When, in 1626, a serious
attempt was made to use it against Buckingham the monarch
would have to resort to rather more desperate evasive action.
On the other hand, the Commons' part in the case, especially
in its later stages, was fairly small, despite the fact that Yelverton did not enjoy the protection provided by membership of
the Lords; and neither Coke nor Selden thought the case worth
mentioning in their discussions of judicature.

While the Lords had been debating with the king over
Yelverton's case the Commons had become involved in a
similar and equally significant controversy arising out of their
sentencing of Edward Floyd. This produced disagreement within
the House and argument with both James and the Lords,
leading to a definition of the Commons' part in judicature
which was of great importance. Floyd in many ways provided
the Commons with their Rubicon, as Yelverton had the Lords,
but the lower House proved less successful in crossing it than
were the peers. They failed to extend their own judicature, as
they had similarly failed in 1610; and the case reminded them
of the very limitations on their power which had compelled
them to turn to the Lords earlier in 1621.

Edward Floyd was a Catholic lawyer who, by order of the
Council, was a prisoner in the Fleet. Early in January 1621 he

[18] Gardiner, *Debates 1621*, 85-90; *C.S.P. Ven. 1621-3*, 55. The case did not ruin
Yelverton. He was reconciled to Buckingham who forgave him his share of the
fine, and he was later made a judge: Rushworth, i, 34; *L.J.* iii, 125.

[19] Nevertheless, Buckingham was probably strengthened by his escape. He had
been found 'Parliament proofe' which, reported Chamberlain, was 'no small
comfort to him': Chamberlain, ii, 374.

had slanderously insulted the king and queen of Bohemia and although this was reported to the Warden of the Fleet it was not until the examination of the warden, late in April, that Floyd's words became public.[20] The Commons reacted violently: on the 28th Floyd was ordered to appear before them on the following Monday. He denied having made the remarks and the Commons ordered the examination of witnesses and a search of his possessions in the Temple and at the Fleet. In a poorly attended afternoon session, from which both Coke and Noy were absent, argument started over the best course of procedure: some members wanted to refer the case to the king; others suggested collaboration with the Lords; but finally the House decided to proceed to punishment itself.[21] If there were no precedent the Commons would make one, rather than let the case slip out of their hands. With great zeal the House fixed on a punishment and arranged for it to be carried out on the following morning, 2 May.[22]

Before this could be done, however, the king intervened, ordering a stay of execution. He asked the House a number of questions: whether it was a court of record with judicature on matters unconcerned with its privileges, its members or the public grievances of the kingdom; whether—if this right existed—it should inflict punishment on a person who protested

[20] The Warden was accused of maltreating his prisoners and charging them high fees. Although he evidently did not receive a full hearing by the Commons, they resolved to send him to the Lords; but they do not appear to have done so. Shortly before the prorogation in June, some of the Warden's prisoners, who had also petitioned the Commons, addressed a complaint against him to the Lords. He must have been bailed during the summer, because he answered to his bail at the start of the second session in November, but nothing further seems to have happened: *C.D.* iii, 273-5; iv, 405; *L.J.* iii, 157-8, 163, 174.

[21] Those such as Digges who advocated co-operation with the Lords were chiefly, of course, the moderates, but it was also suggested that the Commons alone were not able to inflict a sufficiently harsh punishment. On the other hand, some members evidently resented the handing over of offenders to the Lords, and in deciding as it did the House followed the advice of Sir George Moore, Strangways and Seymour. During the debate of 27 February on Mompesson's case, Moore had supported action independent of the Lords, if such were within the power of the Commons: Nicholas, *Proceedings*, i, 370-4; *C.D.* ii, 146; iv, 278; Relf, pp. xv-xvi. It may have been the rather different issues at stake in the case, which was somewhat more general and political in nature than others in 1621, that persuaded the Commons that they had the right to act alone.

[22] Williams, *James I*, ii, 252; *C.D.* iv, 278, 281-2; v, 126ff; Nicholas, *Proceedings*, i, 371, 373, 374.

his innocence, without first taking evidence on oath; whether it could punish a non-member for an offence not committed during a parliamentary session; and whether the House would not have been better advised to ask his pleasure before dealing with his prisoner—a question reminiscent of a criticism James had made of the Commons' proceedings against Proctor. The king also laid before the Commons an ordinance made during the first year of the reign of Henry IV: in this the House had abandoned all power of judicature and judgment, both then and in the future. James concluded his onslaught by thanking the House for its tenderness towards his family, promising to confirm what had been done if it were shown to be legal.[23]

The King's position was an effective one and the ensuing debate showed the extent to which his challenge had thrown the House into confusion. There was an uneasy feeling that their privileges were under attack; disquiet was increased by the realisation of the difficulty of defending them in this instance. Noy questioned the Commons' claim to the power they had assumed, and supported the king's right to suspend judgments, quoting precedents for this.[24] In his view the Lords should have dealt with the case. Alford wanted a royal pardon for Floyd 'since our Ship hath touched on a Rock'. Digges and others wanted the king petitioned to confirm the sentence; Montagu and Moore suggested that a bill be passed to do this, but Crew objected on the ground that to strengthen their sentence in this way detracted from it. Poole proposed a search of the precedents but Hakewill retorted that this would do no good as none appeared to exist.[25]

However, the House did its best to pull itself together. The validity of the king's medieval precedent was questioned on the grounds that it was merely an ordinance, not a statute, and that it was the product of special circumstances—the trial of Richard

[23] Nicholas, *Proceedings*, ii, 2; *C.D.* iii, 134ff; iv, 290-1; v, 131-2. James did not normally have precedents readily available. Perhaps he obtained unaccustomed help at this moment.

[24] *C.D.* ii, 337-40; iv, 291ff. Particularly the precedent of Latimer.

[25] Nicholas, *Proceedings*, ii, 5-8. The proposal of Montagu and Moore, like the bill against Proctor in 1610, is an interesting foreshadowing of the revival of attainder in 1641.

II, with which the Commons did not want to be associated. Members wondered whether it mattered that no oath had been administered during the examination of Floyd. Coke asserted that the House was a court of record, and that it was entitled to deal with an offence committed outside parliamentary sessions but denied in parliament, because the denial constituted a renewal of the offence. He was, of course, going back completely on what he had said barely two months earlier—when different circumstances prevailed. On 9 March he had declared that the Commons alone had no power to punish any but members and their dependants, itself almost certainly in contradiction to the position the House had adopted in punishing Michell. From this shaky position, unsupported by precedent, the Commons sought and were granted a royal audience.[26]

Before they went to the king they held another debate in which they did their best to convince themselves of the legality of their actions. They found fault with James's precedent, asserting that the very existence of the Commons' power of judicature over their own members and those who offended them showed that the precedent had not been followed, Cranfield injected a gloomy note into the debate by saying that the Lords would probably claim that their power had been usurped: this would compel the king to judge impartially between the Houses instead of showing the leniency towards the Commons that might otherwise have been expected. In the afternoon the king made a predictable reply to the Commons' appeal to the law of reason and to their assertion that the House was a court of record. He disputed their claims but reserved a full answer until their precedents had been written down, and he warned against 'challenging an omnipotency or . . . erecting a judicature which is not known how far it may reach'.[27] It was a reasoned challenge which the Commons would never have been able to meet satisfactorily.

Perhaps James realised that it would be unwise to alienate

[26] *C.D.* iii, 144; iv, 292-3; v, 133-5; *C.J.* i, 546. Coke claimed that precedents existed for the Commons' action but he did not substantiate his contention with effective examples: *C.D.* iii, 138-9. Hakewill was no more successful a few days later: *C.D.* iii, 177-8.

[27] Nicholas, *Proceedings*, ii, 13-14; *C.D.* ii, 343; iv, 296.

the Commons by making his victory clearer; perhaps he altered his plans in order to end the whole issue as quickly as possible. The outcome of the examination of Floyd ordered by the king supports the latter surmise. Floyd so annoyed the king by his confession that James determined to punish him at least as heavily as had the Commons. He therefore told the Commons that he was proposing to send Floyd to the Lords.[28] This announcement precipitated another round of excited discussions in the Commons as the House saw its unique right to present cases to the Lords under attack. Roe argued that the Lords had no authority to take cognisance of a public grievance unless the Commons presented the matter to them, and warned the House that the king's proposal might endanger this privilege and lead to their exclusion from such business. Other members bemoaned the lack of precedents and resolved that arrangements should be made for the preservation of records. More immediately, they appointed a committee of eight to set down their proceedings against Floyd. In consequence, the entry for 4 May in the *Commons Journal* states that Floyd was 'impeached before the Commons assembled in this Parliament'.[29]

As far as we know this is the first and only occasion on which the word 'impeached' is used in 1621 of the parliamentary trials of that year. Yet the case of Floyd is less like an impeachment, if this term is used to describe a trial by the Lords of charges or evidence transmitted to them by the Commons, than virtually every other case in this parliament. The Lords had taken no part in the proceedings which the Commons were describing in their entry. On the other hand, the committee responsible for advising the House on this consisted of men such as Coke, Phelips, Noy, Alford and Samuel Sandys, who are likely to have weighed their words carefully. What did members mean and why did they choose to express themselves in this way, using phraseology which was not taken from the medieval records so assiduously studied, and which was not to be repeated

---

[28] The diarists vary in the tone they attribute to the king's message. The majority report it as a proposal, indicating the course of action he will adopt unless the Commons have any other suggestions. According to Smith, the Commons were left with far less opportunity for making proposals: *C.D.* iii, 164; iv, 303; v, 366; vi, 400.

[29] Nicholas, *Proceedings*, ii, 19-23; *C.J.* i, 608.

in 1626 when the formula for impeaching Buckingham was to be drawn exactly from the fourteenth century? It seems hardly possible to provide a wholly convincing explanation. It may be that the verb 'impeached' bore no particular or technical significance in 1621, and there is no doubt that it was in general use at this time to mean 'accused'. Only five years later, however, it had acquired technical significance, at least in the mind of Selden, untypical though he may have been of the average member; and those who determined to 'accuse and impeach' Buckingham probably had some reason for using language which was apparently absent in 1624 or 1621. Perhaps 'impeached' had a different meaning in 1621 from that which it had acquired only a short time later. If so, we are unlikely ever to know what this was, and it can only have had a brief period of currency, for the familiar meaning was emerging by 1626. Perhaps the entry in the *Journal* deliberately used the word 'impeached', knowing that it referred to a judicial process, in an attempt to maintain a belief in the existence of a unicameral judicature by the Commons in such cases. Again, it may be that 'impeached' had a respectably antique ring to it, which, coupled with a vagueness about its technical meaning deriving from its apparently infrequent use in this sense, stood the House in good stead. Certainly, one of the diarists consciously or unconsciously lends assistance in this respect by omitting all mention of the Commons from his account of the proceedings and simply says that Floyd was 'impeached in Parliament', adding that 'the Parliament adiudged' him.[30] Furthermore, even members who found the Commons' behaviour difficult to justify recognised that the House had brought the case to some sort of conclusion. Shortly before the judgment was entered in the *Journal* Noy recommended that it should be 'putt in the forme of a Judicature and to be drawne presently; and not in the words of Question in it, but positively as Judgments are'.[31] It may be that by describing Floyd as 'impeached' the House was merely recording what it believed it had done. If this is true, it is hardly surprising that this word was not used of other cases where a very different procedure was followed. Yet despite such explanations, it must be

[30] *C.D.* iii, 170.   [31] *C.D.* iii, 168.

acknowledged that the entry made in the *Journal* on 4 May still remains something of a puzzle.

The next development in the case was that the Lords, with a timing which cannot have been accidental, asked for a conference with the Commons. The request arrived on 5 May, and at the conference the Lords insisted that the Commons' claims for their rights of judicature should be examined by judges and king's counsel.[32] Some members of the lower House had been worried that the conference would damage the Commons' liberties and jurisdiction and Coke did his best to convince the Lords of the validity of the Commons' position. Edwin Sandys's attempt to appeal to reason led Pym to write in his diary that 'he quickly betooke himselfe to an easyer taske . . .', turning to the zeal the House had shown in dealing with this attack on the king's family. One of the Lords' most effective retorts was to enquire what the Commons' reaction would be if the Lords were to infringe their power to propose subsidies, contrary to the ordinance of 9 Henry IV, as the Commons had infringed the jurisdiction given to the Lords by the ordinance of 1 Henry IV.[33]

The Lords remained unconvinced and when, two days later, they debated what the Commons had said in their defence they agreed that none of the precedents given by the Commons was relevant to this case. The Commons had not shown that they had a right to sentence a man who was not a member of their House for a matter that did not concern them. Consequently, they asked for a new conference. The request produced some grumbling when it reached the lower House. Montagu had been engaged in a search for information about a pursuiv-

---

[32] *C.D.* iii, 173; *L.J.* iii, 110. One of the questions arising from this case is why the Lords had not intervened earlier. Doubtless there had been a great deal of discussion behind the scenes and Miss Relf suggests that Coke and Noy, together with Pembroke, one of the Commons' chief allies in the Lords, used the issue as a means of strengthening the jurisdiction of the upper House. As the peers were embroiled with the king over Yelverton this was probably welcome. Spedding felt that the Lords were frightened to protest, particularly as (until the *Journal* entry of 4 May) they had no official notice of the sentencing of Floyd, and waited for the king's encouragement before doing so. It is important also to remember that the Lords were themselves well occupied at this time, dealing with the Yelverton issue and sentencing Bacon and Michell: Relf, pp. xvii-xviii; Spedding, vii, 274.

[33] *C.D.* ii, 349-50; iv, 313-4.

ant who, though not a member of the Commons, had been punished by them, but the case was more firmly established in his memory than in the records.[34] However, some members at least could see the writing on the wall clearly enough: Edwin Sandys made a conciliatory speech in which he showed that the Lords were not challenging the justice of the Commons' judgment but their power to give it, and that the House had been trying to prove the wrong things at the last conference. This type of approach to the anxious members had its effect: at the conference the Commons quietly accepted criticism of their evidence as well as the statement that the Lords believed their privileges had been infringed. Both Houses politely declared that they wanted agreement. To obtain this they met separately to discuss the appointment of a sub-committee and later arranged that this should meet on 10 May to arrange an accommodation. This sub-committee rapidly produced a settlement: it recognised the Lords' power to deal with Floyd and promised that the action of the Commons would not establish a precedent. It was agreed that the Commons would confirm their promise by drawing up a protestation which would be entered in the *Lords Journal*. Coke even retreated from asking the Lords to punish Floyd, merely leaving him to their wisdom, a withdrawal for which he was subsequently criticised in the Commons.[35]

Both Houses accepted the settlement and the Lords made arrangements to examine Floyd. Half the members of the committee they appointed had been similarly involved in Bacon's case. Their work proceeded smoothly except for one minor fracas with the Commons which nevertheless reveals the insecurity some members of the lower House still felt about the settlement.[36] On the 26th the peers heard Floyd's poor and

[34] *L.J.* iii, 113; *C.D.* iii, 191. Montagu soon gave up: on the 11th, he told the House that he had been in touch with Cotton who told him that the precedents would be best ignored: *C.D.* iii, 229; *C.J.* i, 619.

[35] *C.J.* i, 613; Nicholas, *Proceedings*, ii, 43-5; *C.D.* iii, 229-32, 237-8. There was, however, some doubt as to exactly what the Commons had asked the Lords to do. Edwin Sandys argued that the 'request [was] limitted to the Execution not to the Sentence and examinacion': *C.D.* iii, 230-1; iv, 334.

[36] *L.J.* iii, 125. The dispute was over the Lords' request to the Commons for a trunk containing Floyd's papers. There was a fear that its contents might be used to alter the Commons' judgment, so damaging them: *C.D.* iv, 360-1.

rather insolent reply to the committee's charge and on the
same day sentenced him. The Commons took no part in the
last stage, neither being sent for nor demanding judgment. It
seems that this was because they had already given judgment
upon him. There was certainly a belief that a judgment pronounced by one of the Houses could be reversed only by that
House. Perhaps it was feared that this right might be damaged
if the Commons assisted at the Lords' sentence.[37]

Undoubtedly the Commons had been divided over the case
of Floyd. Some members felt that their privileges would be
endangered by any surrender; others, chiefly the more experi-
enced, felt that their privileges would be endangered by further
persistence. Coke saw the merit in both positions and, for a
time, tried to ride both horses. The dispute caused some bitterness between the Houses which found an echo outside parliament.[38] Yet it led to an important compromise: although their
judgment of Floyd was left standing, the Commons' claim to
sentence any except members or those accused of breach of
their privileges was swept aside. They remained strictly dependent upon the Lords for success in dealing with other defendants,
and they failed to extend their own judicature. However,
disappointing though this was to the more militant members,
they could take comfort from the fact that they had successfully
excluded the king from interfering in what was now becoming
an established process. Although James had not formally
agreed that the Houses might work out a conclusion between
them, his failure to carry out his proposal to present Floyd
to the Lords himself, and his inactivity during the final stages

---

[37] *L.J.* iii, 133-4; Nicholas, *Proceedings*, ii, 107; *C.S.P. Dom. 1619-23*, 253;
C.S.P. Ven. 1621-3, 53; Williams, *James I*, ii, 256; Spedding, vii, 275-6; *C.D.* v,
156, 386. It has been pointed out that if the Lords had no independent power of
original jurisdiction and if the case of Floyd was not an impeachment, the Lords'
punishment was no more justifiable than the Commons' action: Hargrave's
preface to Hale, p. xix; Berkowitz, ch. V, 36.

[38] See Sir Robert Cotton's pamphlet *A Briefe Discourse concerning the Power of
the Peeres, and Commons of Parliament, in point of Judicature* (n.p. 1640), which appeared
at this time. It claims that the Commons' right to participate in judicature would
have been apparent from many precedents had not the keeping of records been
left to the Clerk of the Lords who, either deliberately or through negligence, had
failed to incorporate them in his *Journal*: pp. 5-6. The title of this pamphlet has
been subject at times to slight variation.

of the case, show that he tacitly consented to the arrangement. In doing so, he abandoned not only his implied right to accuse before the Lords, but also a very strong position against the Commons of 1621. The frequency with which, in this parliament, the king was prepared to let his case go by default is strong evidence that he, at least, had little grasp of the potentialities of parliament's revived judicature.

Meanwhile, the Lords had dealt with Michell, whom the Commons, late in February, had sentenced, apparently using a jurisdiction which was even at that time doubtful and which had by now been abandoned. Since then Michell had languished in the Tower. He had been discussed in conference with the Lords, examined by the lower House, and mentioned in written evidence—sent by the Commons to the Lords— about the thread patent, in which he had been associated with Mompesson. Just before the Easter recess the peers were told that he would be sent to them if they so desired, but the Commons do not seem to have taken any initiative in this respect, either then or later. Indeed, it seems that, at this stage, the Lords were more determined than were the Commons to punish Michell, for at the same time they recorded that he had been 'found guilty of many great Misdemeanors . . .', and they discussed what should be done. The Commons, however, had not lost all interest in the matter. On 21 April, they resolved to question the alehouse patentees, Dixon and Almond, and the referees, chief of whom was Mandeville, the Lord Treasurer. This drew from the king the protest that no man should 'be questioned for mistakynge the lawe upon a Reference' and although, after a full debate on 11 May, the matter was quietly dropped, the momentum generated during the previous three weeks perhaps helped to ensure Michell's punishment. No formal charge against him seems to have been sent to the Lords but on 26 April the peers had examined him and the following day went into committee to consider their sentence.[39]

---

[39] *C.D.* ii, 258; iv. 252-3; v, 28, 30, 343, 347; *L.J.* iii, 63, 65; Relf, 35-6; *C.J.* i, 586. The charges against him were read out by Mr Serjeant Crew who later performed the same function in Bennet's case. He shared his responsibility in the cases of Mompesson and Yelverton.

No sense of urgency seems to have possessed them and they soon became distracted by the Yelverton issue, with the result that not until 4 May did the final debate on Michell's punishment take place. Charles, Buckingham and Arundel argued against degradation from knighthood, but this, as well as exclusion from public office, a fine, and imprisonment during the king's pleasure, all formed part of the punishment fixed. The Commons were summoned to the Bar of the Lords to demand judgment on what the peers described as their 'Complaint' against Michell. The Speaker used the form now becoming increasingly familiar:[40]

the Knights, Citizens, and Burgesses of the house of Commons, haveing presented to yowr Lordships one Sir Francis Michell and Sir Giles Mompesson for inormus and gross offendors, heearing that yowr Lordships, after a iudgment before passed on the then Sir Giles, that yow are ready to pronouce sentence on Sir Francis Michell, theay are now comm to demaund it.[41]

Despite these statements by the Lords and the Speaker, there is no evidence in the records that the Commons had ever formally resolved to send Michell to the peers. Still less can Selden's assertion that Michell was 'accused and impeached' by the Commons be justified from contemporary evidence.[42] Nevertheless, whatever the part played by the Commons in securing Michell's condemnation by the Lords, it is interesting to note the Speaker's claim that the Commons had presented Michell to the peers as an offender. Now Maude Clarke argued, quite convincingly, that in 1621 'the Commons had done little more than to demand inquiry; though summoned to hear judgement, the whole conduct of the trial was outside their control.' This seems to be valid, but it is partly based on another opinion which may be debatable. She goes on to state that not until 1626 was the idea of indicting a man of an offence plainly understood, and she accurately points out that in

---

[40] *L.J.* iii, 89-90, 95, 108-9; *C.D.* v, 353; Nicholas, *Proceedings*, i, 341; Gardiner, *Debates 1621*, 64-5. The wording was similar to that used when the Commons demanded judgment against Bacon: *L.J.* iii, 106. For Mompesson the formula had been rather different: *L.J.* iii, 72. For the ceremony before the Earl Marshall's commissioners at which Michell was degraded from his knighthood, see Camden, ii, 657.

[41] *C.D.* iii, 170.   [42] Selden, *Of Judicature*, 30.

Middlesex's case in 1624 'not the man but the articles of accusation were *presented*'.[43] Perhaps the Speaker in 1621 was merely telling the Lords that the Commons had handed Michell over to them: as the Commons appear not to have drawn up a charge his words may have had no particular significance, but it is just possible that they did and that the Commons of 1621 understood well enough the process of indicting a man of an offence.

The Commons were fortunate, especially in view of the confusion over Floyd, that the Lords, before sentencing Michell, did not choose to question their early activities in the case.[44] If they had done so, the case of Michell might have become more important than it did. The slow pace both Houses adopted shows not only how insignificant Michell was compared with parliament's previous victims but also how certain the Houses now were of success whenever they acted jointly.

Michell's case was the last one to be brought to a successful conclusion in the parliament of 1621, but right up to the end of the first session on 4 June both Houses were continuing to investigate abuses and complaints. Many of these had come to light during the course of the earlier trials and might themselves have ended in judgments but for the interruption in June. Of these, two cases reached the point at which the Commons laid evidence before the Lords: that against Bennet took the form of an accusation which the Lords started investigating and which would undoubtedly have led to Bennet's punishment; the evidence concerning Theophilus Field, bishop of Llandaff was not formed into an accusation, partly because Field, like Bacon, was a member of the house of lords, but the Lords did investigate it. No great harm came to Field but the Commons did secure one minor scalp.

Bennet's case was straightforward and raised no new issues, though it gave rise to some discussion of the Commons' authority. Judge of the prerogative court of Canterbury,

---

[43] Clarke, 'Origin of Impeachment', 268.
[44] But as early as 22 March the idea was current in the Lords that Michell was committed by the Commons for contempt: Harl. MS 158, f. 239; *L.J.* iii, 63.

K

Bennet was accused of corruption, and evidence was accumulated by the Commons' committee during the Easter recess. By the moment when this was handed over to the committee for abuses in courts of justice an ominously large amount had been collected.[45] The Commons had declared that members of the house of lords could appear before their committees as witnesses in the case after Coke had assured them that this was in accordance with the precedents.[46] During the third week in April the Commons debated the procedure to be followed with a care and caution which makes all the more surprising their precipitate action against Floyd ten days later.[47] Speakers discussed the extent of the Commons' power: 'There is iudgment of fact which is ours, Judgment of paine which is the Lords',[48] a statement by Samuel Sandys which was forgotten or ignored during the opening of the attack on Floyd. Pym declared that when parliament was divided into two Houses its power was also divided: inquisition to the Commons, judgment to the Lords. But he added that the Commons still had some share in the judgment and should beware of handing over to the Lords too much of their power of inquisition. Shrewdly, he advised the House to present to the Lords only the evidence that was fully proved. The debate shows that there was still much room for argument about the best procedure, but the House agreed that Bennet should answer on the following Monday, either in person or by counsel. A select committee was appointed to prepare matters, and the heads of charges, though not the names of witnesses, were given to Bennet.[49] On 23 April, having heard from Coke of the fate of judges who, in the past, had taken bribes, the Commons expelled Bennet and placed him under house arrest.[50] They approved the

---

[45] *C.D.* iv, 214, 218-23, 236. But Chamberlain still believed that Bennet's friends would carry him through: *C.S.P. Dom. 1619-23*, 248.

[46] *C.D.* iii, 13. He does not appear to have named his precedents. Attempts in subsequent parliaments to secure the attendance of the peers, Middlesex and Buckingham, led to difficulties.

[47] Especially as, unlike Floyd, Bennet was a member of the Commons. A possible explanation is given below: p. 138n. 60.

[48] *C.D.* iii, 53.

[49] *C.D.* ii, 303; iii, 42, 53; iv, 238.

[50] This caused controversy, as it was claimed to be without precedent, but it was defended on the increasingly familiar ground that in cases of necessity there

accusation drawn up by their committee and arranged to ask the Lords for a conference at which it might be handed over. It was while these decisions were being reached that Hakewill commented, 'I have observed when we have gone to the Lords it hath been by impeachment, clamor or accusation', a remark which presumably indicates that he believed that more than one method of approach to the Lords was possible.[51]

Unfortunately, we do not know whether members agreed with Hakewill who, in any case, probably thought that the Commons were acting precipitately: 'He is but barely accused yet.'[52] Still less do we know which method the House adopted. At the conference with the Lords which took place on the 24th, Sackville declared himself 'Commanded by the Lower house to complain of Sir John Bennet . . .'; while Coke wound up: 'We have given nothing but an opinion, your lordships must give the judgment.'[53] The judgment was never given. During the remaining weeks of the session the Lords granted Bennet bail and examined the witnesses but displayed no appearance of haste. Nor is there any evidence to show that the Commons became impatient. The Lords eventually gave Bennet until the next access of parliament to reply to the charges against him but by then both Houses had lost interest in him.[54] However, this conclusion emphasises the difference in the treatment Bennet had received compared with some of his

---

was a great right to make a precedent. The necessity arose from the fear that Bennet would flee abroad through 'his match with the Dutch' (i.e. his third wife): *C.D.* ii, 314; iv, 245-9.

Coke mentioned Chief Justice Thorpe (24 Edward III) who was found guilty of corruption. He was not hanged, contrary to what Coke stated: *C.D.* ii, 313.

[51] *C.D.* ii, 314. For a discussion of this remark, see p. 48, above.

[52] *C.D.* iii, 55.

[53] *C.D.* iii, 74-7. Sackville seems to have presented at least some of the objections in writing: *C.D.* vi, 394. Selden says that the Commons 'accused' Bennet: *Of Judicature*, 31.

[54] *L.J.* iii, 87-8, 130-1, 146-8. Though on 15 December Perrot did complain in the Commons that he had been neither cleared nor sentenced. The Lords told the petitioners against Bennet that they still intended to deal with him but at the next access of parliament: at that moment they were too busy: *C.J.* i, 664; *L.J.* iii, 197-8. He was eventually sentenced in the Star Chamber: G. A. Harrison, ed. 'The Diary of Sir Simonds D'Ewes, deciphered for the period January 1622 to April 1624' (unpublished M.A. thesis of the University of Minnesota, 1915; a microfilm of this thesis is deposited in the library of the University of London), 97-100.

predecessors. The headlong rush to conviction was absent, while the decision to send him the heads of the charges is indicative of an approach which was willing to give him a reasonable chance to defend himself. The case shows that procedure was still flexible and capable of modification.

The Commons showed rather more eagerness to see an end to the case against Field, largely because their own prestige and standing were involved. In March they had been told by Davenport that Field had received a recognisance from Edward Egerton. This promised Field payment if he succeeded in persuading Bacon to grant Egerton a favourable decree. Field had failed to obtain this and, according to Davenport, had refused to surrender the recognisance. The Commons had suggested to the Lords that they should investigate the matter and punish Field if he were found to be guilty. They made no formal charge against him[55] but the Lords did investigate Davenport's accusations. They were found to be groundless and the Lords, apart from hearing a proposal that a reproof be administered to Field, let the matter drop.[56]

There the case rested until 14 May when the Commons, still smarting in the aftermath of their defeat over Floyd, debated it. Davenport had denied, on oath, before the Lords what, unsworn, he had declared to the Commons. The Commons felt that they had been made to look foolish and were worried that Davenport's example would find its imitators whenever the Commons examined without first administering an oath. Furthermore, the Lords had neither asked the Commons to demand judgment on Field nor told them the grounds for the judgment. Hakewill then proposed that the Commons should abandon the practice followed during the session by which they waited for an invitation from the Lords before demanding judgment. He urged the House to assert its right to demand it uninvited, and Alford complained that because they were not told the basis of a sentence given by the Lords they did not know which charges had been proved nor whether a punishment was fair. He advocated an examination

---

[55] But they did talk about their 'Complaint' against him: *C.D.* ii, 149, iii, 271, 356; iv, 352; v, 164; Nicholas, *Proceedings*, ii, 83. Selden does not mention the case.
[56] *L.J.* iii, 53-5; Relf, 52.

of the ancient manner of demanding judgment, and claimed that the precedents gave the Commons the right to demand another judgment if they found the first unsatisfactory. Brushing aside Hakewill's objections that Davenport was the Lords' prisoner and that all their information was based on unofficial reports, the House committed Davenport to the custody of the serjeant to be released on bail and set up a committee to conduct the enquiry proposed by Alford. The following day the House received, presumably from this body, the reassuring if slightly irrelevant information that in the cases of Neville and Latimer they had not only demanded judgment but had even selected some of the punishments.[57] On the 16th the Commons agreed to send a message to the Lords asking whether they were ready to give judgment, because the Commons intended shortly to demand it, in accordance with their ancient rights and customs. Sackville was chosen to deliver the message; he reported the Lords' answer that they would deal with the case as soon as they had time.[58]

In fact, the Lords ignored the Commons' hint that they wished to be called upon to demand judgment and the Commons did not assert what they had implied was their right to demand it without invitation: the proposed change in procedure had failed to materialise. On the 30th the Lords simply informed the Commons that they had asked the archbishop of Canterbury to admonish Field: although not faultless, he had not been found guilty of any bribery. At the same time they handed their examination of Davenport to the Commons, thereby inviting the lower House to deal with a matter which was no concern of the peers. The Commons heard Davenport's apology and excuse that, when faced with the oath, he realised that he had no proof of what he had claimed against Field. They listened to precedents for punishment and on the last day

[57] *C.D.* ii, 368; iii, 249-50; v, 165; vi, 156; Nicholas, *Proceedings*, ii, 69. The information was accurate.

[58] *C.D.* ii, 372, 373; v, 377. In his definition of impeachment, as opposed to complaint, Elsynge said that judgment was not to be given until the Commons demanded it: p. 302. In applauding the Commons' decision of the 16th, Roe and Sackville said that it would 'refresh our old custom of demaunding iudgment, that so things commended to the Lords may not lye ther uniudged': *C.D.* iii, 271.

of the session sentenced him to a month's imprisonment in the Tower.[59]

One of the impressions that the cases of Bennet and Field leave behind them is that both Houses were somehow less determined in pursuit of their victims now than earlier. Perhaps, as Spedding suggested, they were satiated.[60] But if the Commons had really lost some of their initial enthusiasm two difficulties arise which make it seem likely that Spedding's explanation is too simple.

The first difficulty is that during the last three weeks of the session the Commons began to investigate allegations of extortion brought against two more men. These were John Lambe, chancellor of Northampton, destined to be knighted a few weeks after the close of the session, and Richard Craddock, justice of the peace and chancellor of the bishopric of Durham. Members agreed that the evidence should be handed to the Lords after the usual investigations and, with an optimism not, however, shared by all, arranged that these should continue after the end of the session. One might reasonably have expected that the interruption in sittings would cause the House to lose interest in Lambe and Craddock, but this was not so. Unlike Bennet, the two chancellors were still subject to the investigations of the Commons when the autumn session opened, and the House showed itself still anxious to proceed with the case. Shortly before that session ended they were invited to be present at the next access of parliament and there was a clear intention to continue the attack unless they gave a satisfactory answer.[61]

The second difficulty arises from the extent to which some members, at any rate, realised the significance of what had taken place during the first session. Doubtless many of them

[59] *C.D.* ii, 410-1; iii, 356; iv, 416-7.

[60] Spedding, vii, 248. Chamberlain, writing to Carleton on 2 June, felt that parliament was becoming more lenient. He pondered on the reason, suggesting that its first fury was over and that it was loath to impose further fines until those already inflicted were better employed: Chamberlain, ii, 377. The lack of urgency in dealing with Bennet may be explained by the popularity he enjoyed in the Commons: Roberts, 32.

[61] Nicholas, *Proceedings*, ii, 59-61, 362-3; *C.D.* iii, 260ff, 384; *C.J.* i, 668. They were still in the Commons' mind in 1624: Bodl. Rawlinson MS B. 151, f. 103v; Erle, ff. 166v, 190-1.

thought that they had merely been investigating isolated but important grievances. These are the members whose enthusiasm would have declined. But at least one member, an influential one, saw things in rather deeper terms. Speaking in the long debate of 30 May on the threatened adjournment Pym commented on the achievements of this parliament. 'Judgment, the which hath slept theis 300 yeears and is the greatest benifit that may be, is now revived.'[62] Having struggled to revive this judgment he, and those members who thought like him, were unlikely to lose their enthusiasm for it.

Satiety seems therefore unlikely to be more than a partial explanation for the decline in the tempo of judicature. An additional explanation may well lie in the fact that, by the late spring of 1621, the process was no longer struggling for survival. Indeed, the main answer seems to be revealed by comparing the importance of these cases with each other: there can be little doubt that the earlier cases were more important than the later ones. Miss Relf has argued that parliamentary judicature was 'an effort to restore to Parliament its place in the system of courts which it had occupied in the fourteenth century, or even more to put it above the courts of equity which had superseded it'.[63] This view harmonises well with the belief that there was a gradual extension of several types of judicature within parliament in the early seventeenth century, and Miss Relf has, of course, set her interpretation alongside the study she has made of the growth in the unicameral judicature of the Lords. If the reason she gives for the revival of parliamentary judicature is correct, it is reasonable to expect that more work was required to achieve success in the earlier cases than in the later ones, and that the first victories were more important than the subsequent ones.

It is also possible to examine the comparative importance of the cases of 1621 from a political standpoint, and perhaps to explain the decline in judicial vigour in terms of the political

---

[62] *C.D.* iii, 353.

[63] Relf, p. xiii. Cf. Mrs Foster's view that the Commons of 1621 and 1624 undertook the investigations of patents and monopolies because there was no adequate remedy in the courts or the Privy Council: 'Patents and Monopolies', 77. In the context of Miss Relf's opinion, a Lord Chancellor was a superb victim.

insignificance of the later victims as opposed to their earlier counterparts, for there can be little doubt that men like Floyd and Bennet were of less consequence than Mompesson or Bacon. Yet too much can be made of the political overtones of these cases.[64] One may suspect that a few of the more sophisticated members, and perhaps those who, in February and March, had pursued the referees most hotly, were aware of the political significance of what they had done;[65] but the charges brought were concerned primarily with grievances and offences against the law, rather than with political attacks or suggestions of governmental mismanagement. Members were more preoccupied with administering justice than with political opposition. Moreover, James's own attitude helps to confirm this. He would hardly have permitted the session to continue if he had suspected that the trials were politically motivated, and he would surely have regarded the earlier trials with more hostility than the later ones if he had worried about their political implications. In fact, as the weeks passed he increasingly felt that the Commons were not keeping strictly to their brief of investigating grievances. For him Easter was a watershed: until then, he told them on 4 June, all had been well, but since Easter the Commons had taken up 'extravagant matters and out of Parliamentary causes'. He was probably thinking mainly of the Floyd case, though his leniency to Bacon and the arrests made after the session ended are an indication of what he thought of the fairness of some of parliament's decisions.[66] But although his speech of 4 June shows that James had no inkling of the real danger and significance of the manner of Bacon's fall, it does exhibit his growing appreciation and understanding of one aspect of the situation. James regarded the proceedings before Easter as bearable because he still

[64] Relf, p. xiii.

[65] Lambe, who is of course likely to have made the most of this, wrote to the king about his antagonists: 'The Complainantes are underhand sett on and countenaunced by greater persons in this Countye that thorough me, ayme att your Majesty's Ecclesiasticall Jurisdiction': *C.D.* vii, 608.

[66] *C.D.* vi, 409; Gardiner, *Debates 1621*, 79; *Cabala*, 307-8; Nicholas, *Proceedings*, ii, App. Lionel Cranfield told James that in his view the earl of Southampton's circle was almost wholly responsible for the raising of grievances in this parliament: *C.D.* vii, 616.

believed, then, that he could control the House, but as time
went on and he lost one skirmish after another, his optimism—
and with it his contentment and self-confidence—slipped
away. For, throughout the session, the crown suffered from the
lack of effective support in either House. It was a black day
for the apostle of free monarchy when the only vote against the
sentence on the man he had appointed as his Lord Chancellor
was given by a person of the calibre and reputation of Buckingham.

Some of the conclusions of this chapter and the previous
one may now be summarised. Although the procedure adopted
by the Commons and Lords in the trials of 1621 is, in broad
outline, similar in each case, there are clearly substantial
and important variations in detail. There was, for example,
no fixed juncture at which the Commons agreed to present
evidence to the Lords. Sometimes they prepared a detailed
charge, passed by a vote of the whole House, and began to
impose penalties upon the offender; when they went to the
Lords they were merely looking for confirmation of what they
had already decided and, possibly, for a harsher punishment.
Sometimes the Commons drew up no formal charge and made
no pronouncement upon the correctness of the accusations:
they laid the evidence before the Lords, with or without comment: they were relying heavily upon the Lords who, for-
tunately for the Commons, usually rewarded their confidence.
This variation in procedure can be largely explained in terms
of the importance of the victim—though this hardly accounts
for the Commons' circumspection in dealing with Bennet—
and of the changing claims made by the Commons between
February and June 1621.

On a less important level, another example of the diversity
of procedure is to be found in the ceremony in which the Lords
announced their punishment. Normally the Commons were
asked to be present to demand judgment, but in the cases of
Yelverton and Field they merely heard or were told what had
happened.

Procedure was influenced by the Commons' attitude to the
man they were attacking. Michell and Floyd were dealt with

much more summarily than the remainder, though the system adopted in 1621—collection of evidence by committees before which the defendant did not appear—allowed little opportunity for a reasoned defence because committee reports tended to be adopted unquestioningly by each House.[67]

Another influence upon procedure in 1621 was that of precedent. Something has already been said of the extent to which records of medieval parliamentary judicature were available to members, and there is no doubt of the respect with which precedents drawn from these were regarded, despite the meaningless and irrelevant way in which they were sometimes dragged into debates. But the absence of precedents did not seriously impede the Commons. Members might bemoan the lack of precedents but they were prepared to supply the deficiency with grandiloquent appeals to the law of reason: necessity was the mother of invention; they might make, as well as follow, precedents.[68] On the other hand, they liked to have at least the apparent support of precedent. The storm over Floyd showed what could happen when the Commons became too adventurous, and the day after the House had agreed to that settlement it received a warning from Noy when it was considering procedure in the cases of Lambe and Craddock: 'When wee goe in new wayes wee are like to goe astray. Lett us keepe the ould waye.'[69] Precedents were used whenever they might be useful—in determining the powers of the Commons, in attempting to decide procedure, in fixing punishments. But while they provided guidance they also provided justification, a fact which points to greater maturity in the exercise of its judicature than this parliament has usually been credited with.[70] Misuse of precedents normally passed unchallenged because of the impotence of the defence, but the fact that they were misused and, in Floyd's case, shown to be worthless in supporting the Commons' claims, makes it necessary to ask whether they were used merely cynically in 1621, in an attempt to blind the uninitiated with legalistic science. The chief exponent was Coke—though he had his imitators—and he was perfectly capable of turning round in

[67] Spedding, vii, 246.   [68] C.D. ii, 68; vi, 347.   [69] C.D. v, 169.
[70] Cf. Clarke, 'Origin of Impeachment', 268.

his tracks. Nevertheless, for him as well as for other members the traditional path was a serious matter and to accuse them of cynicism would be to miss the point. For conditions in 1621 were conspicuously different from those in the late fourteenth century.

The medieval impeachments were an open attempt to control the king's government by attacking his ministers; the parliament of 1621 was certainly not thinking in these terms, even if there may be occasional hints of it. This parliament acted as it did in response to the conditions of 1621, not in an attempt to revive, for their own sake, the glories of its ancient judicature. Yet in the records of that judicature was displayed a procedure which well suited the requirements of 1621 and which was therefore worth following. Naturally, the precedents would not fit exactly, and naturally the men of 1621 regarded these through the distorting mists of their own unhistorical approach to the ancient powers of parliament. But the accusation of cynicism can be dismissed because while many of them were lawyers, for whom the means is at least as important as the end, they were also politicians, for whom the end must have prime appeal.

Two final points remain to be made about the use of precedents by this parliament. The first is that the king himself confirmed the importance of these searches among the records: following Selden's work for the Lords during the first session, he was examined and his papers were seized at James's command.[71] The second point is that the Commons needed to turn frequently to the precedents and to defend their right to search the records.[72] This need arose from the fact that parliamentary judicature was still a tender growth in 1621. Among the records, the Commons could find examples of successful judicature and it was, above all, success that was required in the early weeks of this session.

Although in 1621 there was a variation both in procedure and in the extent to which precedents were followed, there is

[71] Nicholas, *Proceedings*, ii, App; Gardiner, *Debates 1621*, 99-101; *L.J.* iii, 176. Edwin Sandys and the earl of Southampton were examined on their parliamentary activities at the same time as Selden. Questions put to all of them, together with the answers made by Southampton, are given in Petyt MS 538/19, ff. 1-3v.   [72] *C.D.* ii, 208.

little evidence to suggest that members, or at any rate their leaders, were noticeably inconsistent. The question whether or not to send a defendant to the Lords provides quite a good test. Of course, in some cases this question never seems to have been put and we lack alternative information on this issue, but in four cases—those of Mompesson, Bacon, Bennet and Floyd— evidence of attitudes does survive.[73] Both Coke and Digges advocated co-operation with the Lords against Mompesson, Bacon and Bennet. Coke advised the same course against Floyd after the rash decision in which he took no part; while Digges adopted this position from the start. But after the Commons had passed judgment on Floyd, Digges responded to the new situation by suggesting that the case should be quietly buried. Phelips is less predictable: he proposed an approach to the Lords in the cases of Bacon and Bennet, but he strongly advocated the punishment of Floyd by the Commons. When their right to do so was challenged, he suggested that the king should be asked to confirm the sentence and a few days later he was responsible for advancing the view which Digges eventually adopted. Noy seems to have believed in the efficacy of an approach to the king: he placed faith in this solution to the confusion over Floyd and he proposed that the Commons should take this step after transmitting Bacon to the Lords. But he made no such suggestion when he spoke in favour of sending Bennet to the peers. The attitudes of Edwin and Samuel Sandys are interesting but distinct. Edwin supported the Commons' judgment upon Floyd on the grounds that the Lords were too busy to be troubled with him, but after the king's challenge he became an advocate of an approach to the peers. Samuel remained an unrepentant supporter of what the Commons had done, and was even prepared to contemplate an appeal by Floyd from the decision. But neither man opposed the presentation of Bennet to the Lords, which Samuel eventually advocated, though they did raise some objection to the timing of this. Whether or not men like Roe and Hakewill were consistent is difficult to say because

[73] In the case of Marshall (see above, p. 84 n. 3), which was of a rather different type from these four, Samuel Sandys advocated an approach to the Lords while Noy opposed this: *C.D.* vi, 116-7; Nicholas, *Proceedings*, i, 366.

they appear to have stated their attitude in only one of the four cases. Roe supported Floyd's punishment by the Commons, but also thought that they should complain to the lords of the Council, whose prisoner he was. A few days later, when the House was wondering what to do next, he said that, as the Commons had by-passed the Lords, they could not now approach them. Finally, Hakewill's view emerges in the case of Bennet when he supported the approach to the Lords.[74]

The position can be summarised in another way. None of these men seems to have spoken against sending Mompesson, Bacon or Bennet to the Lords. The passions aroused by Floyd's behaviour led to a few inconsistencies, but some of the proposals offered were forced upon their authors because of the peculiarities of a case in which matters had progressed beyond the point at which reference to the Lords normally took place.

The cases which have been considered in this chapter have long been called impeachments. As we have seen, except for the proceedings against Floyd, they are not given this name in the contemporary records, while there is evidence that some members believed that there were various procedures which the Commons could adopt to approach the Lords. At some stage, probably later, Selden and Elsynge analysed these procedures, seeing them in terms of two main types and using the words 'complaint' and 'impeachment' to distinguish one from another. In 1621 the Commons use the first of these terms on some of the occasions when they present charges or evidence to the Lords. But it would be wrong to conclude that a case so described is a 'complaint' in the rigid sense intended by Selden or Elsynge. These cases cannot easily be fitted into the Procrustean beds set up by those two writers, and the fact that Coke apparently made no classification of the parliamentary trials in which he took part must act as a warning to any attempt to do so now. Moreover, 'complaint' like 'impeachment' was in common enough use in a general sense at the time.

Nor can we be sure that contemporaries did not think of these cases as impeachments without actually ever saying so.

[74] C.D. ii, 148, 314; iii, 53-5, 123, 138, 166; iv, 116, 166-7; v, 359, 363; C.J. i, 532, 560, 561, 587, 604, 605, 608; Nicholas, *Proceedings*, i, 283, 284, 298, 370-1, 373; ii, 21-2.

Although the term must have presented itself to any member who looked at the medieval records, its use may have been deliberately avoided for fear of alarming the king. Yet this theory has its difficulties. It argues a degree of management by the leaders of the Commons which was otherwise hardly attained until the trial of Strafford, and secondly it overlooks the fact that members were perfectly prepared to refer, by name, to medieval cases which were bound up with the fates of the 'sillie weake' kings of whom James so hated to be reminded.[75] But this second objection may not destroy the theory: perhaps to James it mattered more how a thing was said than what was said. It may be that members did deliberately avoid using the term to spare the consequences, but if so it seems an inescapable deduction from this theory that 'impeachment' had some special and probably political significance to both the king and leading members of parliament. There is no evidence to suggest this in the records of 1621, where the charges and evidence are indeed of a largely non-political character; but if 'impeachment' did then carry the political overtones which have subsequently been associated with it, the character of the cases of 1621 would explain why the term is used in connection with only one of them.[76]

All, therefore, that can safely be said is that there is little justification for describing the trials of 1621—with the possible but curious exception of Floyd's—as impeachments, particularly because most writers on the subject have, as Miss Relf has pointed out, 'considered impeachment only as a political measure'.[77] Yet fundamentally disputes about terminology have a restricted importance. What is much more important to notice about the cases of 1621 is that various procedures were tried and that the Commons learnt from their mistakes. In 1624 and 1626 procedure was further developed and modified. These changes are obscured when all the cases are described as impeachments.

[75] See above, p. 102.

[76] It might be suggested that, despite Floyd's insignificance, his offence was more political in character than many in 1621.

[77] Relf, p. xiii. M. A. Gibb regards with scepticism the claims of the cases of 1621 to be regarded as impeachments, but she allows this fate to Middlesex: *Buckingham 1592-1628* (London, 1935), 158 and n.

In other words, parliamentary judicature was developing in the 1620s, just as unicameral judicature was evolving in much the same period and earlier. The cases of 1621 may look forward to the impeachment of Buckingham in 1626 and even of Strafford in 1641, but they are not necessarily identical in type to these. They may resist classification because they ante-date the age of the classifiers and the theorists: they may simply be examples of the 'due proceeding of Judicature'.[78] Perhaps they bear the same relationship to their successors as Lee's trial in 1368 bears, in Maude Clarke's view, to the impeach-ments of 1376. Although, as we have seen, her interpretation has been challenged, she believes that procedure by petition against Lee gave way to procedure by indictment in 1376, and she makes two points which are relevant to the present discussion. She draws a comparison between Lee's trial and the cases of 1621, stating that in the latter proceedings took place

at the *prayer* of the Commons or on their *complaint*; the charges against them were forwarded by the Commons and supported by particular accusers . . . In fact, as in Lee's case (1368), the Commons had done little more than to demand inquiry; though summoned to hear judgement, the whole conduct of the trial was outside their control.[79]

Though she says that the Commons 'impeached' their victims in 1621 it is an implication of her argument that she should not have done so, because her second point is that the idea of indictment, with which she believes impeachment to be closely connected, was only 'becoming clear' in 1624 and not 'at last plainly understood' until 1626.[80] Her arguments may not be wholly convincing, but taken in conjunction with the evidence from 1621 they must give food for thought.

Yet whatever the precise character of the cases of 1621 parliamentary judicature had been revived. The work of James's first two parliaments is likely to have helped, and the powers granted to their committees provided those bodies with much of the authority which, in 1621, enabled them to under-

---

[78] Coke, *Fourth Part of the Institutes*, 23.
[79] Clarke, 'Origin of Impeachment', 267-8.
[80] Ibid. 268.

take detailed work ranging from the examination of witnesses and condemnation of patents to advice on procedure and the framing of charges. But the judgment 'which hath slept theis 300 yeears' and of whose revival Pym spoke in June 1621, was on a different scale from the judicature exercised between 1604 and 1614. By a judicious mixture of precedent, common sense and the luck that frequently attends the bold, the two Houses ended the first session of 1621 with a weapon of remarkable value and potential.

CHAPTER VI

The Fall of Middlesex

When Clarendon wrote his *History of the Rebellion* he said that Buckingham entered upon the parliament of 1624 with the destruction of Middlesex[1] as one of his objectives, confident that in this he would have Prince Charles's support.[2] There is no reason to quarrel with this view, but it leads to the observation that, as a victim of the growth of parliamentary judicature in the reign of James I, Middlesex shares with Yelverton in 1621 the dubious distinction of being odd man out. Both incurred the disfavour of the dominant interest at Court and, unlike all the other men who suffered from this judicature, both were brought down partly or substantially because of the power of this interest. At first sight this consideration might seem to detract from the significance of both cases in the development of parliamentary judicature, and particularly from the significance of that of Middlesex which, unlike Yelverton's, was the leading case of its session. But in fact that development was to be strengthened in 1624 by the proceedings against Middlesex as it had been in 1621 by those against Yelverton. Various procedural advances were made, and methods became rather more complex and sophisticated in 1624, but the Commons were to end the session rather dissatisfied with their achievement.

---

[1] Lionel Cranfield was created Baron Cranfield in 1621 and earl of Middlesex in 1622. I shall refer to him henceforth by his territorial title rather than by his family name. Details of his financial deals, including those which figured in his trial, have been most carefully and thoroughly worked out by Mrs Prestwich.

[2] Edward, earl of Clarendon, *The History of the Rebellion and Civil Wars in England begun in the Year 1641*, ed. W. D. Macray (Oxford, 1888), i, 27-8. John Hacket said that contemporaries referred to it as 'the Prince's Undertaking': *Scrinia Reserata; A Memorial Offer'd to the Great Deservings of John Williams* (London, 1693), 190. Clarendon's view is confirmed by R. C. Johnson, 'The Public Career of Lionel Cranfield, Earl of Middlesex 1575-1645' (unpublished Ph.D. thesis of the University of Minnesota, 1956; a microfilm copy of this thesis is deposited in the British Museum), 290.

Despite the favourable political circumstances, they would find that they were unable to secure the result they desired. Possibly it was to remedy this situation that further procedural changes were made in 1626, to give the Commons greater control over the process of parliamentary judicature. But be that as it may, the lower House was to gain useful experience from the trials of 1624.

Although the omens did not favour Middlesex when the parliament of 1624 opened, the hostility of the prince and the duke was by itself insufficient to secure his overthrow, particularly as in the early stages of the parliament James showed no sign of abandoning his Lord Treasurer. Specific accusations had to be made and these were not forthcoming until after the Easter recess. But in the early days of April almost simultaneous attacks were launched in both Houses. On the 2nd the Lords heard a report that at a meeting of the committee for munitions, which was investigating the defences of the kingdom, evidence damaging to the reputation of a member of their House had been produced. It soon became clear that this member was Middlesex, so that, from the start, this case differed from its predecessors in 1621, because the attack originated as much in the Lords as in the Commons. On the same day Sir Edwin Sandys presented to the lower House a long report from the committee of trade. This dealt with reasons for the decline of trade and indicated three types of impositions with which Middlesex was soon to be associated.[3] The Lords arranged for a sub-committee of the committee for munitions to take examinations, but the Commons merely resolved to continue to debate the report on the following day. However, three days later the lower House was offered information of a more explosive character. On the 5th Sir Miles Fleetwood, Receiver-

[3] *L.J.* iii, 286; *Notes of the Debates in the House of Lords, officially taken by Henry Elsing, Clerk of the Parliaments, A.D. 1624 and 1626*, ed. S. R. Gardiner (Camden Society, new series, xxiv: London, 1879), 50; Erle, ff. 112-112v. (Erle's diary gives Sandys's report under 26 March, but the diarist misplaced his account by a week at this point and did not correct his error until 12 April.) Buckingham was a member of the committee for munitions: Johnson, 'Career of Cranfield', 298. Sandys not Phelips, as Zebel states, was chairman of the committee of trade: S. H. Zebel, 'The Committee of the Whole in the Reign of James I', *American Political Science Review*, xxxv (1941), 951.

General of the Court of Wards and one of Middlesex's sub-
ordinates as Master, accused him of manipulating the king's
revenues, altering the orders of the Court of Wards, and of
taking bribes. A debate followed in which Sir Edward Coke
referred to the allegations as 'a Grievance of Grievances', but
Sandys counselled caution and Noy said that if the accusations
were not proved Middlesex's accusers should be punished.
However, Poole reminded the House that to examine the greatest offenders was its ancient right, and the Commons resolved
to refer the whole charge to its committee of grievances, of
which Coke was chairman, for examination that afternoon.[4]
This committee at once realised that as Middlesex was a
member of the Lords it could not require his presence unless
he chose voluntarily to answer before it; but the fact that it was
prepared to contemplate this procedure against a peer suggests
an assertiveness lacking in 1621, when committees of the
Commons had normally not heard defendants in cases of
parliamentary judicature. The committee also seems to have
determined to conduct its proceedings as fairly as possible,
because it resolved that if copies of the charges against Middlesex were to be freely available to members of the Commons
the accused should also receive them.[5] During the next few
days it conducted a detailed investigation of Fleetwood's
charges, paying particular attention to the allegation that
Middlesex had accepted two bribes of £500 each from the
farmers of the great and petty customs. The witnesses presented
to it were not uniformly satisfactory, as their evidence was
inclined to improve on reflection and after contact with other
witnesses; but by 9 April the House and its committee were
ready to debate the next step.[6] On that day the Chancellor
of the Exchequer proposed that as the House had heard
accusations against Middlesex it should now hear his answer
and any witnesses he might produce to clear himself. This

---

[4] *C.J.* i, 755; Johnson, 'Career of Cranfield', 301; Holles, ff. 118v-119v; Spring,
192. My references are to a microfilm transcript of Sir William Spring's diary,
kindly made available to me by Yale University library and I use it by permission
of Harvard College library.

[5] Nicholas, Diary, f. 112.

[6] *C.J.* i, 758; Holles, ff. 122-124v, 127v-128; Nicholas, Diary, ff. 118v-123v,
130v-133; Holland (Tanner), f. 89; Erle, ff. 128v-129.

suggestion produced some division of opinion: Sir Thomas Jermyn maintained that the House was not the proper place in which to hear Middlesex's answer. The Commons were 'the grand Jury to finde the busynes', but having investigated it they should transmit it to the Lords, where Middlesex should answer. Brooke disagreed: 'The Tresorer desyred as muche an acquytall in this hows, as ye upper.' Sir Humphrey May, chancellor of the Duchy of Lancaster, supported Brooke in a speech which suggests a link in his mind between 'clamour' and 'complaint' but tantalisingly leaves it unexplained: 'Ye antient style of ye complaints of this hows, was called ye clamor of ye Commons (yt word then beeing taken in better sence then now) but now it would iustly be called a clamor, if we should only hear his accusation, & not his defense.' The House eventually resolved to hear Middlesex's answer the following afternoon,[7] but there was clearly still doubt about the procedure to be followed and the function of each House in cases likely to involve co-operation between both of them.

On the same day as this debate took place the Commons heard another report from Sandys's committee of trade. This involved Middlesex in responsibility for two types of burdens: he had benefited personally from the duties on sugar, and he had inflicted an unwarranted composition on groceries in the outports. The report led Spencer to propose the appointment of a select committee to collect information for presentation to the Lords, that 'according to the example of our ancestors' the offenders might be punished. He also reviewed what had been done in the past with authors of impositions, mentioning Latimer 'impeached of the same Offence' as Lyons, to whom he also referred. His speech, which is recorded in the *Commons Journal*, shows that Spencer, at any rate, was prepared to refer to impeachment by name, although the word itself appears no more frequently in the records of 1624 than in those of 1621. If fears of provoking the king explain the abstinence of 1621, they did not inhibit Spencer in 1624. His speech also raises the question whether or not he was thinking of the case, which was building up against Middlesex, as an impeachment. His reference to Latimer does not necessarily suggest this, and

C.J. i, 761; Nicholas, Diary, ff. 130v-131; Holles, f. 127v.

he does not say that Lyons was impeached. He may have quoted these cases merely to provide examples of men whose situations paralleled Middlesex's, rather than of procedures which were similar. However, his remark may perhaps be seen in the light of Selden's discussion of Middlesex's case in his treatise, *Of the Judicature in Parliaments*. Selden says that Middlesex was 'accused and impeached', though as will be seen he subsequently described procedural developments which, taking place in the course of the trial, prevented the case from fitting into his own definition of impeachment. Now, in stating that Middlesex was 'accused and impeached' Selden used language which nowhere appears in the records of the case but which is, of course, the medieval formula. It may be that Selden, probably writing after the trial of Buckingham when this formula was used, remembered more clearly the details of the medieval cases he so assiduously studied than the exact procedure employed against Middlesex; but it is also possible that members like Spencer did believe, at least in the early stages of Middlesex's trial, that they were impeaching him.[8]

After Spencer's speech it was Coke's turn to remind the House of what its ancestors had done. He listed the cases of Latimer, Lyons, and the duke of Suffolk, maintaining that Latimer had been punished although 'hee had excused himselfe by authority from the king', a defence which the Commons were soon to encounter. Previously, Sir Arthur Ingram, Middlesex's partner in many business deals, had tried to defend his friend, but the House adopted Spencer's original proposal and appointed a select committee. This committee was charged with finding out the projectors and advisers of the impositions on sugar and groceries as well as on wines, a duty with which Middlesex's name had not originally been connected but which had been laid at his door by the Secretary, Sir George Calvert, during the debate.[9] When this committee reported to the House on the 12th it confirmed Calvert's information, and

[8] *C.J.* i, 759; Selden, *Of Judicature*, 31. It is, of course, normal for modern accounts to refer to Middlesex as having been impeached: for example, Prestwich, 423 etc; R. H. Tawney, *Business and Politics under James I; Lionel Cranfield as Merchant and Minister* (Cambridge, 1958), 231; but on p. 238 Tawney says 'We do not know by whom the word impeachment was first pronounced.'

[9] *C.J.* i, 760; Spring, 219-21; Holles, ff. 125v-127; Erle, ff. 125v-128v.

the Commons adopted its proposal that all three impositions should be referred to the committee of grievances.[10] By this date, therefore, the committee of grievances was responsible for all the Commons' investigations into the accusations against Middlesex, and it was also ready to hear his answer. But whereas in 1621 it had been almost wholly responsible for many investigations from the beginning, in 1624 a good deal of preliminary work had been done in other committees: the procedure was becoming more complex.

While these developments had been occurring in the Commons, the Lords' committee for munitions had been investigating charges that Middlesex was responsible for the neglect of the ordnance, to which was later added an accusation of fraudulent dealing in the lands of Sir Roger Dallison, a former Master of the Ordnance Office.[11] On 5 April Middlesex exhibited some of the arrogance which earned him so many enemies by claiming that he was the victim of a plot—an allegation which he subsequently failed to substantiate. By the 12th the archbishop of Canterbury was ready to report from his committee and the House gave Middlesex an opportunity to reply to the report. It then asked the sub-committee of the committee for munitions to draw up heads of charges against the Lord Treasurer.[12]

The parallel progress of developments in both Houses up to this point suggests a carefully co-ordinated campaign. But now a hitch occurred. Middlesex was soon to answer the Commons' charges against him, but he had not obtained the permission of the Lords to do so. This led to a debate in the upper House on the 12th, but the matter was quickly resolved in favour of permitting Middlesex to answer. Significantly, Buckingham intervened to state that no one should be blamed for the failure to seek the peers' approval, but the Lords ended the debate by reaffirming that members of their House should not answer complaints in the Commons without licence.[13]

[10] *C.J.* i, 763; Nicholas, Diary, ff. 140v-142.
[11] *L.J.* iii, 299-300.
[12] *L.J.* iii, 290, 296, 301; Gardiner, *Debates 1624 and 1626*, 60-2; *H.M.C Report on the Manuscripts of the Duke of Buccleugh and Queensberry* (London, 1899-1926), iii, 235-6.
[13] *L.J.* iii, 299; Gardiner, *Debates 1624 and 1626*, 65-6.

The realisation of this procedural error may have been one of the reasons why Middlesex did not answer in the Commons' committee on the 10th as originally arranged, but obviously it was not a reason he could make public without creating further difficulties for himself. Before the committee met, therefore, Brooke delivered to the House a message from Middlesex asking for a postponement of his reply on the grounds that he had received the charges on only the previous evening and that he had been occupied in preparing an answer to the Lords' enquiries. This message provoked some criticism: the committee had sent to Middlesex only those charges concerning bribes, and Lord Cavendish complained that, as these were matters of fact, the Lord Treasurer should not require much time to consider whether he should admit or deny having received such gifts. As a consequence, the House refused to alter the arrangements and ordered that Middlesex's answer should be given to its committee that afternoon. Naturally enough, when the committee assembled it received no word from Middlesex, and Fleetwood at once tried to capitalise on this by proposing that the House should forthwith discuss his charges and arrange for their transmission to the Lords. But this suggestion seems to have received no support and shortly afterwards the Chancellor of the Exchequer brought another message from Middlesex asking that he should be permitted to answer on the following Monday afternoon, 12 April. Several members, including Fleetwood, at once supported this request and despite some further debate it was later granted by the House.[14]

Because of this postponement, Middlesex had obtained the consent of the Lords to answer before the Commons' committee of grievances before he actually did so. His secretary brought the reply, which was not admitted until he had

[14] *C.J.* i, 762; Nicholas, Diary, ff. 136v-138v; Erle, f. 130; Holland (Rawlinson), ff. 3, 5-5v. Holland's diary is in two parts: the section in the Rawlinson MSS covers the period 10 April-15 May, 1624; that already cited in the Tanner MSS stops at 9 April.

Fleetwood's abrupt change of mind, in which Cavendish joined, may be a further indication that the real reason for the agreement to Middlesex's request was that he and others now realised that the Lords had yet to give permission for Middlesex to answer.

certified that Middlesex had dictated it to him. Not unreason-
ably, the Lord Treasurer confined himself to explaining his
dealing with the farmers of the customs and denying that he
had received bribes from them. But in the ensuing debate many
of the other matters cited against Middlesex were considered
and Sir John Eliot contributed to the drama of the occasion by
declaring him 'unworthy the favour of his country unworthy the
countenance of his prince and ripe to be commended up to the
Lords'.[15] When Coke reported to the House it resolved that
five separate types of charge should be presented to the Lords:
the two bribes from the customs farmers; malpractices in the
Court of Wards, which included altering its orders, extorting
higher fees, and permitting the use of a stamp of Middlesex's
signature; the misuse of the sugar duties; the collection of
duties on groceries from the outports; and the imposition on
wines. The House then referred the whole matter to a select
committee of twenty-six members for preparation.[16]

There seems to have been no opposition to the proposal to
go to the Lords, so it is difficult to know exactly why this course
was chosen. That it was not absolutely obligatory, the case of
Anyan, later in the session, seems to show. Part of the answer
no doubt lies in the fact that Middlesex was a peer, but a
remark of Digges's during the debate on the 12th suggests that
there may have been another reason. He drew a distinction
between the offence concerning the bribes, which he thought
too unimportant to be sent to the Lords, and matters harmful
to the Commonwealth, which should be transmitted to the
peers. A day or two later the House adopted the same position
when it refused to transmit to the Lords someone who was
thought to have forged evidence against Middlesex, because it
was considered that the offence was too petty.[17] These two
pieces of evidence indicate that some members were coming to
regard transmission to the Lords as a procedure to be reserved
for the more important offences. Perhaps they had felt this
previously, but there is no evidence that in 1621 they had been

---

[15] Erle, f. 133; Holles, f. 129v; Holland (Rawlinson), ff. 12-12v.
[16] Nicholas, Diary, ff. 144v-145; Holles, f. 129v; Holland (Rawlinson), f. 12v;
Tawney, 241; C.J. i, 764.
[17] Nicholas, Diary, f. 143v; Holland (Rawlinson), f. 12; Pym, f. 4v.

unwilling to present to the Lords any of the information that Bacon had taken bribes.[18]

To return to Middlesex's case: during the debate on the 12th Phelips had argued that the chairman of the committee of grievances should deliver the Commons' accusation to the Lords, thus following the precedent set in Bacon's case. Digges had disagreed, proposing that as in Mompesson's case the matter should be distributed among several members. When the select committee reported on the 15th the House modified Phelips's suggestion and arranged that Coke and Sandys, chairmen respectively of the committees of grievances and trade, should deliver its charge to the Lords. However, before sending a message to the upper House asking for a conference the Commons listened to speeches from the two men. Coke surveyed the matters for which he was to be responsible—the accusations concerning the bribes and the Court of Wards; while Sandys dealt with the more hazardous business of the duties and impositions. Here the problem was to avoid any questioning of the right to impose, with its implications of challenge to the royal prerogative, and the House rapidly adopted Sandys's proposal that the word oppression should be substituted for imposition. It also resolved that it did not intend to cast aspersions on any member of the Privy Council apart from Middlesex; and Seymour played a valuable part in clearing away the rather wild allegations that the Lord Treasurer was responsible for suggesting the collection of benevolences and the dissolution of the last parliament.[19]

With these preparations completed the whole house

[18] However, a remark by Moore in the case of the commoner, Bennet, should be noted. He said that, if the accusation was not weighty, it was not worth sending to the Lords: *C.J.* i, 583.

[19] Spring, 233; Erle, ff. 140-2; Holland (Rawlinson), f. 27v; Pym, f. 6v; *C.J.* i, 767. The king took upon himself sole responsibility for the exaction of benevolences and on 16 April the Speaker received a letter from him stating that Middlesex had begged him to continue the last parliament: Harrison, 271; *C.J.* i, 768. Roberts says (p. 38) that Sandys disobeyed the Commons and referred to the dissolution and the collection of benevolences when he made his speech to the Lords. His source is Harl. MS 4289, ff. 191-5, but this record of Sandys's speech is a copy and in the margin of the section dealing with these two charges is a note that they had been deleted in the original: f. 192. Neither charge appeared in the final accusation and there therefore seems to be no reason to suppose that Sandys exceeded his instructions.

assembled that afternoon at Whitehall for the conference with the Lords. In his introductory remarks Coke declared that the Commons

appear for Multitudes, and bind Multitudes . . . They are the Representative Body of the Realm; for all the People are present in Parliament by Person Representative; and therefore, by the Wisdom of the State, and by Parliament Orders, the Commons are appointed the Inquisitors General of the Grievances of the Kingdom . . .

In referring to the Commons' function as representatives of the realm to enquire into the grievances of the kingdom, Coke was justifying their action in the same way as their proceedings against patents and monopolies had been justified in 1621. Grievances were particularly the province of the Commons: the Lords were too exalted to be much troubled by them. It was an idea which was not new even in 1621: in 1610 an unidentified member had made much the same point.[20]

After this introduction, Coke stated that in their inquisition they had uncovered 'many great, exorbitant, and heinous Offences' committed by the Lord Treasurer, and that no member of the Commons had been prepared to declare him not guilty. He followed this with details of the charges and ended by reciting Middlesex's oaths of office. Sandys followed Coke, displaying all the caution he had shown earlier in the Commons, and the case concluded with 'the Knights, Cittizens, and Burgesses, humbly pray and demand iustice of your Lordships.' The peers then referred the case for examination to their sub-committee for munitions, which they increased in size from ten to fifteen members.[21]

This sub-committee worked hard during the next week but not until the 24th was it ready to make a first report. On that day the archbishop of Canterbury reported that, having examined many witnesses, the sub-committee had drawn up

[20] Foster, 'Patents and Monopolies', 62, 75; Foster, *Parliament 1610*, ii, 146. See also above, p. 87. This concept assumes greater significance when set in the context of the growth in size of the electorate in the early seventeenth century. The evidence for this expansion and the part played by the house of commons in achieving it have been discussed by J. H. Plumb, 'The Growth of the Electorate in England from 1600 to 1715', *Past and Present*, no. 45 (1969), 90-116.

[21] *L.J.* iii, 307-11; Erle, ff. 142v-143v.

part of the charge. This was an amalgam of the accusations collected by both Houses, and it consisted of six sections. The first three were concerned with the taking of bribes from customs farmers and seem to have included a bribe which did not figure in the Commons' accusation. The fourth section referred to the abuse in the sugar farm and the fifth to the levying of the composition on the outports. The sixth section combined the malpractices in the Court of Wards with the neglect of the ordnance and the fraudulent dealings in the lands of the Dallison family.[22] The Lords ordered that a copy of the charge should be sent to Middlesex, but they were careful to note in their *Journal* that this should not be used as a precedent to break the normal practice by which parties accused received their charge at the Bar. Middlesex was told to present to the House the names of any witnesses he wished to have examined, and to attend himself at the Bar on 29 April to answer the charge. He was also warned that his charge might be added to later from among other matters still under examination.[23]

Middlesex now embarked on a period of intense activity, designed to win for himself every possible advantage in the crisis that was fast approaching. On the 26th he wrote to the king imploring him to persuade the Lords to grant him longer time for the preparation of his answer. Three days later he followed this with a petition in which he said that the king could save him by being present to hear his cause, adding that 'There must be somwhat in it more than ordinarye that there is so great paynes taken to ruyne mee.'[24] On the

---

[22] *H.M.C. Buccleugh*, iii, 237; *L.J.* iii, 318-9; Johnson, 'Career of Cranfield', 315. Since this sub-committee began its work the Lords had received two further petitions about Dallison's lands. One was read after Abbot's report: *H.M.C. Buccleugh*, iii, 237; *L.J.* iii, 320.

[23] *L.J.* iii, 319, 320. The charge was sent to Middlesex because the absence of many lords for the celebration of the Feast of St George meant that the House would be poorly attended for the next few days. This gave Middlesex a respite which otherwise he might well not have had: *C.S.P. Dom. 1623-5*, 223. The Lords' order about the charge begins 'Whereas, by the ancient Customs of this House, the Parties accused and complained of are to receive their Charge at the Bar . . .'

[24] *Cabala*, 267-8; Kent Record Office, Maidstone: Sackville (Knole) MSS series 1, Cranfield Addenda, Bundle IV. The bundle is labelled 'Cranfield MSS Impeachment'. I am indebted to Lord Sackville for permission to make reference to his manuscripts.

27th and on each of the next two days he also sent petitions to the Lords. He first asked for counsel to be assigned to him to assist him in making his answer, and he suggested that the examination of witnesses should be deferred until he had done this. The Lords had apparently anticipated the first request because on the previous day they had asked their sub-committee for privileges to search the precedents and report how those accused before them in the past had answered. They now told him that he could use what counsel he pleased but that they would not be permitted to attend at the Bar; they also refused to postpone the examination of witnesses, a list of whom Middlesex had attached to his petition. In his second petition he pleaded with the Lords for more time in which to prepare the interrogatories on which these witnesses were to be examined, and he also asked to be sent copies of the depositions made on both sides without which he maintained that his defence would be severely handicapped. The Lords' reaction was hostile: Middlesex was told that to send witnesses for examination without accompanying interrogatories showed disrespect, and his second request was dismissed as wholly unsuitable. He was reminded that they expected him to answer before them on the following morning. However, instead of doing so, the Lord Treasurer sent yet another petition: asserting that he was ill, he asked for a postponement of the hearing and he repeated his request for copies of the depositions. The answer was a good deal milder than might have been expected: having heard the previous two petitions and their answers to them re-read, the Lords adopted the prince's motion that the request for delay be granted. Middlesex was told that if his health permitted he was to appear on 1 May, bringing his answer with him; if not, he was to send his answer in writing, submit his interrogatories within the next two days, and appear in person on 7 May for the final determining of his cause.[25] Unless the Lords took Middlesex's illness at its face value, which seems unlikely, there are two reasons which may account for their readiness to accede to his request: it is possible that the king may have brought pressure to bear on their leaders as a consequence of Middlesex's letter to him of the

[25] *L.J.* iii, 321, 323, 325-7; *H.M.C. Buccleugh*, iii, 239.

26th, but if so it is likely that the petition of the 28th would have received a different reply. It therefore seems more probable that shortly before the 29th they became aware of deficiencies in one, or possibly two, of the charges already sent to Middlesex and seized upon the opportunity of a deferment with alacrity. At any rate, as soon as the reply granting Middlesex's request had been despatched, the Attorney General read an addition to the charge concerning the sugar duties, and a new accusation relating to profiteering as Master of the Great Wardrobe; and when Middlesex received these he commented that it was as well that the first charge had been altered because it had previously been utterly mistaken.[26]

With the help of this revised schedule the case now proceeded rather more smoothly. On 1 May Middlesex sent to the Lords his answer to the charges. In this long and elaborate document, undoubtedly prepared with the assistance of his two counsel, Nicholas Hyde and William Hakewill, he denied many of the accusations and explained away others, declaring himself ready to justify all that he had written. He also sent interrogatories on four sections of the charge, petitioning to submit the remainder on the following Monday, the 3rd. He renewed his request for copies of the depositions, claiming that he had never expected to receive them before he had made his own answer; and at last, on the 3rd, believing that they were ignoring all the precedents, the Lords granted Middlesex's wish.[27]

Meanwhile the Commons had settled a small but important piece of procedure. On 23 April they had received a petition complaining that Middlesex had placed an extra imposition upon hops. In due course the committee of trade recommended that the matter should be sent to the Lords, but two members, Poole and Moore, wanted it examined by the House first. However, the Commons decided to be guided by their memory

---

[26] *L.J.* iii, 327, 328; Johnson, 'Career of Cranfield', 323. Johnson regards the king's letter as the cause of the granting of Middlesex's request. It is also, of course, possible, as Tawney suggests (pp. 246-7), that the Lords realised that their original schedule was too tight, though what he regards as stages unavoidable before the trial could open would readily have been avoided if Middlesex had confessed to the charges as Bacon had done in 1621.

[27] *L.J.* iii, 329-35, 337-8; *H.M.C. Buccleugh*, iii, 239; Chamberlain, ii, 555.

that in Bacon's case all petitions presented againt him 'after the transferment' had been immediately sent up to the Lords without further examination. Accordingly, this new matter was transmitted 'not as a thinge iudged by them but to be considdered by the Lords as theye sawe Cause'.[28]

On 4 May, the archbishop of Canterbury told the Lords that the examination of Middlesex's witnesses had been completed.[29] Nothing now remained but for the House to await the Lord Treasurer's appearance at the Bar on the 7th. At this point the king intervened. Summoning the Lords to him he delivered a speech which excelled in the art of sitting on the fence. He began by telling them that as 'I am the Judge, in whose Room you are to exercise Judgement' he thought it necessary to advise them lest their judgment conflicted with his views in the matter. Although he acknowledged that they were 'the most Honourable Jury of England'[30] yet it was necessary to point out that because Middlesex, unlike Bacon, had justified himself in answering the charges, they must take great pains to uncover the truth. James then commended to them Middlesex's application and good service, maintaining that all good treasurers must, of necessity, be hated; but he also reminded them that Middlesex was appointed 'upon a Reformation' so that if he had himself transgressed he was doubly to blame. James took upon himself responsibility for some of the items in the charge—though he did not specify these—because he said that they were done with his knowledge and consent, but he ended by declaring that he would never maintain a man in a bad cause. At no point in his speech did the king do more than hint at the political pressures which were so largely responsible

[28] Nicholas, Diary, ff. 170-170v; Erle, ff. 165v-166; Pym, f. 28; D'Ewes, f. 116; *C.J.* i, 696.
[29] *L.J.* iii, 341. Dudley Carleton told his father that Middlesex had produced forty witnesses, twelve of whom had deposed directly aginst him: *C.S.P. Dom. 1623-5*, 232. The number of witnesses gives some idea of the scale of the task that faced the Lords.
[30] *L.J.* iii, 343. Later in the *Journal* account of the speech James said 'The Informers are the Lower House, and the Upper House are the Judges': p. 344. Bodl. Rawlinson MS B. 151, f. 67v. has 'Jurie' in places of 'Judges' here, but this is of small consequence: the Lords, of course, fulfilled the function of both judge and jury, one of the characteristics which gives this type of judicature its unique quality.

for Middlesex's ruin, and it is hardly surprising that Chamberlain reported to Carleton that opinion was divided as to whether James had spoken in favour of, or against, his Lord Treasurer.[31]

When the hearing opened on 7 May the Lord Keeper, Bishop Williams, presided and the case against Middlesex was presented by Sir Randolph Crew, Chief Justice of the King's Bench, and Sir Thomas Coventry, Attorney General, two of the lawyers attendant upon the Lords. Middlesex was brought to the Bar without his Staff and knelt until told to stand. Crew opened the charge: 'The Commons, being the general Inquisitors of the Sores and Grievances of the Kingdom, have presented to the Lords their Complaint against this great Lord and Officer; whereof, and of other Misdemeanors, their Lordships have taken Cognizance.'[32] This introduction requires some discussion. It indicates, first, that, while the Commons' peculiar right to investigate grievances was acknowledged, the evidence thus discovered was not to be the only basis for the trial. Middlesex was also being charged with 'other Misdemeanors', those which the Lords' own enquiries had revealed. The case against him had, from the very beginning, been the result of the work of both Houses, a factor which makes this trial exceptional among the cases of parliamentary judicature being studied. Yet in spite of this, the charge itself had been drawn up by the Lords. In Selden's view this duty was forced upon the peers, because the Commons had presented their accusation orally at a committee of the two Houses. In explanation, he says that they had departed

from the Ancient Course in this, they delivered not their Accusation in writing (he being absent;) Had it been in the open House, an Impeachment by word of mouth had been sufficient, and the Suit had been theirs: but it being at a Committee, how could the Lord Treasurer take notice of their Impeachment? wherefore the Lords of necessity did draw up a Charge against him out of their Accusation,

---

[31] *L.J.* iii, 343-4; Chamberlain, ii, 559; Erle, f. 174. James came closest to referring to the pressures exerted by Charles and Buckingham when he warned the Lords not to permit any man's particular aims to establish a precedent which might prove prejudicial to them and their heirs: *L.J.* iii, 344.

[32] *L.J.* iii, 344.

and then it became the Kings Suit, and they were abridged of their power to reply, or demand Judgment.[33]

Now it will be remembered that Selden, who had earlier stated that Middlesex was 'accused and impeached', defined impeachment as a procedure in which the suit belonged to the Commons, while one characteristic of a complaint was that the proceedings were *ex parte regis*. Elsynge's treatise also makes this point and adds that in an impeachment the Commons have the right to reply to the accused's defence, while 'Judgment is not to bee given till they demand it.'[34] It therefore seems as though Selden believed that by a certain stage Middlesex's case had ceased to be an impeachment. This is not, of course, to say that the Commons or the Lords shared his view, even though he was now a member of the lower House. But there may be some significance in Crew's reference to the Commons' accusation against Middlesex as 'their Complaint'.

A final point may be made about Crew's introduction. He states that the Commons' complaint was presented to the Lords, and Maude Clarke considered this important: '. . . not the man but the articles of accusation were *presented*'. But she contrasted this with the concept of the Commons as general inquisitors of the grievances of the kingdom, pointing out that Coke had concluded the long speech, which he had introduced with this concept, by declaring that the Commons' 'complaint is of a high lord, the lord treasurer . . .' She therefore concluded that, despite the fact that Middlesex himself was not presented to the Lords, 'the idea of indictment was becoming clear.'[35] However, it may be questioned how far this distinction between presenting the man and presenting his accusation was clearly drawn. There is an account, possibly not contemporary, in the diary of Sir Simonds D'Ewes, of the Commons' decision to go to the Lords. According to this, Sir Thomas Holland, a

---

[33] Selden, *Of Judicature*, 64-5. The Commons did demand judgment, but only when the Lords invited them to do so; they did not employ their 'power to reply' to Middlesex's defence.

[34] Ibid. 14; Elsynge, 302.

[35] Clarke, 'Origin of Impeachment', 268 and n. 2. Many years ago, C. H. McIlwain pointed to the connection between the concept of the Commons as the grand inquest of the nation and their function of presentment: *High Court of Parliament*, 189.

member of the Commons, had told D'Ewes that the House had 'resolved to transmitt himm [i.e. Middlesex] upp with his charge to the Lords as a guilty person to bee censured by them'.[36] This remark suggests that the presentation of the offender was as important to the Commons as the presentation of their accusation; but on the other hand it may be doubted whether Holland knew enough law to appreciate the distinction.[37]

After Crew's introductory speech he developed a procedure which was to be followed throughout the investigations of the next few days: either he or his colleague, the Attorney General, would introduce a particular part of the charge which would then be supported by depositions of witnesses read out by the Clerk. Middlesex would then answer, often calling witnesses in his defence. Following this, the prosecution might reply, sometimes challenging what the defence witnesses had said, and Middlesex might make a rejoinder.[38]

Although an amateur confronted by legal experts, Middlesex fought the case against him every inch of the way. He also stretched the Lords' patience to breaking point: after two full days' hearing, between which he had won a Saturday's respite, he retired to his bed and announced to a delegation sent to visit him that he was receiving un-Christiàn treatment. This delegation reported that he was perfectly well, and he narrowly escaped being sent to the Tower for his impudence. When he reappeared in the House on the afternoon of the 11th he complained about the manner in which the Attorney General had conducted the case, and the Lords had to interrupt proceedings to clear their officer.[39]

Between 7 and 11 May the Lords examined all the charges that had been brought against Middlesex with the exception of that referring to an imposition on wines and the belated

---

[36] Harrison, 271. See also D'Ewes, f. 109v.

[37] *C.D.* i, 90-4.

[38] Tawney, 249. Tawney points out that, unlike Bacon, Middlesex was required to attend at the Bar; but of course Bacon offered no defence.

[39] *L.J.* iii, 360, 371, 373-4; Chamberlain, ii, 559. Middlesex's answer to the charges is given in *L.J.* iii, 349, 358-61, 365-7, 369-70, 374, 376-8. Like Bacon, Middlesex also had a collection of precedents made, undoubtedly to assist his defence: Kent Record Office, Maidstone: Sackville (Knole) MSS series 1, Cranfield Addenda, Bundle IV; Historical Manuscripts Commission, London: Sackville (Knole) MSS series 1, Cranfield Papers, Unnumbered MSS, Bundle IV.

M

accusation of an imposition on hops. In one instance the king had intervened effectively to assert that he had approved the alterations in procedure in the Court of Wards; in consequence that part of the charge had been dropped. But, predictably, much of the case had gone badly for Middlesex and he doubtless recognised this when he made his concluding speech on the morning of the 12th. He very briefly recapitulated some of his earlier remarks and then reminded the Lords of his service to the king and its value. He finished by craving pardon if he had omitted anything or annoyed the House in any way.[40]

The Lords occupied the remainder of the day in debating and voting on each part of the charge. Here again they adopted a set procedure: each part was taken in committee and the Lord Keeper frequently set the tone in his introductory speech. Five or six speakers followed, and the House then resumed to vote whether Middlesex was censurable on that part of the charge. The Lords dealt first with the accusation of mismanagement in the Great Wardrobe. Here they at once had to face the difficulty that Middlesex had received a pardon for pocketing the difference between the running costs of this department and the annual allowance, an action in any case permitted to him by his patent. He had, however, failed to keep accounts, though he was under no legal obligation to do so. While the Lords were making up their minds about the pardon and deciding that none the less Middlesex was still guilty of mismanagement, they censured him for taking bribes from the customs farmers. They also had no hesitation in imposing a censure for the accusations concerning the Ordnance Office and Dallison's lands. On the charge referring to the Court of Wards they were more cautious: the king had already intervened here and the Lords felt able to censure Middlesex only for those sections dealing with the doubling of fees for liveries and the use of the signature stamp; they declared that it was not proved that he had appointed his Secretary to take fees for petitions or that he had benefited from concealed wards. However, when they stepped back to view the complete charge at the end of their debate they decided that he deserved a

[40] *L.J.* iii, 375, 378.

censure for the whole thing. Rather uneasily, they let him off
the charge concerning the sugar duties because the king had
acknowledged that he knew the extent of Middlesex's gains
from the lease, but Charles warned the House not to forget
that the king had suffered financially because of the Lord
Treasurer's behaviour. Finally the charge about compositions
on groceries in the outports failed because Middlesex was able
to justify himself from precedent.[41]

When the Lords met on 13 May they first sent a message to
the Commons warning them to expect a further message of
importance shortly. They then had read out the charges and
the votes passed on the previous day. Next, they went into
committee to obtain guidance on punishment from a whole
galaxy of medieval precedents. Before fixing on this they
debated Middlesex's claims to good service, belittling some
and rejecting others. Then by means of seven questions they
resolved on the Lord Treasurer's punishment. They declared
that he should lose all his offices and be excluded from holding
any in future. He was never to sit in parliament again and was
to be prohibited from attendance at Court. He should be
imprisoned in the Tower during his majesty's pleasure and pay
to the king a fine of £50,000. There was some feeling that the
financial penalty was too low and Saye proposed linking a
higher fine with confiscation of Middlesex's lands. Other
members, including the prince, thought that the Lord Treasurer
should be compelled to make restitution to those he had
wronged; but the Lords merely accepted an offer by the Lord
Chamberlain to introduce a bill making his lands liable for
his fine.[42]

The final scene in the destruction of Middlesex was closely
similar to that in which Bacon had been the central figure
three years earlier. The Lords despatched Crew and Coventry

---

[41] *L.J.* iii, 379-81; Gardiner, *Debates 1624 and 1626*, 74-84; *H.M.C. Buccleugh*,
iii, 241-2.

[42] *L.J.* iii, 382-3; Gardiner, *Debates 1624 and 1626*, 84-91. Saye suggested a
figure of £80,000; the Commons had apparently thought in terms of £200,000:
C.S.P. Dom. 1623-5, 244. Chamberlain, who was invariably hostile to Middlesex,
thought it remarkable that the Lords did not degrade him. He also noted the
similarity between the sentences of Middlesex and Bacon: Chamberlain, ii, 560;
Johnson, 'Career of Cranfield', 165.

to the Commons to tell them that they were ready to deliver judgment on Middlesex if the lower House would come to demand it. With the peers and the Speaker in their robes, the Lord Treasurer, dressed in black, was brought to the Bar. The Speaker declared that the Commons had 'transmitted unto your Lordships several Offences against the . . . Lord High Treasurer of England' and duly demanded judgment.[43] The Lord Keeper then pronounced the censure, after which the Lords appointed a committee to acquaint the king with the sentence and to ask him to take away the Staff from Middlesex.[44]

The Commons were not pleased with the sentence or with the final stages of the attack on Middlesex: they had expected a harsher penalty and a censure more specific to the charges. They may first have been provoked by the omission from the list of charges of the imposition on wines, an accusation which the Lords perhaps ignored in order to avoid any conflict with the royal prerogative.[45] But whether or not because of this omission, the Commons, prompted by Robert Phelips, realised on 11 May that they possessed no independent record of the charges transmitted to the Lords. They therefore resolved that Coke and Sandys should set down the charges as presented lest there should be 'as in the case of the Lo: Chancelor Bacon, no memorialls remayning'. On the 13th, before the Commons went to the Lords, Phelips reminded them of his motion but although Coke went over the charges for which he had been responsible Phelips hardly seems to have got his way if the skeletal record in the *Journal* is any guide. Moreover, although the Speaker was apparently instructed to repeat to the Lords every head of the charge presented and to demand judgment on all of them, he did not do so.[46]

When the Commons returned from the Lords, angered by

---

[43] Two accounts substitute 'Compaints' for 'Offences' in the Speaker's statement: Holland (Rawlinson), f. 87v; Nicholas, Diary, f. 199v.

[44] *L.J.* iii, 383; Gardiner, *Debates 1624 and 1626*, 92.

[45] Spielman, 95-6; *H.M.C. Buccleugh*, iii, 243; D'Ewes, f. 121v.

[46] *C.J.* i, 787-9; Erle, f. 179; Nicholas, Diary, f. 197. Nicholas records this instruction to the Speaker; it does not appear in the *Commons Journal*. Sandys does not seem to have delivered to the Commons his part of the charge until 28 May: *C.J.* i, 797; Nicholas, Diary, f. 233.

the sentence, Phelips again tried to prod them into action. He complained that the lords 'did decline from the auntient mann [i.e. manner] of iudging in parlmt, for it was a use that evy iudgemt given here and transmitted ov by us to the lords did receave its weight and particler iudgemt above with their lordshipps'.[47] He told them that if a sentence fell short of what the Commons expected, they had in the past demanded an additional censure—and he cited the case of Michael de la Pole as an example. He proposed that Noy and Selden be asked to search the precedents. Noy tried to bring the discussion back to the immediate issue by moving that committees of both Houses should meet to record the judgment against Middlesex; but the only resolution adopted was that a search of the precedents be undertaken to determine how such judgments had been made in the past 'by the Lords upon Complaint made by the Commons'. A committee of antiquaries (Coke, Cotton, Noy, Phelips and Selden) was appointed and, apart from the addition of a further member a few days later, that is the last we hear of it or of the Commons' grievance—both doubtless overtaken, the one by the end of the session and the other by the enfeebling influence of the passage of time.[48]

As the session drew to a close the Houses cleared up the remnants of their case against Middlesex. The Lords laid down procedure for the future in consequence of proposals made by their sub-committee of privileges on 28 May. Proceedings before them were to be 'clear and equal'; a defendant was to receive copies of all depositions sufficiently in advance of the hearing to give time for preparation, and, if he asked for it at the appropriate moment, he was to receive the assistance of learned counsel.[49] If there is little in this order from which Middlesex had not benefited, it is nevertheless significant that the Lords

[47] Nicholas, Diary, f. 200.

[48] C.J. i, 789, 791; Erle, ff. 183-183v; Nicholas, Diary, f. 200; D'Ewes, ff. 121-121v.

[49] L.J. iii, 418. From the Lords' order it is not clear whether they were now prepared to allow counsel to plead for a defendant, or merely, as they had permitted to Middlesex, to advise him. Selden indicates that they had intended the former and believes that, in denying Middlesex the full benefit of counsel, they had shown a misunderstanding of the precedent in Michael de la Pole's case: Of Judicature, 103.

were attempting to guarantee and institutionalise their reviving power of judicature. As for Middlesex himself, the Lords embarked on an investigation of demands for restitution, and both Houses passed the bill to make his lands liable for the payment of his debts, though in the Commons Phelips protested about the precedent that was being created. When James gave his assent to this bill at the prorogation, he tried to make use of the opportunity to reassert his own authority. He told the Commons that though they might present general grievances they should not be too eager to hunt them out, nor should they determine on a remedy until he had had 'the hearing and allowing of it'. He declared that he would not in future permit 'any officer of his to be complained of in Parliament without leave', and he reminded them, quite correctly, that the sentence, some parts of which he rejected, was subject to his confirmation. But his speech might have carried greater conviction had he been prepared to give more assistance to his Lord Treasurer both during and after the trial. In fact, the severity of the sentence was reduced more slowly than many people expected, and a great deal more slowly than Middlesex found comprehensible; there was probably some truth in the Venetian Resident's cynical report to his superiors that the advantages to be derived from the sentence, such as the redistribution of Middlesex's offices, would 'console him [the king] for the treasurer's fall'.[50]

If the attack on Middlesex originated in the personal hostility towards him of Charles and Buckingham, the Commons and Lords did not develop it merely as disciples of this leadership. They accused him of crimes and of other activities with an enthusiasm which was clearly not second-hand.[51] Moreover, while it is possible to question the fairness of some of the case

---

[50] *L.J.* iii, 396, 420; *C.S.P. Dom. 1623-5*, 259; *C.S.P. Ven. 1623-5*, 325, 343; Chamberlain, ii, 561-2; Nicholas, Diary, f. 232v; Erle, ff. 205-205v. On 13 May Dudley Carleton had written to his father that everyone expected the king to remit Middlesex's fine: *C.S.P. Dom. 1623-5*, 245. For Middlesex's attitude, see, for example, *C.S.P. Dom. 1623-5*, 318, 481.

[51] However, it is perhaps going too far to agree with Eusden that for the first time the Commons were able to carry through an action against a minister of state on their own initiative and authority: J. D. Eusden, *Puritans, Lawyers and Politics in Early Seventeenth-Century England* (New Haven, 1958), 152.

against Middlesex,[52] a detailed and specific charge had been brought against him. As in Bacon's case, the accusation was not, in itself, political—whatever the pressures that inspired it— and it reflected only indirectly on Middlesex's competence as a minister. While it is true that, for the second time in three years, parliamentary action had ruined an important minister of the crown, and while some of the implications of this may well have lain behind James's speech at the prorogation, the accusation was of a different character from that levelled against Buckingham in 1626.[53]

Apart from these general considerations, the process of judicature was refined, sharpened, and to some extent modified in the course of this case. The use of committees by the Commons became more complex: the committee of grievances was employed to continue and complete work begun in other committees; while its invitation to Middlesex to answer before it represented an extension of its powers. The Commons presented to the Lords definite charges against Middlesex whereas in 1621 they had merely handed to them without comment information about Bacon. Although they were bolder in dealing with Mompesson they required a whole series of conferences with the Lords for the purpose, whereas in 1624 one conference sufficed. But while they had handed to the Lords the written evidence they had collected against Mompesson, their delivery of the charges and supporting information in the case of Middlesex was purely oral: in this respect they did not advance from their position in Bacon's case.[54] However

[52] See Tawney, 250ff. and Prestwich, 455ff. Selden maintained that Middlesex harmed himself by withdrawing from the House, 'for he might have stayed there until Judgment, unless when his own Cause came in agitation': *Of Judicature*, 101. Elsynge substantially confirms this (p. 302): a member of the Lords accused of misdeamours might remain in his place until judgment, except during examination of his cause or while his censure was debated.

[53] It is, however, necessary to avoid being influenced by Clarendon's intriguing but unauthenticated story of James's warning to the prince and the favourite of the consequences of their parliamentary activities in 1624: Clarendon, i, 28; Spielman, 92.

[54] Hargrave isolates four examples of procedural immaturity in Middlesex's trial, but only one of these, the oral presentation of the case, can be accepted without qualification: preface to Hale, p. xxxv. In pointing to 'irregularities' in Middlesex's case, Tawney (p. 248) seems to have accepted too uncritically Hargrave's analysis.

the prospect of duelling with a peer and a high officer of state did not inhibit them as it must have done in 1621; they invited Middlesex to appear before their committee of grievances to answer their accusations, though doubtless in doing so they did not overlook the advantages of the acquiescence of Charles and Buckingham. Finally, the Lords in 1624 developed a feature of parliamentary judicature which had shown some signs of existence in 1621—that of investigating and drawing up charges of their own, quite separate from those framed by the Commons against the same man. In 1621 it is arguable that the Commons' initiative was responsible, as for example in the case of Yelverton, for the Lords' action; but in 1624 the timing of the Lords' enquiries precludes this explanation of the investigations of their committee for munitions. Their work through this committee compels us to make some modification of the traditional view that the Lords' part in parliamentary judicature is exclusively that of judge and jury. Certainly they were dealing with a peer but they were undertaking part of the Commons' function of acting as informers.

The Commons gained in confidence as a result of the accusation against Middlesex, and proceedings advanced in formality. Hesitations and uncertainties remained, forms were not clearly established, but it was soon to prove possible to contemplate what would probably have seemed unattainable in 1621—an attack through the processes of parliamentary judicature on a man of the stature of the duke of Buckingham.[55]

Two other cases in the parliament of 1624 are of some significance for the development of parliamentary judicature. They are those of the bishop of Norwich, Samuel Harsnett,

[55] A further dimension might have been added to parliamentary judicature in 1624 if some advice of Cotton's had been implemented. Apparently, the Spanish ambassador had accused Buckingham of planning to use parliament to place James under restrictions and to transfer the government to Charles. Cotton advised the duke to complain to the Lords and then to withdraw from the House. The Lords would then ask the Commons for a conference and a message would be taken by the Speakers of both Houses to the ambassador, requiring him to produce his charge and proofs: Harl. MS 304, ff. 40-40v. I am grateful to Mr Roger Lockyer for drawing my attention to this material.

and the master of Corpus Christi College, Oxford, Dr Anyan. The bishop, a man of Arminian views, was first complained of to the Commons before Easter, by the citizens of Norwich.[56] For several weeks little happened,[57] but after the committee of grievances had freed itself of the charges against Middlesex it began to investigate the matters alleged against the bishop. There was the usual variety: he had suppressed preaching, extorted higher fees, failed to register institutions to livings, introduced popish practices and punished the disobedient, and set up over the font an image of the Holy Ghost in the shape of a dove which 'by certen engines' was designed 'to come downe in the time of Baptisme, and hover over the water'. From the beginning members were divided about what should be done: Brooke felt that the matter was outside the Commons' jurisdiction and should be referred to the archbishop of Canterbury; Perrot and others thought that they should direct their main attentions to the king; but Coke claimed that the House might legitimately deal with the matter, and Sherland and Rich proposed that, because it was a grievance, it should be presented to the Lords.[58] This final suggestion was adopted and a charge in six parts was drawn up. The business was again delayed by the Lords' preoccupation with Middlesex but the charge was finally presented at a conference on 19 May, when Coke claimed that 'it was ordinary for the Commons to complain of the Governors of the Church. . .' After the archbishop of Canterbury had reported to the Lords, the bishop at once denied virtually the whole charge in a long and apparently able speech.[59]

The Lords then discussed their next step. Saye wanted the

---

[56] J. Ballinger, ed. *Calendar of Wynn (of Gwydir) Papers 1515-1690* (Aberystwyth and London, 1926), 196; *L.J.* iii, 388.

[57] Because the Commons were awaiting confirmation from the mayor of Norwich: *L.J.* iii, 388.

[58] *C.J.* i, 784; Erle, ff. 167-9; Holland (Rawlinson), ff. 71, 72v, 73v; Pym, ff. 31-31v. The varying points of view appear in debates on 16 April and 3 May: Holland (Rawlinson), ff. 36, 74v-75.

C.J. i, 784, 786, 790; *L.J.* iii, 384, 388-90; National Library of Wales 9059E Letter no. 1226: Letter of 24 May from Henry Wynn to his father. According to Locke, the bishop's answer was so satisfactory that the accusation would have been dropped had not he asked for an examination, but this view is not confirmed by other accounts: *C.S.P. Dom. 1623-5*, 252.

appointment of the normal type of examining committee, but Charles proposed that only the charges concerning fees and institutions to livings should be examined by the Lords, suggesting that the remainder—of a more purely religious character—should be referred to the High Commission. Spencer supported Saye; Sheffield countered the Lord Steward's criticism that a reference to the High Commission would endanger the Lords' privileges unless the court reported to the Lords, by saying that in the past the House had referred matters complained of for final determination in other courts. Finally, Saye produced an acceptable compromise by which all six parts of the charge were to be referred to the High Commission for a report on which the Lords would pass a judgment. Charles then declared that this was what he had intended in his original proposal.[60] One wonders whether this debate made Charles realise that the Lords were not always as biddable as only a few days earlier he might have thought.[61]

The Commons took exception to the procedure the Lords had adopted. Some disquiet seems to have been expressed on the following day but there is no record of real anger until the 27th. On that day Robert Phelips, who had been concerned about the lack of an adequate record in the lower House of its charge against Middlesex, drew attention to the fact that the Lords had sent the bishop to the High Commission. He said that this represented an indignity to the Commons, they having voted the matter worthy of the Lords' examination: they should not 'be patient att such slightings'. Whether the Commons agreed with Phelips and whether either House did anything further about the bishop of Norwich the record

[60] Gardiner, *Debates 1624 and 1626*, 96-7. According to *L.J.* iii, 390, the Lords took this decision because of the shortage of time but Gardiner's source (Elsynge) shows that this is too simple an explanation.

[61] The attack on the bishop displeased the king, who regarded the puritans as responsible. Unless Charles's success as the idol of parliament had gone completely to his head he can hardly have disagreed here with his father. Had the session lasted longer, the refusal of the Lords to abandon the case completely to the High Commission could have proved embarrassing for both James and Charles. For James's opinion, see *Diary of Walter Yonge*, ed. G. Roberts (Camden Society, xli: London, 1848), 75; *C.S.P. Dom. 1623-5*, 265, 267.

does not reveal, but Phelips's comments do seem to have persuaded the Commons to change course in dealing with Anyan.[62]

At the end of April Spencer had delivered to the Commons a petition against Anyan from the fellows of his college. It was referred to a select committee from which Selden reported on 20 May. Whether or not Anyan had appeared before the committee we do not know, but it had found him guilty on four counts—misuse of the college endowments, avoidance of the visitor's examinations, negligent administration, and wanton behaviour—and recommended, without apparently giving a reason, that these be transmitted to the Lords. At this point Sir Henry Poole, influenced perhaps by the Lords' decision of the previous day in the case of the bishop, asked the Commons whether they were not wronging themselves by leaving all judicature to the Lords. He was quickly silenced by Sandys who said that it was inappropriate to raise such questions so near the end of the session; and the committee's recommendation was adopted. But on the 27th, after his criticism of the Lords' behaviour, Phelips reverted to Poole's speech and said that the Commons should not confirm the Lords' 'clayme of Judicature'. Pym pointed out that the Commons could not disguise the fact that they lacked this right, but the House reversed its previous decision to go to the Lords. It was, however, Pym, supported by Sandys, who proposed the alternative course which the Commons adopted—that they should petition the king for Anyan's removal.[63] In his speech of prorogation James objected to the Commons' 'Complaint' on the grounds that their oath of supremacy forbade them to deal with church matters, and that they had complained against Anyan without hearing

[62] Erle, ff. 186v-187; Nicholas, Diary, f. 224v; Bodl. Rawlinson MS B. 151, f. 68v. The Commons did, however, order Pym to write down the heads of the charge against the bishop and these were delivered to the Clerk on 29 May: C.J. i, 714, 715, 798; Erle, f. 196. Why Pym was chosen is not clear: Coke, as the man who had presented the charges to the Lords, was the obvious choice. Perhaps Pym's intervention in the debate about Anyan on the 27th had something to do with it.

[63] C.J. i, 692, 707, 791, 796; Erle, ff. 164v, 186v-187; Spring, 272-3; Bodl. Rawlinson MS B. 151, f. 68v.

him. From parliament's point of view the complaint ended there.[64]

The decision to adopt the well-established course of petitioning the king seems to make Anyan's case a commentary upon the disappointments suffered by the Commons in their attacks on Middlesex and the bishop of Norwich. Apparently lacking effective means of remedying the situation in these two cases, they chose to deliver a snub to the peers by refraining from sending Anyan to them. In so doing, they demonstrated their awareness that alternative means were available to them for dealing with cases important enough to be sent to the Lords. But in addition their attitude in the closing stages of all three cases perhaps provides an explanation of the procedural modifications adopted in 1626. In the proceedings against Buckingham, the Commons were to be more assertive than previously. Doubtless this was because the representatives of the realm were growing in confidence, and appreciated the need for great resolution if they were to achieve any success against a man of Buckingham's eminence; but it also seems likely that such changes were made in an attempt to avoid a repetition of the disappointments of 1624.

It may be that it is as dangerous to apply to the cases of 1624 as it was to those of 1621 the rigid distinction between impeachment and complaint drawn by Selden and Elsynge. Although in the accounts of these trials the former term appears hardly at all while the latter figures frequently, we cannot be sure that any such distinction was recognised in 1624.[65] On the other hand, the procedure followed in that year—whatever it may be called—gave the Commons insufficient control of a case after its transmission to the Lords to ensure a result which satisfied them. Furthermore, Selden's analysis of Middlesex's

---

[64] *L.J.* iii, 424. Anyan was the subject of further accusations to the Commons in 1626 but these do not seem to have progressed beyond the investigatory stage: R. F. Williams, ed. *The Court and Times of Charles the First* (London, 1848), i, 91; Whitelocke, Diary (12.22), f. 29v.

[65] Gardiner talked about the revival of impeachment in connection with the case against Middlesex: *History*, v, 230. Selden described the bishop of Norwich as 'accused and impeached', but the records do not contain this phrase. Selden did not mention Anyan: *Of Judicature*, 32.

case seems to confirm this by stating that the Commons' power to reply to Middlesex's defence was removed as a result of the form adopted for the accusation against him. In 1626 when circumstances were far less favourable to the Commons than they had been in 1624, the House not only declares that it is impeaching its victim but it also assumes an interest in the case, after the transmission to the Lords, which it has not previously claimed. The cases of 1624 mark a further, but not the final, stage in the development of parliamentary judicature.

CHAPTER VII

The Impeachment of Buckingham

As the parliament of 1624 drew to a close the earl of Kellie wrote to the earl of Mar that it was apparent from 'the courss that is now caryed that if the Parlament did leaste onye time that their is verrye few or noe officer that wold scaipe their hands . . .'[1] While his comment testifies vividly to the increased authority of parliament it is also true that dissolution and prorogation, or the threat of either, had often effectively deterred members from reviving on a subsequent occasion the grievances of a previous session. After 1624, however, this manifestation of the royal prerogative lost its power to interrupt permanently a case of parliamentary judicature: investigations begun in one parliament would be resumed in the next. There are many reasons for this change, several of them obvious enough: more frequent parliaments meant that the burning issues of one assembly were not extinct before the next met; members were gaining in confidence and experience, and no longer assumed that grievances had only to be complained of to be remedied. But the change of monarch also provides part of the explanation. James had been prepared to give some encouragement and assistance to those of his ministers and servants whom parliament chose to attack, but there was a point beyond which he would not go in their defence. Dissolution did on occasion interrupt investigations, but frequently not before parliament could feel that it had achieved a good deal. If James responded inadequately to parliament's complaints he did, at least, respond. Charles, although recognisably the son of his father, rapidly showed himself to possess substantially different attitudes towards parliament.

In the parliaments of 1625 and 1626 investigations which

---

[1] *H.M.C. Supplementary Report on the Manuscripts of the Earl of Mar and Kellie* (London, 1930), 202.

ultimately involved, or would have involved, the exercise of parliamentary judicature were conducted into the actions of the duke of Buckingham and Dr Richard Montague. The details of both cases help to illustrate Charles's attitude to parliament and the extent to which it differed from James's, but, more importantly, it is possible that the attitude of the new monarch helped to determine the form that the proceedings against Buckingham took.

The attack on Buckingham in 1626 can hardly have been unexpected. Already, in the parliament of 1621 there had been indications that he was too intimately connected with some of the grievances complained about, and there would doubtless have been more distinct mutterings in 1624 had he not put himself at the head of the forces of criticism in that session. But in the parliamentary session at Oxford in 1625 his opponents found their voice. On 11 August, in a House worried on account of the plague and increasingly uneasy about the government's foreign policy, Seymour, supported by Phelips, openly accused Buckingham of incompetence. This was no chance occurrence: it seemed to contemporaries like the beginning of an organised attack, the first to be made by the Commons on a minister whom they did not accuse of breaking the law.[2] As a consequence Charles dissolved parliament.

If the king hoped that his action would produce a quiescent Commons in the next parliament he was not long to remain undeceived. Salvetti, the Tuscan Resident, predicted in September that a new parliament would insist on resuming

<hr />

[2] H. Hulme, *The Life of Sir John Eliot 1592-1632* (London, 1957), 93; S. R. Gardiner, ed. *Debates in the House of Commons in 1625* (Camden Society, new series, vi: London, 1873), 118; Roberts, 51; Rushworth, i, 195; *H.M.C. Mar and Kellie*, 232. Shortly before Seymour's speech Cotton and Eliot seem to have been collaborating on a speech which was never delivered. Full of precedents of royal favourites whose behaviour had almost ruined the country, it may nevertheless have circulated among members in manuscript form: Hulme, *Life of Eliot*, 92; J. N. Ball, 'The Parliamentary Career of Sir John Eliot 1624-1629' (unpublished Ph.D. thesis of the University of Cambridge, 1953), 112, 115; J. N. Ball, 'Sir John Eliot at the Oxford Parliament 1625', *Bull. Inst. Hist. Res.* xxviii (1955), 113-27, especially 121-5; *Cottoni Posthuma*, 273-81. I am grateful to Dr Ball for permitting me to refer to his thesis.

where the last had left off by demanding enquiries into the conduct of those who had spent the war supplies; and the Venetian Resident, reporting in mid-January, said that there was talk among parliamentarians of refusing supplies 'unless he [Buckingham] is put down'. Some uneasiness may even have clouded the duke's horizon because in a further despatch a week later the same Resident said that his dependants were trying to secure a strong party for the forthcoming parliament. Moreover, the government disqualified several of the leaders of the previous parliament from sitting by pricking as sheriffs men like Coke, Seymour, Phelips and Alford.[3] Whether the absence of such members materially affected the course of events in 1626, we cannot say: we do not know what would have happened had they been present. But the lack of Coke's leadership may have permitted some fresh thinking on procedure, and it is reasonable to suppose that other men filled the breach. Members like Pym and Selden achieved greater prominence than before.

When parliament met on 6 February it did not at once launch an attack on Buckingham, and his name was not mentioned in connection with any complaint until 22 February.[4] On that day Eliot reported from a select committee which had been set up to consider the seizure and arrest of English property in France. The committee had discovered that the French action had largely stemmed from the capture of one of their ships, the *St Peter of Newhaven*, by the English fleet during the previous autumn. Although the ship had been released, it had been rearrested on orders from Buckingham as Lord Admiral, on the ground that it was carrying Spanish goods. During the debate on the report the House had its attention concentrated more closely on the duke by Lord Cavendish, who read a letter stating that Buckingham had refused to examine proofs of the legitimate character of the *St Peter*'s cargo. As a result of the day's work the Commons and its

---

[3] *H.M.C. Eleventh Report* (London, 1887-8), App. i, 31; *C.S.P. Ven. 1625-6*, 298, 311; Hulme, *Life of Eliot*, 92 n.4. Hulme suggests (p. 102) that in December 1625 Eliot may already have been planning the charge against Buckingham.

[4] Nevertheless Mead regarded Eliot's speech of 10 February as aimed at Buckingham: Williams, *Charles I*, i, 82; Hulme, *Life of Eliot*, 105-7.

select committee embarked on an investigation of witnesses.[5]

Three days later the Lords produced their first challenge to Buckingham. They adopted a proposal made by their grand committee of privileges that after the end of the session no lord should be permitted to hold more than two proxies. The duke, with thirteen, opposed the suggestion and Chamberlain wrote that he had had 'one feather pluckt from his wing . . .' According to Pesaro, the Venetian Resident, the Lords' decision greatly encouraged the Commons.[6] Whether or not for this reason, the Commons began to broaden the scope of their investigations: by means of a committee of the whole, under the chairmanship of Christopher Wandesford, they determined to enquire into evils, then to discover their causes, and finally to suggest remedies. On the 27th this committee, which subsequently took its name from its three objectives, resolved that there were two evils—the reduction in the honour and strength of the kingdom and the stopping of trade—and immediately began an investigation of their causes. During the course of its work on the following day Sir Robert Harley proposed that 'single or unsound councell' might be a cause. Corriton supported this and Harris suggested blaming 'Men unable put in places . . .' In pursuance of these propositions the committee resolved to examine the Council of War which had been appointed to supervise the spending of the subsidy granted in 1624.[7]

Although the Commons had no difficulty in securing the attendance of members of the Council of War they were less successful in obtaining clear answers to their questions. These were designed to establish whether the Council's advice had been followed, but after the House had listened to a variety of reasons why its questions could not or should not be answered

[5] *C.J.* i, 823; Whitelocke, Diary (12.20-1), ff. 70v, 74v. Written interrogatories were drawn up for the examination of at least one of these witnesses: already the Commons were employing greater formality than previously: *C.J.* i, 824.

[6] *L.J.* iii, 507; Gardiner, *Debates 1624 and 1626*, 114-5; Chamberlain, ii, 630; *C.S.P. Ven. 1625-6*, 352.

[7] *C.S.P. Ven. 1625-6*, 352; Harl. MS 6445, ff. 3v, 6v-7v, 9-10; Whitelocke, Diary (12.20-1), ff. 60v, 59v, 58v. (Whitelocke has written part of his account by starting at the back of his notebook and working towards the front. This explains the form taken by some of my references to his folios.)

it abandoned the examination.[8] The Commons fared little better in their enquiries into the history of the *St Peter*. The committee found evidence to suggest that part of the ship's cargo had been confiscated for the benefit of the duke, and although the House was not prepared to adopt Eliot's motion that this be declared a grievance, it did despatch a messenger to Buckingham demanding to know within three days why the ship had been arrested a second time. Its enthusiasm led it straight into the procedural difficulties from which Buckingham himself had helped to extract the House in 1624. Members had again forgotten to apply to the Lords first before requiring an answer from a member of their House. So when Buckingham asked for leave to make his answer to the Commons, the peers remembered their dignity and asked their committee of privileges for advice on procedure. Naturally, this committee reminded them of the order made in 1624, and the Commons had to retrieve the situation by maintaining that their order had been wrongly entered by the Clerk and that they had intended only giving Buckingham notice that a complaint had been received about the *St Peter*. Honour having been satisfied, Buckingham's attorney appeared in the Commons on 6 March with the duke's answer. In this he denied that the ship's cargo had been touched, and he declared that the second arrest could hardly have been responsible for the seizure of English goods in France as the latter event had preceded the former by a month. He admitted having ordered the rearrest but stated that he had done so at the king's express command. This defence brought the Commons face to face with a familiar difficulty: nothing that they might say or resolve must reflect upon the king because the king could do no wrong. If errors were committed his councillors must be to blame: evil advisers were the obstacle between the undoubted wisdom of the monarch and the unquenchable love of his subjects. As recently as 28 February Digges had proposed to the committee for evils, causes and remedies, that it should clear the king of responsibility for any of the causes; and if the constant reiteration of the righteousness of the monarch was beginning to make the more

[8] *C.J.* i, 829, 832, 833; Harl. MS 6445, f. 17; Whitelocke, Diary (12.20-1), f. 29.

adventurous minds question its validity there is no doubt that even these continued to render formal loyalty to the doctrine. On this rock, sharpened by the technical difficulties of a complex enquiry, the *St Peter*, as the repository of the Commons' hopes, began to founder. On both 11 and 16 March Eliot failed to persuade the House to declare the matter a grievance and on the second occasion Digges proposed that it should rest. It was not to be revived until 1 May.[9]

By the middle of March, therefore, the Commons had devoted a good deal of time to the exploration of two lines of attack on Buckingham, neither of which had proved very fruitful. Moreover, the government was trying, with some success, to persuade them to turn to the more general and less dangerous issues of the safety of the kingdom and the international situation.[10] However, in the committee for evils, causes and remedies, they had continued to investigate the causes of the evils besetting the land. On 6 March they had debated the inadequate state of the naval defences and Spencer had criticised the sending of badly needed ships to La Rochelle. At the end of that debate they had resolved that the coasts had been insufficiently guarded since the dissolution of the treaties with Spain: at least these general questions were more speedily resolved than intricate matters like that of the *St Peter*. Then on 10 March, Dr Meddus reported to his correspondent, the Rev. Joseph Mead, that he had heard that a member of the Commons had thirteen articles prepared to present against a very great man, which would lead either to his ruin or to their dissolution. His information was not quite accurate but on the following day Dr Turner, member for Shaftesbury, told the committee for evils, causes and remedies, that 'there should be a causa generalissima stated, which should be the Mother of ye rest, ye Common fame presents one man to be this cause . . .' He then put six questions: was not the duke responsible for the loss of the king's regality in the Narrow Seas; were not the

---

[9] *C.J.* i, 827-8, 830, 831, 835; *L.J.* iii, 513, 514, 515-6; Gardiner, *Debates 1624 and 1626*, 118; Hulme, *Life of Eliot*, 110-11; Whitelocke, Diary (12.20-1), ff. 45v, 42v, 52, 53; Harl. MS 6445, f. 8.

[10] *C.J.* i, 832; Whitelocke, Diary (12.20-1), ff. 39v, 38v; B. M. Lansdowne MS 491, ff. 146v-148v.

gifts made to him and his relations a reason for the decline in the king's wealth; was not the accumulation of offices in his hands and those of his friends and kin, some of whom were incapable of filling them, a reason for the evil government besetting the commonwealth; had he not secretly favoured recusants; had not the sale of offices which he had arranged led to evils; did not his failure to sail with the last fleet help lead to its misfortunes?[11]

Turner's speech was the lineal descendant of Seymour's at the end of the 1625 parliament.[12] Both men helped to alter the whole character and authority of parliamentary judicature. Hitherto when ministers appointed by the Stuarts had been accused in parliament, they had been charged with offences perpetrated in the execution of their duties: it had not been suggested, whatever might have been thought, that they were not competent to perform those duties. Behind the illusion of the competent minister, dismissed for peccadilloes, the doctrine that the king could do no wrong could survive; it could not long survive attacks on ministers for incompetence.

Charles reacted to Turner's speech by sending a message to the Commons demanding satisfaction. He said that Turner's attack on Buckingham was unsubstantiated by proofs and was in reality an attack on his and his father's government, and he repeated James's contention that he could not permit enquiries about the meanest of his servants. He also complained

---

[11] Whitelocke, Diary (12.20-1), ff. 18[a], 18[b], 37; B. M. Sloane MS 826, f. 24; Williams, *Charles I*, i, 89-90; W. A. J. Archbold, 'A Diary of the Parliament of 1626', *E.H.R.* xvii (1902), 732; L. Pearsall Smith, *The Life and the Letters of Sir Henry Wotton* (Oxford, 1907), ii, 294n. In his account of this episode Gardiner described Turner as a man 'otherwise of no note'. While in a general sense this is no doubt true he had already contributed usefully to this parliament, once at an earlier meeting of the same committee and once with some apposite remarks during the debates on the *St Peter*: Harl. MS 6445, ff. 4v-5; Whitelocke, Diary (12.20-1), f. 53v; Gardiner, *History*, vi, 76. Professor Hulme, *Life of Eliot*, 114n. and Dr Ball, 'Parliamentary Career of Eliot', 165-6, 169, have disposed of the old theory that Turner was a spokesman for Eliot, and Ball has pointed out that Turner was a dependant of Pembroke whose relations with Buckingham were strained in 1626. This doubtless encouraged him to speak as he did, but there is, of course, no reason to suppose that he was not largely motivated by personal conviction. For other connections perhaps partly responsible for the sources of the attack on Buckingham in this parliament, see Prestwich, 483-4.

[12] See p. 179, above; and Roberts, 51.

about a seditious speech of Clement Coke, son of Sir Edward, and said that this had emboldened Turner. On the following day, 15 March, the House sitting as a grand committee cleared Coke of uttering sedition and appointed a sub-committee to frame a reply to the king; on the 16th they turned to the more important matter of Turner's speech. They first heard Turner again: he began by protesting his loyalty and then discussed the criticism Charles had made of the weakness in his attack on Buckingham—that it was not based on proofs provided by the evidence of witnesses. He said that he believed that common fame was a legitimate and parliamentary basis for a presentment. The committee held an inconclusive debate, finally agreeing to adjourn for two days to give Turner time to prepare a fuller reply. Little more progress was made on the next occasion but on 22nd, after a debate in which Spencer made the nice point that the complaint about Turner's speech was itself based upon common fame, the committee reached a decision. It resolved that the accusation against Buckingham was indeed grounded upon common fame and it decided that it would next debate whether this was a parliamentary form of proceeding.[13]

This leisurely pace shows the Commons being deliberately obstructive and the king eventually complained bitterly about it. But it doubtless helped to divert attention from the real progress made in the committee for evils, causes and remedies. Here, under the inspiration of Turner's six questions, causes of two evils from which the kingdom was suffering were rapidly identified, and a sub-committee under Eliot's chairmanship was set up to enquire into the cause of these causes. On 25 March Wandesford delivered a detailed report from his committee to the House. He listed ten causes upon which the committee had agreed and stated that so far Buckingham had been found responsible for four of these. The House formally approved the committee's original findings on the two evils and accepted nine of the proposed causes, holding the tenth over for further consideration. It then arranged a day for the consideration of those causes with which the

[13] *C.J.* i, 835, 837; Whitelocke, Diary (12.20-1), ff. 43, 51, 53, 54, 75, 76, 185; Add. MS 22474, ff. 12-12v.

duke's name had been connected, and sent him word of its intentions.[14]

Buckingham's adherents had failed to stop the headlong progress of the committee for evils, causes and remedies, and Charles was still awaiting a reply to his message about Coke and Turner. On the 27th the Commons debated the king's request for a subsidy and Eliot seized the opportunity to compare their predicament with some of the darker episodes of the late middle ages. Largely under his influence the House resolved to pass a subsidy bill as soon as it had heard the king's answer to its grievances.[15] At this point Charles intervened in a situation that was rapidly getting out of hand.

On the day appointed for a further meeting of the committee dealing with Turner's speech he ordered the Commons to attend him with the Lords at Whitehall on the following morning and in the meantime told them to suspend all further business. Largely through the Lord Keeper, Charles addressed them on that occasion in tones of considerable bitterness. He complained that they had ignored his request for justice against the two members and that their committee had 'walked in ye stepps of Turner, and ... [had] proceeded in an unparliamentarye inquisition'. After lavishing praise on Buckingham he ordered them to cease their examinations and to obey his previous commands. He then turned to the question of supply, pointing out that only two days in twelve had been devoted to its discussion and objecting to the manner in which it had been made dependent upon redress of grievances. He warned them that the sum proposed—three subsidies and three fifteenths—was inadequate and that unless they increased it

---

[14] Whitelocke, Diary (12.20-1), ff. 18ᵇvff, 55ff, 84ff; H. Hulme, 'The Leadership of Sir John Eliot in the Parliament of 1626', *Journal of Modern History*, iv (1932), 371; Archbold, 736; *C.J.* i, 841-2. The Lords, however, on 28 March, refused Buckingham permission to answer the Commons: *L.J.* iii, 543.

[15] Whitelocke, Diary (12.20-1), ff. 5v, 93. Eliot referred to Hugh de Burgh and Michael de la Pole, associating them with the misfortunes of their respective kings, Henry III and Richard II. Ball says that Eliot was careful to avoid giving the impression that such ministers had been 'impeached': 'Parliamentary Career of Eliot', 181. When, a few days later, Eliot compared the attack on Buckingham with that on de la Pole, he emphasised that his use of this precedent was not intended as a reflection upon Charles or his government: Whitelocke, Diary (12.20-1), f. 119v.

unconditionally within three days he would not promise to continue their sitting.[16]

The Commons took exception to this speech and, after hearing Wentworth say that they would need all their wisdom to protect their liberties, suspended all other business and resolved themselves into a grand committee to consider it. They heard Eliot declare that their investigations had been soundly based and that 'this place ever had the course of questioning, examining the subject', but before they had reached any conclusions they were interrupted by a message from the Lords asking for a conference. When, as a committee of the whole, they assembled in the Painted Chamber, they found the government intent on conciliation. Through Buckingham, Charles cancelled the threats and limitations surrounding the subsidy and gave them leave to continue their investigation of grievances 'in the auntient wayes of your predecessors, and not so much to seeke faults as the meanes to redresse them'. The duke then entered into a long justification of his own actions, ranging widely over the ten causes which the Commons' committee had enumerated. On their return to their own House the Commons seem to have dealt with the duke's ill-timed answer by ignoring it, but in committee they debated whether a remonstrance was required to protect their liberties. Some members argued that the explanation just given rendered this unnecessary but Digges and Wentworth helped to have a sub-committee appointed to draw one up.[17]

The fight between the government's supporters and its critics was continued at this sub-committee, which spent some time reviving the issue of the legitimacy of common fame as a basis for an accusation. Members were as usual quick to deny any intention of casting aspersions upon the king, but when the

[16] *C.J.* i, 843; Whitelocke, Diary (12.20-1), ff. 103v-106.

[17] *C.J.* i, 843; Add. MS 22474, ff. 22ff, 31-31v; Whitelocke, Diary (12.20-1), ff. 107-107v, 109vff, 117-117v, 118v; Diary of Sir Nathaniel Rich, frame 75. (The original manuscript of this diary has disappeared. However, Cornell University possesses a photostat copy of the manuscript and my references are to the frames of a microfilm made from this copy.)

Herbert was chairman of the grand committee, Glanville of the sub-committee, though on at least one occasion Pym reported from the latter: Whitelocke, Diary (12.20-1), f. 121; *C.J.* i, 843.

remonstrance was presented to the House it was framed in determined, if loyal, language. It denied that Coke had spoken seditiously and said that he had, in any case, at once explained his few unwise words, adding that the House would have dealt with both speeches had not the king's message to attend him interrupted proceedings. On the more important issue of the Commons' investigations it maintained their claim to examine anyone found responsible for grievances and it asserted that 'whatsoever wee shall doe accordingly this parliament, we doubt not but it shall redound to ye honour of your Crowne, & welfare of your subjects.' On the Tuesday before Easter the remonstrance was presented to the king, who replied that he would not at once give an answer but would like the Commons to adjourn for eight days as the Lords had done. The motion to do so was passed by a majority of only thirty in a vote of two hundred and seventy.[18] The Commons were clearly in no mood to be deflected from their objective.

Meanwhile, a situation which was soon to prove embarrassing for the government, while encouraging to its opponents, had been developing in the house of lords. The earl of Bristol, ambassador to Spain at the time of the marriage negotiations, had fallen from favour and had been placed under restriction on his return home. No charges had been brought against him and his attempts to receive a hearing had been refused. When parliament was called in 1626 the earl was not sent a summons, and when he petitioned the Lords on 22 March for assistance in his plight it was to this in particular that he drew their attention. His petition led to the issue of a writ but, when he also received a letter ordering him not to attend, he again appealed to the House. In this second petition he placed the blame for the treatment he had received on Buckingham's head, and said that if the Lords would hear him he would explain how the duke had abused the king and his father, the state and both houses of parliament.[19]

[18] *C.J.* i, 844; Whitelocke, Diary (12.20-1), ff. 119-120, 122v, 124.

[19] J. O. Halliwell, ed. *Letters of the Kings of England* (London, 1848), ii, 230; *L.J.* iii, 537, 544, 563. A comparison between Bristol's case and the medieval appeal of treason would be worth making. On 9 May Digges referred to Bristol's accusations as an appeal: Grosvenor, 70 (references are to a typescript of this manuscript). If it was, why did not Charles intervene with the statute of 1 Henry

It was out of this situation that there grew Bristol's charges against Buckingham and the king's counter charges against Bristol. These accusations have little direct part in the history of parliamentary judicature, for although the Commons clearly derived encouragement from this additional challenge to Buckingham, the case itself was almost wholly confined to the house of lords. However, it will require some attention as, to an extent, it affected the development of the trial of Buckingham. Furthermore, it must have worried the duke: up to Easter his support in the Lords had seemed firm enough, but during the recess he was apparently considering a proposal to strengthen his position there by securing the creation of twenty new peers.[20]

When the Commons reassembled on 13 April the king sent them a message renewing his request for rapid supply and stating that he did not intend to reply to the remonstrance because of the shortage of time. There was some protest but, possibly because a number of members had still to return, no action was taken. The absence of members, which it was thought might benefit Buckingham, was certainly the reason why the committee concerned with his affairs did not resume work until the 18th, but when they did so it was with unabated vigour. New allegations, such as Buckingham's extortion of money from the East India Company, were investigated, while further examinations were made of subjects like the misuse of the king's revenues and the sending of ships to La Rochelle,

IV, cap. 14, which prevented the hearing of appeals of treason in parliament? Did he know that, on occasion, this statute had been disregarded? (For a breach of the statute, see Bellamy, *Law of Treason*, 147.)

Gardiner said that Bristol was impeached. Apart from a solitary remark of Bristol's (for which see below, p. 196 n. 33), the only evidence to support this is provided by a marginal heading in the *Lords Journal*. Some of these headings occur in the manuscript Journal and are therefore contemporary; others, including this one, do not, and were provided when the Journals were prepared for printing: S. R. Gardiner, ed. 'The Earl of Bristol's Defence of his Negotiations in Spain', *Camden Miscellany*, vi (Camden Society, civ: London, 1871), p. ii; *L.J.* iii, 632. Another marginal heading, similarly absent from the manuscript Journal, states that the 'E. of Bristol impeaches the Duke of Buckingham to the Commons . . .': *L.J.* iii, 580.

[20] *C.S.P. Ven. 1625-6*, 390. Pesaro also reported that Buckingham had approached many members with inducements to help his cause.

which had been first discussed before Easter. When yet another message about supply arrived from Charles, the Commons' answer was a resolution to set aside all business other than Buckingham's: they argued that the sooner they completed it, the sooner they would be able to satisfy the king's requests for money. By the 21st work was sufficiently advanced for the House to accept Digges's proposal that a select committee be appointed to consider the state of the 'great Business now in hand', to reduce it into form and to survey the relevant precedents. Twelve members were appointed, including the chairmen of the various committees and sub-committees which had dealt with the case since the beginning of the parliament. That same afternoon, Glanville, on behalf of the select committee, asked whether the House would decide if 'common Fame [was] a Ground for this House to proceed upon; because it conduceth much to the Business now in hand'. No longer could the Commons avoid dealing with this fundamental issue: they resolved to debate it on the following morning and instructed the lawyers to be present with their precedents and their officers with the records.[21]

When the debate opened, Mallett, as so often in this parliament, gave the government view. He produced a whole series of reasons why common fame should not be accepted as a basis on which the Commons could proceed: their methods should not resemble those of a grand jury; a party accused on common fame would have to answer both the fame and the accusation; if he was cleared he would have no redress against his accuser; common fame would be more frequently employed by lesser courts if parliament had been accustomed to accept it; the Lords had rejected the Commons' case against the bishop of Durham in 1614 because it was grounded upon common fame.

[21] Whitelocke, Diary (12.20-1), ff. 126v, 139v, 147vff, 150; *C.S.P. Ven. 1625-6*, 387; *C.J.* i, 846, 847; Hulme, *Life of Eliot*, 127. The members of this select committee were Eliot, Herbert, Pym, Hoby, Digges, Selden, Erle, Glanville, Lake, Wandesford, Whitby and Sherland. In the early stages of its work Glanville often reported from it and was chairman on at least one occasion. Later, Digges was the usual reporter. It is not entirely true to suggest, as Mrs Spielman does, that Glanville reported on procedural matters while Digges dealt with the actual subjects of the impeachment: Spielman, 124 n.52; *C.J.* i, 847, 849, 850, 853, 856; Whitelocke, Diary (12.20-1), f. 159v; Grosvenor, 29.

His arguments were hardly answered in the speeches which followed, but these did not lack persuasiveness. Wilde claimed the authority of Bracton for saying that all suspicion must be grounded upon common fame, adding that some presumptions did not admit to proof. He pointed out that, to be acceptable, the fame must arise among men of 'the better Sort' and Littleton supported him, saying that there was a great difference between common fame and rumour. Littleton also declared that the Commons were 'not a House of definitive Judgment, but of Information, Denunciation, or Presentment; for which common Fame sufficient'. Sherland adopted the most advanced position, arguing that if fame was a sufficient basis for accusations concerning the life of one man, it should also be permissible in those relating to the life and soul of the commonwealth. But Wentworth and Selden had already put the really influential argument, political rather than legal: only upon common fame might men safely accuse the great; 'The Faults of the Gods might not be told, till the Goddess Fame born.' For this reason the Commons resolved that common fame was a proper ground for their own proceedings and for any transmission of the case that might be made, either to the king or to the Lords.[22] Without this decision the case against Buckingham would have failed then and there, because no one had yet come forward prepared to present specific information against the duke. In this respect it differed significantly from the cases of 1621 and 1624, in which detailed evidence had been secured from particular witnesses.

During the next week, the committee for evils, causes and remedies, and its sub-committee for the cause of causes, wound up their business, and the select committee busied itself examining witnesses and continuing investigations. The House offered Buckingham a further opportunity of a hearing and, when the Lords refused to permit this, proceeded to vote him responsible

---

[22] *C.J.* i, 847-8; Whitelocke, Diary (12.20-1), ff. 152v, 154v. As Mrs Spielman points out (p. 126), Sherland's speech looks ahead to the trial of Strafford in 1641. No one in the debate seems to have mentioned the concept of notoriety, which common fame closely resembled, but three weeks earlier Noy had said 'Ther is a proceeding on a notoriety of ye fact & uppon c. fame': Whitelocke, Diary (12.20-1), f. 119.

for eight causes.[23] It then received from the select committee the astonishing news that, contrary to the advice of the royal doctors, Buckingham had administered medicine to James during his last illness. This seemed to confirm rumours which had been circulating for some time, that the duke had poisoned the king, and the Commons at once referred it to a grand committee for consideration. Very rapidly, this committee confirmed the report but avoided suggesting that treason had been committed. Ignoring the vigorous protests of the chancellors of the Exchequer and the Duchy of Lancaster, the House added the accusation to the duke's charge as an 'act of a transcendent Presumption, of dangerous Consequence'.[24] On the following day, the king, probably making a virtue of necessity, asked the Commons to conclude the case in whatever way they chose but to do so as quickly as possible. The House thanked him and promply arranged to revive the matter of the ship, *St Peter*.[25]

On 1 May the House voted that the duke's behaviour in the rearrest of the *St Peter* was a grievance: its adoption of a course vainly urged by Eliot in March shows how far opinion had moved against Buckingham. During this debate Rolle advanced an argument which was to be used more forcibly

[23] Whitelocke, Diary (12.20-1), f. 155; *C.J.* i, 848-9; *L.J.* iii, 570-1; Hulme, *Life of Eliot*, 127. Four of the causes had been successfully laid at Buckingham's door by Eliot's sub-committee in March: *C.J.* i, 841. In refusing Buckingham permission to answer, the Lords referred back to their order of 28 March: see above, p. 186 n. 14.

[24] *C.S.P. Ven. 1625-6*, 13; *C.J.* i, 850-1.

[25] *C.J.* i, 851; Lowther, 10; Whitelocke, Diary (12.20-1), f. 168. Ball, 'Parliamentary Career of Eliot', 179, suggests that Charles probably withdrew his opposition to the Commons' proceedings to avoid the awkward constitutional implications that could be read into an impeachment made without royal consent. This seems to argue a greater degree of understanding of a constitutional situation than Charles in fact possessed, as well as an equally uncharacteristic anxiety to show respect for the proprieties of the law. That he had not forsaken strong-arm tactics is revealed by the pressure to which Cotton was subjected at this time to cease supplying the Commons with precedents, and by the arrests of Digges and Eliot which were soon to occur: Williams, *Charles I*, i, 98. The bishop of Mende reported to d'Herbault that the charge concerning the death of James had worsened Buckingham's position because, hitherto, he had always believed that parliament could be dissolved to save him. If Charles now chose this course before the charge was dealt with, it would be assumed that he was implicated in his father's death: Paris Archives, Baschet's Transcripts, P.R.O. 31/3/63, f. 66.

later when he said that, even though the king commanded the rearrest, Buckingham should not have obeyed to the point of breaking the law: if an officer of the crown did so, he should be punished.[26]

On the following day, Digges, supported by Glanville, reported that the select committee of twelve had approved ten causes of the two evils afflicting the kingdom and had determined that Buckingham was the cause of all these. From its investigations of these the committee had drawn up thirteen articles against the duke and it now laid them before the Commons. A strenuous attempt was made to persuade the House to present the articles to the king, but it resolved to follow 'ye old way' and transmit them to the Lords. It would perhaps have decided thus anyway, but Strangways may have settled the matter by arguing that this was the normal course and by warning the House not to show distrust of the Lords. Accordingly, the select committee was given the task of arranging how the decision should be carried out.[27]

The committee made two recommendations which represented a departure from recent practice. It proposed that the accusation should be divided among eight members, who would be responsible for its presentation to the Lords. Each of these members would have two assistants who would help with the presentation of his section, but not speak. This proposition was accepted without demur and, when the Commons' case was eventually transmitted to the Lords, Digges and Eliot, respectively, presented the preamble and epilogue, while Herbert, Selden, Glanville, Sherland, Pym and Wandesford divided the articles of the charge among themselves. All these men had been members of the select committee.[28] However, that

---

[26] *C.J.* i, 852; Grosvenor, 9. Eliot adopted a similar position on 10 May: T. B. Howell, ed. *A Complete Collection of State Trials and Proceedings for High Treason and other Crimes and Misdemeanors* . . . (London, 1816), ii, col. 1368.

[27] *C.J.* i, 853; Whitelocke, Diary (12.20-1), ff. 173-173v; Lowther, 11-13; Grosvenor, 16, 23. Of the ten causes many had already been reported to the Commons and voted on: see, for example, *C.J.* i, 849 (account for 24 April).

[28] *C.J.* i, 854; Lowther, 13; Add. MS 22474, f. 104. Sherland replaced Whitby who fell ill before his part was delivered: Sherland had previously been one of Whitby's two assistants: *L.J.* iii, 590. It appears that the select committee originally proposed that Erle should deal with the part eventually delivered by Glanville. No reason is given for the change: *C.J.* i, 854; Add. MS 22474, f. 104.

committee's second recommendation met opposition. As Digges read the draft of the preamble to the Commons it became clear that, in addition to the customary oral transmission of the case, he was proposing that the charge should also be embodied in a bill. Sandys at once objected that one method was sufficient and that to present the accusation in writing was a new way of delivering it. The proposal was referred back to the committee, which, if it bothered to reconsider it, did not change its mind. So when, on the 6th, the committee presented its last major report, detailing the complete charge and showing how it was to be distributed, the chancellor of the Duchy of Lancaster, Sir Humphrey May, took up the cudgels. He asked the committee to explain why 'we goe in a new way: calling this a bill different from the late way'. Selden answered him: 'we used to make the accusacion of those persons accused by word of mouth: and that a good course. But as true that when accusacions are of many parts; this course was also used: as 50 Ed. 3: 28 H. 6: there a large accusacion is called a bill . . .' Another diarist gives part of the same speech more cryptically, and raises again the problem of the meaning of the word clamour: 'Some excused [accused] by clamour of ye commons, some by mouth of ye commons.'[29] The precedent-worshipping Commons accepted Selden's guidance but this leaves unexplained why the committee had recommended adding procedure by bill to the normal method. Certainly the case was complex, but some of its predecessors had not been exactly simple, and in the past the Commons had been anxious to avoid committing themselves in writing. Clearly the accusation was of great importance, but this had been equally true of that against Middlesex in 1624, and if procedure by bill had then been thought a suitable method the Commons would surely have had no difficulty in using it. One is left wondering whether the bill was in some way a cloak behind which the intention to proceed by impeachment could hide until the last

[29] *C.J.* i, 856; Lowther, 13-14, 17; Grosvenor, 29, 53; Whitelocke, Diary (12.20-1), f. 181. Selden's references are, probably, to the impeachment of Latimer in 1376 and, certainly, to the impeachment of Suffolk in 1450. In both cases bills (or petitions) were employed in the Commons' accusation, and, in the case of Suffolk, over twenty charges were listed by this means. For Latimer, see above, p. 15; for Suffolk, see *Rot. Parl.* v, 176-83.

possible moment, or whether it was regarded by the committee as an essential part of this procedure. There is some evidence to support both possibilities, but it is first necessary to consider their implications. They assume, of course, that impeachment had some special significance, at least to the committee, and that it was thought necessary to disguise the intention to impeach Buckingham. Why secrecy might have been regarded as important we can only guess, but it may be that to use the term would have destroyed the contention of men like Eliot that they were not intending to attack the king or his government. As for the assumption that impeachment had some special significance, we know from Selden's treatise, probably written at about this time, that he believed this. Now, it is interesting that it was Selden himself who answered May's criticism of the committee's decision to proceed by bill, as well as orally, against Buckingham. For it will be remembered that it was, in his view, the failure of the Commons to present their accusation against Middlesex in writing that lay at the root of the process by which they lost the power, in that case, to maintain their own suit—a power which was, to Selden, one of the characteristics distinguishing a Commons' impeachment from a Commons' complaint. Though Selden might be a theorist, believing in distinctions which, to the average member, may have meant nothing, he was at this moment in a position to influence the development of parliamentary judicature from the standpoint of a practising politician.[30] Furthermore, the fact that he chose to make a distinction between impeachment and complaint suggests that some, at least, of the Commons' leaders were aware—or were becoming aware—not only that there were various procedures available to them but also that impeachment was a recognisable and, within limits, definite process which offered distinct advantages to those choosing to use it.

As for the wording of the bill itself, it is, of course dangerous to argue from the silence of the records, but when Digges on 3 May read to the Commons the draft of his preamble Buckingham merely stood accused. The select committee did not report

[30] In his treatise Selden says that the Commons 'accused and impeached . . . Buckingham . . . and delivered their Declaration in writing, that the said Duke might be put to his Answer': *O Judicature*, 32.

its final work on the charge until the afternoon of Saturday, the 6th, and the engrossed articles were not read to the Commons until the morning of Monday, the 8th—the very day of the presentation of the charge to the Lords. Even at the last minute some minor alterations were made to these articles and not until this was done was the message sent to the Lords asking for a conference.[31] This message contains the first open acknowledgement to appear in the record that the Commons were impeaching Buckingham: it is possible that at the last minute the word impeachment was slipped into the bill. Of course, if there were evidence that the intention to impeach Buckingham had become widely known before the introduction of the bill, the suggestion that the bill was a means of keeping this intention secret would at once collapse. But the records give little indication that any such knowledge was widespread. Occasionally, before the transmission of the charge to the Lords, the proceedings are described as a complaint,[32] but in the records of the case before 8 May, there is only one reference to impeachment. Moreover, this reference is cryptic and negative, suggesting that impeachment was not being contemplated. During the discussion of the accusation that Buckingham had administered medicine to James, Marriott maintained that the committee, which had already recommended adding this to the duke's charge, did not intend to 'impeach him so dear to the King . . .'[33]

---

[31] *C.J.* i, 856, 857; Lowther, 14. The guess that the bill was the means by which impeachment was surreptitiously introduced perhaps receives support from Sandys's apparent failure to renew the strong objection he had first raised, when the debate was resumed on the 6th. He was not a member of the select committee and so might not at first have known what was afoot.

[32] Add. MS 22474, f. 22. The term also appears occasionally after the charge was sent to the Lords: *L.J.* iii, 615, 649; Rushworth, i, 377.

[33] Lowther, 9. On 1 May the word was used in the Lords, probably imprecisely, in Bristol's case. There is nothing in the charges either by or against him to suggest an impeachment, and yet he desired not 'to be impeached until his Charge of so high a Nature be first heard': *L.J.* iii, 576. The charge against him was brought by the king, and the Commons were in no way responsible for it. According to the calendared version of Salvetti's despatches to the Florentine court, he had reported in March that the Commons wished to proceed against Buckingham 'by impeachment'. But the use of this term cannot be justified from the Italian transcript of his despatch. This merely states that the Commons wanted to bring a process (*un processo*) against the duke: *H.M.C. Eleventh Report*, App. i, 51; Add. MS 27962, iv, f. 142v.

If impeachment had some special significance which led to the need for secrecy, why was there no eruption of anger when the intention did become known? Two answers are possible. First, if the plan remained secret until the morning of 8 May, there was no time to whip up opposition before the Commons met the Lords that afternoon. Secondly, after the Commons had impeached Buckingham there was little point in conducting a post mortem: it would simply underline the extent to which the government's supporters had lost control of the situation. Moreover, Charles doubtless felt that his attack on Eliot and Digges, soon to take place, was a fairly satisfactory revenge.

In any case, it was doubtless of limited interest to Charles whether or not his favourite was impeached, even if he attached any special significance to the term. To him what mattered was that Buckingham was under attack, and during the first week in May little happened in either House from which he could draw comfort. He had tried to prevent Bristol's charge against Buckingham from getting under way in the Lords by accusing the earl of high treason, but the Lords had decided to hear the charges from both sides and Bristol had retaliated with a charge of high treason against the duke. When the news that Buckingham had been accused of treason reached the Commons, Eliot moved that they should ask the Lords to commit him to prison. At that moment the House refused to listen, but a few days later it reconsidered the proposal and eventually adopted it. Moreover, through his son, Bristol delivered to the Commons a copy of his charge against Buckingham. This contained allegations that the duke had shown strong inclinations towards Catholicism and had plotted the conversion of Charles. Hearing this, the Commons promptly revived their unfinished investigation into the duke's part in encouraging papists, ignoring a demand from the king that they should end their inquisition and present the charge, and even examining a witness who more properly belonged to the Lords.[34]

On the afternoon of 8 May the two Houses met in committee

[34] *L.J.* iii, 578; *C.J.* i, 853, 855, 857; Williams, *Charles I*, i, 99; Lowther, 11, 15; Hulme, *Life of Eliot*, 132; Whitelocke, Diary (12.20-1), ff. 178-9. The committee for evils, causes and remedies was reconvened to conduct the revived investigation.

o

in the Painted Chamber and Digges introduced the Commons' impeachment of Buckingham.[35] The lower House had clearly aimed at making the occasion as impressive as possible: it had ordered that places should be reserved for the eight speakers and their assistants, and that those not appointed to deliver the charge should remain silent. In addition, the phrasing of the bill shows how much bolder the Commons had become since 1621 and 1624; while the concept of an indictment which Maude Clarke believed essential to any impeachment, is apparent:

For the speedy Redress of great Evils and Mischiefs, and of the chief Cause of these Evils and Mischiefs, which this Kingdom of England now grievously suffereth, and of late Years hath suffered . . . the Commons . . . do, by this their Bill, shew and declare against George, Duke, Marquis . . . [a long list of his titles and offices is given] . . . the Misdemeanors, Misprisions, Offences, Crimes, and other Matters comprized in the Articles hereafter following; and him the said Duke do accuse and impeach of the said Misdemeanors, Misprisions, Offences, and Crimes.[36]

Each article was read out and the member responsible then spoke to it. Eight articles had been dealt with when the Lords announced themselves 'wearied with the heat' and asked for an adjournment. In consequence, the remainder of the charge was delivered on the 10th, and Eliot concluded the Commons' case by reserving their right to add subsequently any further accusation or impeachment, to reply to the duke's defence, and to offer any necessary further proof. His final request was that Buckingham should be put to answer all the articles, and that every one of them should be considered in the course of the proceedings and judgment.[37]

[35] *C.J.* i, 857. The Lords gave the Commons a meeting, not a conference, 'bicause they will only lend us their eares', but Whitelocke persists in calling it a conference: Diary (12.20-1), ff. 96, 182. Presumably because of the length of the charge, it was more convenient for the Commons to meet the Lords in committee than to present their case at the Bar of the upper House. If Selden is to be believed (see above, p. 163), to meet in committee in no way impaired the Commons' claim to a continuing interest in the case, provided that the charge was presented in writing—and on this the House had already resolved.

[36] *L.J.* iii, 619; *C.J.* i, 857; Clarke, 'Origin of Impeachment', 268.

[37] Add. MS 22474, ff. 101v, 142; *L.J.* iii, 590; *H.M.C. Buccleugh*, iii, 288; Whitelocke, Diary (12.20-1), ff. 96ff. The thirteen articles were: 1. holding an

On the following morning a delegation from the Commons, headed by Rich, appeared before the Lords to ask for Buckingham's committal to safe custody.[38] Two reasons were given: he had been impeached by the Commons and, as they understood, accused of high treason before the Lords by another peer. This was the outcome of the proposal first made by Eliot on the 4th. Although his suggestion had then been ignored, Kerton had made a somewhat similar proposal, just before the conference on the 8th, when he moved for Buckingham's sequestration on the basis of the Commons' charges.[39] Sandys objected that the House had not asked for the sequestration of either Bacon or Middlesex, and Noy, evidently thinking of Bristol's charges against the duke, declared that it was not for the Commons to direct the Lords what to do in a case before them. But although opposing Kerton's motion, or at least its wording, Selden said that many precedents justified the committal of a man accused of high treason. Presumably because of shortage of time the House arranged to continue the debate on the next day. By then the proposal to sequester had given way to the bolder notion of committal, and the House needed little time to decide that high treason was a sufficient basis for this. However, opinions differed as to whether the Commons might properly ask for a committal on a charge made only in

excessive number of offices; 2. buying the position of Lord Admiral; 3. purchasing the wardenship of the Cinque Ports (these three articles were delivered by Herbert); 4. failure to guard the Channel adequately; 5. The affair of the *St Peter* (Selden); 6. extortion of money from the East India Company; 7. handing over ships to the French; 8. their use against La Rochelle (Glanville); 9. compelling Lord Roberts to buy his honour; 10. sale of the offices of Lord Treasurer and Master of the Wards (Sherland, who replaced Whitby when the latter became ill); 11. procuring honours for the duke's relations; 12. misusing and profiting from the king's revenue (Pym); 13. administering medicine to James in his final illness (Wandesford): *L.J.* iii, 619-24; Add. MS 22474, f. 104; Grosvenor, 53, gives article 6 to Selden but is the only account to do so.

[38] A good deal of argument had previously taken place in the Commons as to the exact procedure to be adopted in delivering this message. Rich had argued that it should be presented by the Speaker at the Bar of the Lords. He evidently felt strongly about this as he made the same point about the presentation of Montague's charges to the Lords: Grosvenor, 71-2.

[39] *C.J.* i, 857, 858; Whitelocke, Diary (12.20-1), f. 182v. Kerton had first proposed sequestration from the Lords and the Court when on the 4th the Commons renewed their investigation of the duke's encouragement of papists: Whitelocke, Diary (12.20-1), f. 178.

the Lords, and, if not, whether their own accusation provided a sufficient basis for such a request. Buckingham's supporters put up a strong fight, but opinion had hardened against him as a consequence of his insolent behaviour during the presentation of the charges on the previous day, and the motion to pray for committal was passed by a majority of 119 votes. But the Commons' efforts were of no avail: the Lords never replied to their message and Buckingham remained in the House.[40]

At the same time, the Commons' ability to protect their own members came under test. Shortly before Rich's delegation had gone to the Lords to ask for the duke's committal, the king had told the peers that he intended to punish certain of those who had delivered the articles of impeachment. Soon afterwards the Commons discovered that Digges and Eliot had been spirited away to the Tower. Digges, who had introduced the accusation, had offended the king with his comments upon the charge concerning James's last illness; while Eliot, in pronouncing the epilogue, had allowed his imagination full rein, blackening Buckingham's character and comparing him with Sejanus, the unscrupulous minister of Tiberius. As soon as they had heard the Vice-Chamberlain criticise these speeches, the Commons suspended all other business and went into committee of the whole to consider what to do. Having been told that the papers of the two members had been ransacked they appointed a sub-committee to draw up a remonstrance. On the next day they resolved that each member should take a protestation that cleared Digges of having spoken as the king had alleged, and shortly afterwards thirty-six members of the house of lords voluntarily made a similar declaration. Thereupon the king released Digges, but Eliot remained in prison where he was subjected to a searching examination.[41]

To begin with, the Commons showed less concern for Eliot's

[40] *C.J.* i, 857, 858, 859; Whitelocke, Diary (12.20-1), ff. 182v-184, 186; Grosvenor, 60-70; Hulme, *Life of Eliot*, 134. For Buckingham's behaviour see Williams, *Charles I*, i, 103. He did subsequently withdraw during part of the proceedings on his case: Gardiner, *Debates 1624 and 1626*, 201-2.

[41] Hulme, *Life of Eliot*, 137n, 141-2; Gibb, 238; Rushworth, i, 362-5; *L.J.* iii, 592, 627; *C.J.* i, 859, 860; Lowther, 22, 24, 25; Harl. MS 383, f. 32; Whitelocke, Diary (12.22), ff. 11, 14v.

misfortunes than for Digges's, perhaps because they felt that he had spoken with excessive violence. But when they were told that the king had arrested him for matters over which the Commons had no jurisdiction, they demanded an explanation, and they began to contemplate asking the Lords for a conference to discuss the whole affair. Eventually, Charles announced that he had accepted Eliot's denial, though of what was never specified, and he was restored to the House which at once gave him an opportunity to clear himself. Though the proposed conference never seems to have taken place, work on a remonstrance, later replaced by a bill, for the protection of the Commons' liberties, continued until the end of the parliament.[42]

After the presentation of the Commons' charges to the Lords, the case against Buckingham made poor progress. Although the Lords seem to have done their best to withstand the pressures upon them, as their kindness to Bristol indicates, Buckingham's continued presence in the House undoubtedly had an intimidating effect. He took part in some of the debates on his case and won the concession that he should answer only the written charges and not the additions, known as aggravations, made to these by the Commons' speakers. Moreover, Charles never wavered in his support for the duke: when the chancellor of the University of Cambridge died, the king secured his favourite's election and withstood the very considerable anger of the Commons that a man whom they had impeached should be so advanced.[43] On 8 June Buckingham handed to the Lords his written answer, a carefully prepared rebuttal of the Commons' charges. The Commons rapidly asked for a copy, which the Lords sent after being told by the Lord Treasurer that the precedents supported the Commons' right 'to reply unto their Accusation'. The lower House referred the answer to the select committee of twelve which at once set to work on it.[44]

[42] *C.J.* i, 860, 861; Lowther, 28-9; Hulme, 'Leadership of Eliot', 377-8; Whitelocke, Diary (12.22), ff. 19, 22, 24-24v, 56v.

[43] *L.J.* iii, 627, 629-30, 631, 650; *C.J.* i, 866; Lowther, 31; Gardiner, *Debates 1624 and 1626*, 193ff; Rushworth, i, 375, 378.

[44] *L.J.* iii, 655-67 (Buckingham's answer), 672; *C.J.* i, 869, 870; Whitelocke, Diary (12.22), ff. 150ff.

By asking the Lords for a copy of the answer the Commons were making an important innovation. No such request had been presented in 1624 when Middlesex had made his answer, and yet the Commons of 1626 seem to have had no hesitation in asking. It seems certain that they knew in advance that the procedure followed against Buckingham entitled them to make such a request.[45] Moreover, as soon as the answer was received, Eliot, who had been responsible for the request, indicated the next stage by declaring that the Commons would have to reply. It is possible that these developments are a further sign of the influence of Selden, who regarded them as essential characteristics of an impeachment, but what is particularly important is that they show the Commons taking a much greater interest than previously in the detailed development of a case after its transmission to the Lords.[46] Perhaps they feared that, without their intervention, the Lords might prove unequal to dealing with Buckingham; perhaps they acted in this way as a consequence of the disappointments of 1624.

There is no doubt that the Commons intended to continue with the impeachment[47] but they were also at work on another form of attack on Buckingham. True to their belief that only evil advisers kept them from their loving monarch, they resolved on an approach to the king himself. A grand committee was set up to prepare a declaration, listing all the hindrances and abuse they had suffered at the duke's hands, and asking for his removal. They dealt with a letter from the king demanding the passing of a subsidy bill within eight days, by tacking to the declaration a promise that they would give supply as soon as they received redress. On the 14th the Commons asked Charles to receive them with the declaration; on the 15th he replied with a dissolution.[48]

[45] Because Eliot, in his speech to the Lords on 10 May, had reserved the Commons' right to reply to the duke's defence: see p. 198, above.

[46] *C.J.* i, 869; Whitelocke, Diary (12.22), f. 46; Grosvenor, 176; Selden, *Of Judicature*, 109.

[47] As Ball has shown: 'Parliamentary Career of Eliot', 208-10. It is also clear from the declaration itself: Rushworth, i, 407.

[48] *C.J.* i, 870, 871; Lowther, 32-3; Rushworth, i, 404-10 is the declaration. Roberts has pointed out the 'revolutionary' nature of the declaration: it 'announced the new principle that there were faults that were not criminal and yet justified the removal from office of those who were guilty of them': p. 63. For the most recent

In 1626, for the first time, a Stuart had dissolved a parliament to save a minister. It is quite possible that, if Charles had allowed the impeachment of Buckingham to run its full course, the duke would have been acquitted by the Lords. By dissolving parliament when he did, Charles appeared to be suggesting that in no other way could he control it. He thus magnified its authority and ultimately harmed his own. But, in fact, an act of parliamentary judicature was not to compel him to choose between surrender and dissolution until 1641. In the parliamentary session of 1628, Charles warned members that a revival of the trial of 1626 would lead to an immediate dissolution, and ten weeks passed without a renewal of the attack on Buckingham.[49] When Coke eventually exploded: 'I think the Duke of Buckingham is the cause of all our miseries', his clarion call that 'that man is the Grievance of Grievances' was followed, not by a revival of the proceedings of 1626, as Selden proposed, but by a remonstrance to the king asking for the duke's removal. Charles virtually ignored it and Buckingham remained, as others in recent years had wrongly thought themselves, 'Parliament proofe'.[50]

However, if the Commons had not yet learned how to coerce a reluctant monarch into dismissing his minister, Charles had had to pay quite a high price for his refusal to accede to their clearly expressed wish. He had lost the subsidy and, in the eyes of the Venetian Resident, he had lost much popularity.[51] His

analysis of Charles's precise reasons for the dissolution, see J. S. Flemion, 'The Dissolution of Parliament in 1626; a Revaluation', *E.H.R.* lxxxvii (1972), 784-90.

[49] Gibb, 295. Four days before the opening of the session, some of the Commons' leaders met at Cotton's house. They seem to have been Coke, Eliot, Holles, Kerton, Pym, Selden and Wentworth. They decided for the present not to renew the attack on Buckingham: Gibb, 300.

[50] Gibb, 307, 310; Gardiner, *History* vi, 305-6; Chamberlain, ii, 374; Rushworth, i, 615 (Rushworth prints this remonstrance: pp. 631-8); Hulme, *Life of Eliot*, 262. Clarendon (i, 9-10) makes the point about the benefit to parliamentary authority which flowed from saving a man by dissolution. J. N. Ball has questioned whether parliament was dissolved to save Buckingham: 'The Impeachment of the duke of Buckingham in the Parliament of 1626', *Melanges Antonio Marongiu; Studies presented to the International Commission for the History of Representative and Parliamentary Institutions*, xxxiv (Palermo, 1968), 46.

[51] *C.S.P. Ven. 1625-6*, 512. The Venetian Resident, Angelo Contarini, had a poor opinion of Charles. When the king declared that he would rather lose his crown than abandon Buckingham, Contarini commented that 'he judges badly in this as in everything else': ibid. 604.

reaction to the attack on Buckingham had been exposed to scrutiny, and if Eliot genuinely believed that Charles would have behaved differently if only the Commons had been able to remove the influence of the duke, John Pym, a man of vastly greater insight, was likely to have made more significant deductions. In particular, if Pym's handling of the impeachment of Strafford in 1641 is any guide, he must have thought deeply about the reasons for the Commons' failure in 1626. The Commons had proceeded too slowly and too publicly; they had missed the opportunity which, in charging Bristol, the king had seized, to frame an accusation of high treason against Buckingham, based on the suspicion surrounding James's death. This might have secured his committal to prison. Instead, Buckingham had remained in the Lords, impeding proceedings against himself and receiving the advice of some of the best available counsel. Strafford was to suffer from very different treatment fifteen years later, although the process used against him was similar to that employed in 1626.[52]

Although the Commons failed to secure the downfall of Buckingham, 1626 marked a further refinement in the technique of parliamentary judicature. The Commons successfully based their charge upon common fame rather than upon specific information arising from petitions presented by named people—the more normal and surer method. In doing so, they acquired the resemblance to a grand jury of the kingdom, to which Mallett had so strongly objected in April. They then indicted Buckingham of offences, whereas in 1624 they had merely presented articles of accusation against Middlesex to the Lords.[53] Whether this distinction, so important to Maude Clarke, was more apparent than real must remain an open question; but there is little doubt that the decision to draw up the charge in writing in 1626 represents the sort of advance in the Commons' procedure and determination which lends support to Miss Clarke's view. In addition, in 1626 the Commons took sole responsibility for the compilation of the

[52] Spielman, 141-2. For accounts of Strafford's impeachment, see C. V. Wedgwood, *Thomas Wentworth, First Earl of Strafford, 1593-1641; a Revaluation* (London, 1964), 312ff; Spielman, 147ff.
[53] Prestwich, 485; Clarke, 'Origin of Impeachment', 268.

charge which, two years earlier, had been partly provided by the Lords. The Lords were about to occupy the position of judge and jury which subsequently has been regarded as their traditional function in an impeachment; when, in 1641, the Commons' managers of the impeachment conference became the prosecutors at the impeachment trial, the lower House, too, assumed what has long since been recognised as its proper share in an impeachment. Again, by demanding a copy of Buckingham's answer, the Commons made an important innovation. Yet this change was so readily accepted in both Houses as to suggest that it was known that the procedure adopted in 1626 entitled the Commons to make such a request. It cannot, of course, be proved that they did not possess this right in 1624, but if they did it is curious that they made no use of it: circumstances were favourable and a copy of Middlesex's answer might have made up for their lack of a record of their charges. Perhaps the Commons of 1624 simply did not know that they had power to make such a request, but it is at least possible that the changes of procedure in 1626 gave them an authority which the apparently rather different procedure of 1624 denied them. Be that as it may, the Commons' request in 1626 shows that what happened to a case after its transmission to the Lords was a matter of increasing concern to them. Ultimately, it was their continuing determination to achieve success in a case after sending it to the peers as much as their vigour while it was still under consideration in their own House which ensured the effectiveness of parliamentary judicature.

As the records describe Buckingham as having been impeached while they do not use this word of his predecessors in misfortune, and as John Selden sat in parliament in both 1624 and 1626, it is legitimate to suggest that Buckingham's case may have been the first impeachment in England in the seventeenth century. Yet such propositions are not capable of definite proof. What is more important is to recognise the clear practical differences between this case and its predecessors, rather than the likely but unproveable theoretical distinctions.

The procedural changes made in 1626 may well have arisen directly from the need for the Commons to have greater control over a case involving a man of Buckingham's stature.

Moreover, it is possible that, quite apart from this consideration, the issues at stake in the case were recognised as differing from those in the trials of 1621 and 1624. In those years men had been accused of crimes and grievances committed in office; in 1626 Buckingham was really being attacked because he was thought incompetent to fill the offices he occupied. Hitherto, the attack had been largely legal in nature; now it had become mainly political. There is some evidence that this distinction was recognised. Warnings without precedent in the seventeenth century were issued to the king—from sources which are, to us, unknown—about the consequences of a successful attack on Buckingham: if he was 'but decourted, it will be the Corner stone on which the demolishing of his Monarchie will be builded'. Charles was warned that if Buckingham suffered for obeying him 'the next attempt will be to call the King to accompt...' The bishop of Mende reported that parliament was deliberately encroaching on the royal authority, and Charles was even told that those attacking the duke wished to destroy the monarchy.[54] However exaggerated some of these utterances may be, the point is that apart from Lambe's comment in 1621 there is no evidence that such warnings had ever been directed at James. He had washed his hands of Bacon and Middlesex in a manner which his son steadfastly refused to imitate. Of course, having acknowledged Buckingham's responsibility as his own, Charles could not then dismiss the duke without admitting his own fault. But however earnestly the Commons believed that Charles was innocent of the sins of his minister and favourite, by attacking Buckingham in this way and in these circumstances they were saying something about the monarch and his government which had not been said previously in the seventeenth century. Even if this was barely realised, the change of emphasis was shown by the decision to base the charge against Buckingham on common fame. Because of his closeness to the king no one was prepared to come forward with a detailed accusation, while the type of charge required against him was unlikely to lend itself to proof based on specific evidence. Finally, one may speculate that if in

[54] *Cabala*, 227; Rushworth, i, 360-1; Paris Archives, Baschet's Transcripts: P.R.O. 31/3/63, f. 85.

the early seventeenth century the term 'impeachment' had a special significance, redolent of the errors of medieval monarchs and the reformation of their governments, it is not surprising that it first reappears clearly and unequivocally in connection with the case against the duke of Buckingham.

The only other case in this parliament that was to have been submitted to the judicature of the two Houses, was that of Dr Richard Montague.[55] He had first come to the notice of the Commons in May 1624 when Pym had reported from the committee of religion the receipt of a petition from two clergymen, complaining of the Arminian character of Montague's book, *A New Gagg for an Old Goose*. The House considered whether to send the petition to the king, but decided to report the matter to the archbishop of Canterbury, George Abbot, who told Montague to revise his book. Montague, however, replied to these attacks by writing a more extreme statement of his views, *Appello Caesarem*, which was licensed for publication by James just before he died.[56] In 1625 the Commons dealt with this defiance of their authority by committing Montague to the custody of the serjeant-at-arms for contempt. Shortly afterwards, Charles appointed him to a royal chaplaincy and tried to take the matter out of the Commons' hands. In a debate during the Oxford session leading speakers maintained the House's right to examine the king's servants, and Montague only escaped further proceedings by pleading sickness.[57]

Before parliament opened in 1626 the king withdrew his objections to the Commons' examination of Montague's opinions, although five bishops had pronounced them in no way contrary to the doctrines of the Church of England and

[55] On 17 April, accusations were brought into the Commons against the bishop of Bangor, Lewis Bayly. An examination was conducted by the committee for religion, but progress was slow and the case was brought to an end, while still before the lower House, by the dissolution in June. The accusations, of which we have few details, included simony, incontinency, licensing incestuous marriages, bribery, extortion, and ordaining unsuitable men. Montague was the bishop's chaplain: *C.J.* i, 845, 850, 851, 853, 856, 862, 863, 865, 871; Williams, *Charles I,* i, 96; S.P. Dom. 16/25, no. 10.

[56] Gardiner, *History*, v, 351-4; Nicholas, Diary, f. 199; Erle, f. 182.

[57] Gardiner, *History*, v, 373, 400; Roberts, 51-2.

had recommended the prohibition of further controversy about them. In the committee for religion the Commons duly set to work to investigate them, surely encouraged by the knowledge that in doing so they were also sniping at one of Montague's chief supporters, the duke of Buckingham. This committee rapidly set up a sub-committee to prepare for a conference with the Lords, but not until after Easter was a full report presented to the Commons.[58] This was made by Pym, whose performance was so masterly that Montague's best friends left the House rather than take part in the divisions. Pym was careful to emphasise that the committee had concerned itself only with the effects, not with the truth, of what Montague had written. It had found that he had caused disturbances in the Church, that he had tended to create sedition by dividing the king from the people and the people from each other, and that he had violated the doctrine of the Church of England and endeavoured to reconcile the people with Rome. Some members—we do not know who—wished to implement at once the committee's recommendation that, as he was a public offender against the peace of the Church, his case should be transmitted to the Lords; but Wandesford and Whitby wanted him to answer in the Commons first, an important confirmation of a growing tendency in these cases. Accordingly, the House arranged to give him notice that it would hear him if he wished, and in the meantime it imposed a fresh duty upon the sub-committee by asking it to frame appropriate questions to put to him. Montague did not accept the Commons' invitation and so, on 29 April, the House resolved on three charges, closely modelled on the findings of the

---

[58] Rushworth, i, 202-3; *The Works of the Most Reverend Father in God, William Laud*, ed. W. Scott and J. Bliss (Oxford, 1847-60), vi, 249; Whitelocke, Diary (12.20-1), ff. 19, 20, 84, 85. On 24 March Erle told the committee for evils, causes and remedies that Buckingham had greatly encouraged Montague, but Fleetwood said that the duke detested Arminianism. If Buckingham's support was waning at this time Meddus saw little sign of an estrangement later: writing on 22 May he described Buckingham as a great supporter of 'Montagutians': Whitelocke, Diary (12.20-1), ff. 84, 85; Williams, *Charles I*, i, 105. For Buckingham's support of Montague at the York House disputation in February, see I. Morgan, *Prince Charles's Puritan Chaplain* (London, 1957), 163. Morgan sees this conference as marking the final disillusionment of Buckingham's puritan friends, after which the real attack on the duke began: pp. 166, 168.

committee. Pym moved for the usual conference with the
Lords, but Rich objected and proposed instead that Pym
should deliver the charge in a message at the Bar of the Lords.
He gave three reasons: this method would be more public than
a conference; it was the ancient way which the Commons had
employed in 1614 against the bishop of Lincoln and which
they must not lose; it would obviate the risk that some of
what was said at the conference might be omitted from the
subsequent report to the Lords. Rich's suggestion was adopted
and the Commons asked the committee to write down the
objections to Montague's books, which would be handed to the
Lords.[59]

The impeachment of Buckingham and its aftermath was
presumably responsible for the slow progress made by the
committee, but early in June several lawyers were added to it.
On the 10th Pym reported the charge and the articles, and the
engrossing of the latter was probably just completed when the
dissolution brought the case to a sudden halt.[60]

It is unfortunate from our point of view that the case against
Montague in 1626 did not advance one stage further. It would
be most interesting to know how Pym would have introduced
it at the Bar of the Lords. Although Rich was correct in his
reference to the case of Neile in 1614, the Commons were
varying the practice of the recent past in ordering Pym to
present a message at the Bar of the upper House. A few days
afterwards they were to make another variation when they
approved procedure by bill against Buckingham; but the
reasons they gave for the changes were not similar and there is
no suggestion that, at any time, they thought of presenting to
the Lords a bill against Montague, although the evidence
against him, but not apparently the charge, was to have been

[59] Williams, *Charles I*, i, 96; *C.J.* i, 845, 851; Whitelocke, Diary (12.20-1),
f. 133; S.P. Dom. 16/25, nos. 10, 87.
[60] *C.J.* i, 866, 871; Whitelocke, Diary (12.22), f. 50v. The case was revived
in 1628 and Montague was invited to appear before the committee for religion.
But although the House eventually ordered the transmission of his case to the
Lords the *Journals* of that House contain no indication that this was ever done:
C.J. i, 889, 911; B. M. Stowe MS 366, ff. 234-234v; Lowther, 42-3; Warwickshire
County Record Office, Warwick: Diary of John Newdegate, MS CR 136/box A,
ii, ff. 29ff.

handed to the Lords in writing.[61] Furthermore, the bill against
Buckingham was presented at a joint committee meeting of the
two Houses, not at the Bar of the Lords. Perhaps in altering
their procedure in both cases the Commons were remembering
their dissatisfaction at the outcome of the trials of Middlesex
and the bishop of Norwich two years earlier; while it may be
significant that Selden believed that the case against Middlesex
ceased to be an impeachment because the charge was not
presented either in writing at the committee with the Lords
or orally at their Bar. But there is no indication that Montague
was to be formally impeached and Selden does not mention
the case in his writings. Nevertheless, the modification in
procedure, unchallenged though it seems to have been, interestingly foreshadows the change made at the same stage during
Buckingham's case, and both point to the continuing flexibility
of the process of parliamentary judicature.

Montague's case raises another question—whether the
house of commons was beginning to claim jurisdiction in
doctrinal matters.[62] When Coke had presented the charges
against the bishop of Norwich to the Lords in 1624, he had
claimed that the Commons possessed the right to make complaints against the leaders of the Church, but the Lords had
decided—to the annoyance of the Commons—to refer the
charges to the High Commission for a report. In doing so, they
appear to have been influenced by the semi-doctrinal character
of some of the accusations. Two years later, when Pym reported
on the examination of Montague's writings by the committee
for religion, he emphasised that the committee had dealt only
with the consequences, and not with the truth, of Montague's
opinions. Nevertheless, the committee had found that he had

---

[61] *C.J.* i, 851; Whitelocke, Diary (12.22), f. 50v. Montague wrote to Cosin on
20 April that he had been told that his pardon would not help him because the
Commons intended to proceed 'by an Act of Parliament which will avoid the
pardon'. Even if he was referring to a bill of the type used against Buckingham, it
would be dangerous to accept his statement in the absence of any corroborating
proof in the parliamentary records or diaries: *The Correspondence of John Cosin*, ed.
G. Ornsby (Surtees Society, lii, lv: London, 1869, 1872), pt i, 88-9. The articles
against Montague are printed in *State Trials*, ii, cols. 1263-6, and Rushworth, i,
213-6.

[62] I am grateful to Mr Conrad Russell for drawing my attention to this
question.

not only disturbed the peace but that he had also violated the doctrine of the Church of England. Furthermore, the charges prepared for presentation to the Lords contain details of Montague's false doctrine, although they end by asking the upper House to punish him for disturbing the peace. Because the dissolution of parliament interrupted further progress on the case, we do not know how the Lords would have dealt with the charges nor with the conflict between the Commons' opinion and that of the five bishops, who had declared that Montague had in no way challenged the doctrine of the Church of England. However, if matters of doctrine were still supposed to be the preserve of the monarch and the bishops, the actions of the Commons in 1626 suggest that they were no longer prepared to respect this position in its entirety. The sources do not enable us to determine whether any such encroachment was consciously or unconsciously undertaken, and how far in reality the House was more concerned with the consequences of false doctrine than with doctrine itself; but it may be noted that a letter from the bishops of Rochester, Oxford, and St David's to Buckingham in August 1625 warned him that the mounting attack on Montague represented a challenge to established doctrinal authority.[63]

If Buckingham's case looks temptingly like the climax of parliamentary judicature in the 1620s, it is not the final case in the series. In Charles I's third parliament one man, Dr Roger Manwaring, who was chaplain to the king, was presented to the Lords by the Commons, and the present study will conclude with an examination of his case. Charles had issued a warning that a revival in 1628 of the proceedings against Buckingham would be followed by an immediate dissolution, but he seems to have made no attempt to interrupt the attack on Manwaring which was well under way before Coke's outburst against the duke. We do not know how nor exactly when the Commons' enquiries began, and some of the dating in two of the printed collections of material is wildly

[63] *Cabala*, 117. The bishops were, respectively, John Buckeridge, John Howson and William Laud.

inaccurate.[64] But there is no reason to doubt the entry for
3 May in Sir Richard Grosvenor's diary. On that afternoon a
member, Rouse, reported from a sub-committee to the committee for religion that Manwaring was aiming at subverting
the commonwealth and overthrowing parliament, robbing
people of their property and condemning those who would not
lend money to the king, and attempting to divide the monarch
from his people. These wide-ranging accusations stemmed from
two sermons preached by Manwaring in which he upheld the
king's right to raise forced loans without the consent of parliament, and castigated as impious and rebellious those who
refused to pay. The committee probably held a debate on the
report and it agreed to a motion of Spencer's 'to have a Bill
to attaynt him'.[65] Doubtless because of a preoccupation with
the Petition of Right, the Commons did not hear of its committee's resolution until 14 May, by which time Manwaring
had preached further sermons reiterating the themes of his
earlier ones. But when Pym made his report Spencer's motion
was the centre of attention and caused some controversy. We
do not know why he had proposed a bill of attainder but he
gained the support of Phelips who seems to have been concerned
about the need for haste. Phelips thought that Spencer's
motion would not preclude the possibility of transmitting
Manwaring's case to the Lords, presumably in the customary
way, at a later stage. But Digges had already objected to the
bill on the ground that it would prevent Manwaring from
receiving sufficient punishment. Why he believed this is not
recorded, but he did propose that the Commons should go to
the Lords. However, a second speech by Pym is more enlighten-
ing. Diverging from his committee's recommendation, he
declared that a bill would debar the Commons from stating

---

[64] The first entry in *State Trials* is dated 23 June, 1629. It consists mainly of a
speech by Pym, probably delivered on 14 May, 1628, though it may also contain
elements of another speech by him of 31 May, and possibly of an earlier speech by
Rouse, to whom *State Trials* credits the whole entry: *State Trials*, iii, cols. 336-8;
H. F. Snapp, 'The Impeachment of Roger Maynwaring', *Huntington Library
Quarterly*, xxx (1967), 221; B. M. Stowe MS 366, f. 204; Grosvenor, 1628, 166-7
(references are to a typescript of this manuscript). A similar account among the
State Papers has been supplied, subsequently, with the date, 11 June, 1628:
S.P. Dom. 16/107, ff. 3-4v; *C.S.P. Dom. 1628-9*, 158.

[65] Grosvenor, 1628, 110-11; *State Trials*, iii, col. 335.

their reasons—presumably for their accusation. He also warned the House that such procedure might provoke the Lords, because of their claim that bills of attainder should begin in the upper House; and he explained that the Lords held this view because the Commons were not empowered to administer the oaths upon which such a bill must be based. His opinion that the House should present itself to the Lords combined with Selden's, who argued that attainder should be used only in cases where the defendant could not be brought before the Commons or where the issue at stake was outside the jurisdiction of the House. The debate concluded with a speech by Rich who advocated sending Manwaring's case to the Lords but asserted that either method was within the Commons' power. The House resolved as most of these speakers had suggested, and thus, exceptionally, in the field of parliamentary judicature, rejected the recommendation of one of its committees. However, it asked the sub-committee of the committee for religion to draw up the charge for presentation to the peers, though it added to this sub-committee five new members including Pym and Selden.[66]

The sub-committee was given power to examine the printer of those of Manwaring's sermons which had been published, as well as the usual authority to call for witnesses and records. Preparation of the charge was nearly complete by the end of May, when Manwaring suddenly announced that he wanted to be heard by the Commons. Eliot, who with Coke seems to have taken little part in this case, pointed out that this could not be denied him, and he was given a day to appear. In fact, there is no indication that he took advantage of the opportunity, and on 4 June a message was sent to the Lords asking for a conference. There is no evidence of any suggestion that the Commons should present their case at the Bar of the Lords as they had done, through Pym, against Montague in 1626. On the contrary, as in Buckingham's case, both Houses appointed

[66] Add. MS 27878 (a 'True Relation', one of many copies), ff. 260-260v; Grosvenor, 1628, 168; Harl. MS 5324, f. 16v; S.P. Dom. 16/97, f. 70v; B. M. Stowe MS 366, ff. 165, 204; C.J. i, 897, 907. Further members were later added to the sub-committee which was soon being described as a committee. They included Noy, Hakewill and Littleton: C.J. i, 898, 907; Snapp, 222. We do not know the names of the original members.

P

committees which met on the afternoon of 4 June in the Painted Chamber. Pym again bore the chief responsibility, though he was probably assisted by Rich, Ball, Rouse and Hampden. But Manwaring's charge was not distributed among several speakers as Buckingham's had been.[67]

Pym began by reading out a declaration against Manwaring, and this was later handed to the Lords. It describes itself as a 'Bill of Complainte' and it does not 'accuse and impeach' Manwaring of offences as the bill against Buckingham had done two years earlier. Its approach is less direct: the Commons pray that he may be put to answer their complaints. They do, however, reserve the right to exhibit subsequently 'any other accusacion or impeachment' against him, to reply to his defence and to offer further proof. The Commons were clearly safeguarding their interests in the later stages of the case and, in fact, writing into their bill many of the requests which Eliot had made in his concluding speech at the impeachment conference in 1626.[68] If different types of parliamentary judicature had previously existed or been recognised, it may be that they were now merging into one.

Having read the declaration Pym then made a long and elaborate speech. Manwaring may have been a relatively insignificant person, but in the year of the Petition of Right the position which he had taken up was of fundamental importance.[69] Pym conducted a detailed examination of Manwaring's opinions and of the reasons for the Commons' objections. The conference ended with the Lords asking for time to consider the matter and promising the Commons an answer.[70]

When on 9 June the Lord Keeper reported the conference proceedings to the peers, the House at once took action. Although it had yet to charge Manwaring, it ordered that he

---

[67] Add. MS 27878, f. 340v; *L.J.* iii, 838; *C.J.* i, 901, 902, 906, 907, 908, 909; Lowther, 35.

[68] *L.J.* iii, 845. The declaration is among the acts of parliament, kept in the House of Lords Record Office, and should be used in preference to the version printed in *State Trials*, iii, cols. 338-40.

[69] Snapp, 217, believes that, from the standpoint of demonstrating the positions of parliament and crown, the case rivals, if it does not surpass, in importance the proceedings against Mompesson, Bacon and Middlesex.

[70] B. M. Stowe MS 366, f. 217v. Pym's speech is given in *State Trials*, iii, cols. 340-51.

should be taken into custody—and thus established for itself a new precedent. On the following day the Lords examined witnesses, including five M.P.s who attended and were sworn with the consent of the Commons. Manwaring himself was brought to the Bar on the 11th and was charged by Mr Serjeant Crew and the Attorney General with the offences contained in the Commons' declaration. In the course of his speech the Attorney General pointed out the similarity between Manwaring's offence and that of Cowell in 1610. Manwaring then denied that he had had any intention of proposing an alteration to the fundamental laws of the kingdom, and he annoyed the Lords by requesting them to refer to the bishops for judgment the logical deductions and inferences to be found in his printed sermons. They did, however, accept his plea for a copy of the charge and time to prepare his answer, and they permitted him to return to his house; but they denied him counsel to speak for him on the legal aspects of his case and they continued to employ a guard to watch over him.[71] Buckingham had been treated far less severely.

Manwaring required little time to decide that a submission would be preferable to a defence. On the 13th he came to the Lords to deny that his sermons had had any seditious or malicious intent or that they had aimed at 'destroying . . . the municipal laws of the land, or slighting . . . parliaments'. His only objective had been 'to persuade those honourable gentlemen, who refused to conform themselves, to yield a supply unto the present and imminent necessities of the state'. He concluded by begging 'pardon and mercy of their lordships, and of the commons . . . humbly beseeching them to accept of this submission'.[72]

This speech did not satisfy the archbishop of Canterbury, who administered a sharp rebuke to Manwaring before the latter withdrew; but the House as a whole showed itself rather less

---

[71] *L.J.* iii, 845, 846, 847; *C.J.* i, 911; *State Trials*, iii, col. 352; Relf, 220n, 221. On the 12th the Lords agreed to a Commons' request to examine Manwaring's printer, to find out on whose authority his sermons had been published: Add. MS 27878, f. 404; B. M. Stowe MS 366, f. 244v; Relf, 221. Manwaring claimed on the 13th that they had been printed at the king's 'special command': *State Trials*, iii, col. 353.

[72] *State Trials*, iii, cols. 353-4.

hostile, and resolved on a sentence which accepted some of his denials. He was to be imprisoned during the pleasure of the House, fined £1,000, suspended from exercising his ministry for three years, prohibited for ever from preaching at Court or from holding any ecclesiastical or secular office, and ordered to acknowledge his offences to both Houses in a manner to be prescribed by a committee of the Lords. In addition, the Lords declared that his book of sermons should be burnt, and they resolved to ask the king to call in all copies and to prohibit any further printings.[73]

Whether the Commons would have exercised the right, mentioned as long ago as 1621, of demanding judgment uninvited, we do not know. For, as so often previously, the Lords rapidly issued the customary invitation and the Commons presented themselves at the Bar. According to the *Lords Journal* the Speaker declared that 'the Knights, Citizens, and Burgesses, of the Commons House of Parliament, have impeached before your Lordships Roger Manwaring . . . of divers enormous Crimes', and one of the manuscript accounts tells us that he demanded judgment against him 'uppon the Complainte before mentioned'.[74] The sentence was then pronounced, and in due course Manwaring formally recognised the justice of his punishment and apologised for his offence in a statement which he read out to both Houses.[75]

From the moment when the Commons considered the possibility of attainder and rejected the recommendation of their committee for religion to proceed in this way, the case exhibits some unusual features. The Commons sent to the Lords a written declaration, although their reason for adopting this course against Buckingham—the length and complexity of the case—hardly applied in 1628. The declaration was not closely modelled on the bill of 1626, although men like Pym and Selden were intimately associated with the drafting work

[73] *State Trials*, iii, col. 356.

[74] Ibid. iii, cols. 355-6; *L.J.* iii, 855-6; Add. MS 27878, ff. 409v, 428; Lowther, 47.

[75] *State Trials*, iii, cols. 357-8; *L.J.* iii, 870; *C.J.* i, 916. The king issued the desired proclamation on 24 June: *C.S.P. Dom. 1628-9*, 175. He pardoned Manwaring on 6 July and conferred on him the rectory of Stamford Rivers: Gardiner, *History*, vi, 330.

in both parliaments. When the Commons' case was presented to the Lords, Manwaring was at once taken into custody, although he had yet to be charged. In the matter of counsel, his treatment was closer to that received by Middlesex than by Buckingham, and the requirement that he should submit in the Commons as well as in the Lords was a significant comment upon the interest of the lower House in the case. Finally, there is evidence that by the end of the case, but not perhaps at its beginning, it was being referred to as an impeach-ment.

How parliamentary judicature would have developed in the years after 1629 if parliament had continued to meet, we can only guess. By the time when Strafford was brought to trial conditions were very different. But there can be no doubt that the trials of 1626 and 1628 consolidated and extended that judicature as a significant and important part of parliamentary procedure.

Conclusion

The parliamentary judicature revived in 1621 was called into existence in response to the needs of the moment. The Commons resolved to go to the Lords when they discovered that their own powers were inadequate to cope with the requirements of the situation. Although, on occasion, they experimented with other procedures, they kept faith with this method and their trust in the Lords was, on the whole, rewarded. Cautiously, parliament was regaining its power to right the wrongs which the courts of equity were increasingly failing to remedy. But this judicature was not to be confined to the private and personal: in 1626 parliament declared Buckingham incompetent to discharge the trust laid upon him.[1] This increased assertiveness was matched by a development in procedure: in particular, the Commons assumed a larger part in the cases of 1626 and 1628 than they had done in those of 1621 and 1624. While the earlier cases resemble more closely the 'complaints' of Selden and Elsynge than their 'impeachments', we cannot be sure that such distinctions meant anything to the majority of members at the time, and there is some evidence that the two terms were being used to describe the same case in 1628. If there had previously been two separate procedures, they were apparently merging by the time when Manwaring was brought to trial. Nevertheless, when Selden and Elsynge distinguish between complaint and impeachment, they point to two main differences—whether or not the Commons present to the Lords articles against the accused, and whether or not the lower House has an automatic right to participate in a case after its transmission to the peers. Now in the cases of 1621 and 1624 the Commons were inclined to leave to the Lords the work of drawing up the articles of the charge. Certainly there are exceptions, but the tendency for the Commons to take

[1] Relf, pp. xii-xiv, xviiiff.

on this work becomes much more marked in and after 1626. Furthermore, the trials of 1621 and 1624 show the Commons playing virtually no part in a case after it had left their House, until the moment when they are called upon by the Lords to demand judgment upon the accused. Here again the trial of Buckingham in 1626 does not exhibit a clean break with past procedure, because on one occasion in 1621 the Commons had threatened to demand judgment uninvited; but in 1626 they inaugurated the practice of asking for a copy of the accused's defence and of claiming the right to reply to this. Moreover, the frequency with which the cases of 1621 and 1624 are described as complaints must be noted; and even though this term is not absent from the records of 1626 and 1628, the appearance of the word 'impeach' during the trial of Buckingham has to command attention.

Nevertheless, whether or not the distinction between complaint and impeachment has any practical application in the 1620s, it is important to emphasise that impeachment did not, as is often assumed, re-emerge in its full form in 1621. Such an assumption obscures the very important developments in judicial procedure which occured in both Houses in the 1620s. Not only do these developments point to the flexibility of that procedure, a procedure which, as Coke said of the medieval precedents, had 'beene with some varietye'; they also yield evidence that the Houses modified their practice, cautiously and perhaps reluctantly, in response to the requirements of the moment, rather than in accordance with any long-term plan.

The judicature which has been the main subject of this study should be seen as a part of the general growth of the judicature of the two Houses separately, which preceded and accompanied its development. The various strands may be regarded as different themes in the same story, of which parliamentary judicature is in many ways the most important aspect. Some, at least, of the other themes helped to determine its development. Much the same may be said about the medieval records which the Commons so eagerly studied. Many members tried to follow precedent and evidently felt that they were picking up the threads of the past, but they were no more bound by precedent than by the rigid rules of contemporary courts of law. Although they were instinctively conservative and backward-looking, they were prepared to modify and adapt procedures. In the absence of any specific theory or philosophy of constitutional action, precedent was bound to assume peculiar importance, but, in addition, like their predecessors in 1388, the Commons applied what they called the 'laws of parliament': these might be age-old or they might be newly created, but they were invoked or ignored as circumstances required.[2] In consequence, although parliamentary judicature showed considerable qualities of adaptability, it also possessed sufficient substance to attain its objectives. To study its power in evolution is to understand more fully the advance in parliamentary authority during the early seventeenth century.

[2] Rushworth, i, 407; Clarke, 'Origin of Impeachment', 269; Coke, *Fourth Part of the Institutes*, 14-15; T. K. Rabb, 'Parliament and Society in Early Stuart England; the Legacy of Wallace Notestein', *American Historical Review*, lxxvii (1972), 706, 709.

This table is intended primarily for reference and should be used only in association with the text, since precedents are presented in a variety of ways, ranging from detailed discussion to a brief, passing reference.

Precedents used in 1621 debates (date given unless this is 8 March)	Precedents used by Coke 8 March 1621	Precedents used by Selden	
		Priviledges of the Baronage of England	Of the Judicature in Parliaments
1368			
Lee	×	×	×
1376			
I Bury	×		×
I* Ellis 19.ii	×	×	×
I* Latimer 19.ii; 26.iii; 2.v; 3.v.	×	×	×
I* Lyons	×	×	×
I* Neville 26.iii; 4.vi.	×		×
I* Peach 19.ii; 26.iii.	×		×
1377			
Gomeniz & Weston	×	?	×
I Perrers 28.ii		×	×
1380			
Ferriers			×
1386			
I Pole 3.v	×		×
1397			
I* Mortimer, Thomas	×		×
1423			
Mortimer, John 28.ii	×		×
1450			
I* Suffolk	×		×
Thorpe, Speaker 28.ii	×		×
		× Cavendish v Pole, 1384 Northumberland, 1404	Despenser, 1321
			Wesenham & Chiryton, 1348
			Perrers, 1376
			I Despenser, 1383
			I* Burley ⎫
			I* Beauchamp ⎬ 1388
			I* Salisbury ⎪
			I* Berners ⎭
			I* Judges, 1388
			Other unnamed cases,[1] 1388
			Appellants,[2] 1397
			I* Cobham, 1397
			Haxey, 1397
			Northumberland 1406
			Somerset ⎫
			Duchess of Suffolk ⎬ 1450–1
			Bishop of London ⎭
			I* Stanley, 1459

Notes

I indicates that a case is described in the medieval records as an impeachment.

* indicates that the phrase 'accuse(d) and impeach(ed)' or 'impeach(ed) and accuse(d)' is used in the records of a case.

[1] The bishop of Chichester was also 'impeached' in 1388.

[2] These are the trials of the lords appellant of 1388. Thomas Arundel, though not one of these appellants, was a brother of Richard, earl of Arundel, who was. Thomas was 'accused and impeached' in 1397.

William of Wykeham, 1376, who does not appear in this table, was also 'impeached'.

TABLE II. *Procedures adopted, 1604-28*

This table must be used in conjunction with the text, for the adoption in different cases of similar procedures may not necessarily be the result of similar circumstances.

    (C) case described in the records as a complaint
    (I)   case described in the records as an impeachment

I Case	2 Commons' committees used (specified where known)	3 Commons' sub-committees used	4 Accused/defendant examined or heard by Commons or their committees
Bristol (C) (privilege)	×		
Cowell (privilege)	Grievances	×	
Proctor (privilege in part)	Grievances		×
Spiller	Grievances		×
Neile (privilege)	Four used		
Mompesson (C)	Grievances; one other		×
Michell (C) (?privilege in part)	Grievances		×
Bacon (C)	Abuses in courts of justice		
Yelverton	×		×
Floyd (I)	×		×
Bennet (?C)	Abuses in courts of justice; two others		Commons offered hearing: not taken up
Field (C)	Abuses in courts of justice		
Middlesex (C)	Grievances; trade; two others		×
Norwich (?C)	Grievances		
Anyan (C)	×		
Buckingham (I; occasionally C)	Evils, causes and remedies; three others	×	×
Montague	Religion	×	Commons offered hearing: not taken up
Manwaring (C; I)	Religion	×	Manwaring asked to be heard. Commons offered hearing: probably not taken up

TABLE II 225

5 Accused/defendant committed to custody/imprisonment by Commons	6 Commons condemn patent	7 Case sent to Lords verbally	8 Case sent to Lords in writing	9 Formal resolution in Commons to transmit case or accused to Lords
		Probably		
		Probably		
			Bill	
		×		
×	×	×		×
×	×	No initiative by Commons		
		Evidence handed over without accusation		See column 7: Commons resolved to do this
		×		
×		×		×
		Commons proposed Lords' investigation		
		×		×
		Almost certainly		×
				Decision later reversed
Commons asked Lords to commit Buckingham to custody		×	Bill	×
In 1625				×
By Lords, on their own initiative		×	Declaration	×

I Case	10 Joint conferences or committee meetings of both Houses	11 Lords' committees used	12 Lords' sub-committees used	13 Accused/defendant examined or heard by Lords or their committees
Bristol (C) (privilege)	×			×
Cowell (privilege)	×			
Proctor (privilege in part)	Only at end of case	×		×
Spiller				
Neile (privilege)				×
Mompesson (C)	×	Four used		Mompesson had fled but Commons' case examined
Michell (C) (?privilege in part)	×			×
Bacon (C)	×	Three used		×
Yelverton				×
Floyd (I)	At Lords' request			×
Bennet (?C)	×			
Field (C)	×			×
Middlesex (C)	×	×	Two used	×
Norwich (?C)	×			×
Anyan (C)				
Buckingham (I; occasionally C)	×	×		×
Montague				
Manwaring (C; I)	×			×

TABLE II   227

14 Commons demand copy of defence and claim right to reply	15 Lords report to Commons	16 Commons invited to demand judgment	17 Other characteristics
	×		
	×		
	×		
			False accuser punished by Commons
	×		Commons' case based on common fame
		×	Commons' written evidence presented to Lords. Both Houses active in accumulating evidence
		×	Both Houses active in accumulating evidence
		×	Lords drew up charge
			Lords added a charge to that of Commons
			Commons resolved to punish
			Lords never gave judgment
	×		Commons threatened to demand judgment uninvited. Commons punished false accuser
		×	Accusation compiled by both Houses. Middlesex made a detailed defence. Commons dissatisfied with sentence
			Lords referred case to High Commission for a report
			Commons petitioned king for Anyan's removal
×			Commons' case based on common fame. Commons made preparations to petition king for Buckingham's removal. (Request presented in 1628)
			Before the dissolution, the Commons had resolved to present the charge at the Lords' Bar, and to hand over their evidence in writing
Commons reserved right to reply		×	He was required to make a personal submission in the Commons as well as in the Lords

BIBLIOGRAPHY

UNPUBLISHED SOURCES

1. *Manuscript sources*

Bodleian Library, Oxford
  Carte 78
  Eng. Hist. C. 286
  Rawlinson B. 151   D. 723   D. 1100
  Tanner 392
British Museum, London
  Additional 18597   22474   26639   27878   27962
  Cottonian Julius C. iii
        Titus B. vii   C. vi   F. iv
  Harleian 158   383   1601   6018   6445
          159   390   4289   6274   6799
          304   481   5324   6383   7207
  Lansdowne 167   173   486   491   513
  Sloane 826
  Stowe 366
Cambridge University Library, Cambridge
  Dd. 2.39
  Dd. 12.20-1
  Dd. 12.22
Cornell University Library, Ithaca
  Diary of Sir Nathaniel Rich for 1626
Hampshire Record Office, Winchester
  Diary of Henry Sherfield
Herriard Park, Hampshire
  Diary of Sir Thomas Jervoise
Historical Manuscripts Commission, London
  Sackville (Knole) MSS series 1
    Cranfield Papers, Unnumbered MSS, Bundle IV
House of Lords Record Office, London
  Braye 11   15   69   89
  Main Papers, 4-27 April, 1621
Huntingdonshire Record Office, Huntingdon
  Diary of Sir Nathaniel Rich for 1628
Inner Temple Library, London
  Petyt 537/8   537/14   537/19   538/2   538/19
       537/11   537/18   538/1   538/7

Kent County Archives Office, Maidstone
  Sackville (Knole) MSS series 1
    Cranfield Addenda, Bundle IV (bundle labelled:
    Cranfield MSS Impeachment)

National Library of Wales, Aberystwyth
  9059E. Letter no. 1226

Northamptonshire Record Office, Northampton
  Finch-Hatton 50

Public Record Office, London
  S.P. Dom. 14/54   14/163   16/25   16/107
             14/156   14/166   16/97
  S.P. 81/30

Staffordshire County Record Office, Stafford
  D. 661/11/1/1
  D. 661/11/1/2

Warwickshire County Record Office, Warwick
  CR 136

Wiltshire County Record Office, Trowbridge
  Diary of John Hawarde

2. *Manuscript transcripts*

Public Record Office
  Paris Archives, Baschet's Transcripts.
Yale University Library, New Haven
  Typescript of Harvard College Library MS Eng. 980.
  Typescript of Trinity College, Dublin, MS 611.
  Typescript of Trinity College, Dublin, MS 612.

3. *Other unpublished sources*

Ball, J. N. 'The Parliamentary Career of Sir John Eliot 1624-1629'. Unpublished Ph.D. thesis of the University of Cambridge, 1953.
Berkowitz, D. S. 'Young Mr. Selden; Essays in Seventeenth-century Learn-
  ing and Politics'. Unpublished Ph.D. thesis of the University of Harvard,
  1946.
Friedlaender, M. 'Growth in the Resources for Studies in Earlier English
  History'. Unpublished Ph.D. thesis of the University of Chicago, 1938.
Harrison, G. A., ed. 'The Diary of Sir Simonds D'Ewes, deciphered for
  the period January 1622 to April 1624'. Unpublished M.A. thesis of the
  University of Minnesota, 1915.
Johnson, R. C. 'The Public Career of Lionel Cranfield, Earl of Middlesex
  1575-1645'. Unpublished Ph.D. thesis of the University of Minnesota,
  1956.

Q

Spielman, D. C. 'Impeachments and the Parliamentary Opposition in England 1621-1641'. Unpublished Ph.D. thesis of the University of Wisconsin, 1959.

PUBLISHED SOURCES

1. *Primary sources*

Archbold, W. A. J. 'A Diary of the Parliament of 1626', *English Historical Review*, xvii (1902), 730-7.

Ballinger, J., ed. *Calendar of Wynn (of Gwydir) Papers 1515-1690* (Aberystwyth and London, 1926).

Bond, M. F., ed. *The Manuscripts of the House of Lords, Addenda 1514–1714*, new series, xi (London, 1962).

Bowyer, R. *The Parliamentary Diary of Robert Bowyer 1606-7*, ed. D. H. Willson (Minneapolis, 1931).

British Museum. *A Guide to a Select Exhibition of Cottonian Manuscripts* (Oxford, 1931).

Cabala, Mysteries of State, in Letters of the great Ministers of K. James and K. Charles (London, 1654).

Calendar of the Fine Rolls, preserved in the Public Record Office 1369-1377 (London, 1924).

Calendar of the Patent Rolls, preserved in the Public Record Office 1374-1377 (London, 1916).

Calendar of State Papers, Domestic Series, of the Reign of James I 1603-1625. Four volumes (London, 1857-9).

Calendar of State Papers, Domestic Series, of the Reign of Charles I 1625-1626, 1628-9 (London, 1858-9).

Calendar of State Papers and Manuscripts, relating to English Affairs, existing in the Archives and Collections of Venice, and in the other libraries of Northern Italy 1613-15, 1619-23, 1625-6. Four volumes (London, 1907, 1910, 1911, 1913).

Camden, W. *The Annals of Mr William Camden in the Reign of King James I.* In *A Complete History of England: with the Lives of all the Kings and Queens thereof*, ed. J. Hughes and W. Kennett. Three volumes (London, 1706).

Chamberlain, J. *The Letters of John Chamberlain*, ed. N. E. McClure. Two volumes (Philadelphia, 1939).

Clarendon, Edward, earl of. *The History of the Rebellion and Civil Wars in England begun in the year 1641*, ed. W. D. Macray. Six volumes (Oxford, 1888).

Cobbett, W. *Parliamentary History of England from the Norman Conquest, in 1066, to the year, 1803.* Thirty-six volumes (London, 1806-20).

Coke, E. *The Third Part of the Institutes of the Laws of England*, 4th edition (London, 1669).

— *The Fourth Part of the Institutes of the Laws of England*, 5th edition (London, 1671).

Collas, J. P., ed. *Year Books of Edward II*, xxv, Selden Society, lxxxi (London, 1964).

Collins, A., ed. *Letters and Memorials of State, in the Reigns of Queen Mary, Queen Elizabeth, King James, King Charles the First, part of the Reign of King Charles the Second, and Oliver's Usurpation*. Two volumes (London, 1746).

Cosin, J. *The Correspondence of John Cosin*, ed. G. Ornsby, Surtees Society, lii, lv (London, 1869, 1872).

Cotton, R. *A Briefe Discourse Concerning the Power of the Peeres, and Commons of Parliament, in point of Judicature* (n.p., 1746).

— *An Exact Abridgement of the Records in the Tower of London* (London, 1657).

— *Cottoni Posthuma; Divers Choice Pieces of that Renowned Antiquary Sir Robert Cotton* (London, 1651).

Cowell, J. *The Interpreter* (Cambridge, 1607).

De Villiers, E., ed. 'The Hastings Journal of the Parliament of 1621', *Camden Miscellany*, xx, Camden third series, lxxxiii (London, 1953).

D'Ewes, S. *The Autobiography and Correspondence of Sir Simonds D'Ewes, Bart., during the Reigns of James I and Charles I*, ed. J. O. Halliwell. Two volumes (London, 1845).

Ellis, H., ed. *Original Letters illustrative of English History; including numerous royal letters: from autographs in the British Museum, and one or two other collections*, first series: three volumes; second series: four volumes; third series: four volumes (London, 1824, 1827, 1846).

Elsynge, H. 'The moderne forme of the Parliaments of England', ed. C. S. Sims, *American Historical Review*, liii (1948), 288-305.

Foster, E. R., ed. *Proceedings in Parliament 1610*. Two volumes (New Haven, 1966).

Galbraith, V. H., ed. *The Anonimalle Chronicle 1333-81* (Manchester, 1927).

— *The St Albans Chronicle 1406-20* (Oxford, 1937).

Gardiner, S. R., ed. *Debates in the House of Commons in 1625*, Camden Society, new series, vi (London, 1873).

— *Documents illustrating the Impeachment of the Duke of Buckingham*, Camden Society, new series, xlv (London, 1889).

— *Notes of the Debates in the House of Lords, officially taken by Henry Elsing, Clerk of the Parliaments, A.D. 1621*, Camden Society, ciii (London, 1870).

— *Notes of the Debates in the House of Lords, officially taken by Henry Elsing, Clerk of the Parliaments, A.D. 1624 and 1626*, Camden Society, new series, xxiv (London, 1879).

— *Parliamentary Debates in 1610*, Camden Society, lxxxi (London, 1862).

— 'The Earl of Bristol's defence of his negotiations in Spain', *Camden Miscellany*, vi, Camden Society, civ (London, 1871).

Goodman, G. *The Court of King James the First*. Two volumes (London, 1839).

Grosart, A. B., ed. *An Apology for Socrates, and Negotium Posterorum: by Sir John Eliot.* Two volumes (n.p. 1881).

Hacket, J. *Scrinia Reserata; a Memorial Offer'd to the Great Deservings of John Williams* (London, 1693).

Halliwell, J. O., ed. *Letters of the Kings of England.* Two volumes (London, 1848).

Hassall, W. O., ed. *A Catalogue of the Library of Sir Edward Coke* (London, 1950).

Historical Manuscripts Commission.

Third Report of the Royal Commission on Historical Manuscripts (London, 1872).

Fourth Report of the Royal Commission on Historical Manuscripts (London, 1874).

Seventh Report of the Royal Commission on Historical Manuscripts (London, 1879).

Tenth Report of the Royal Commission on Historical Manuscripts (London, 1885).

Eleventh Report of the Royal Commission on Historical Manuscripts (London, 1887-8).

Twelfth Report of the Royal Commission on Historical Manuscripts (London, 1891).

Thirteenth Report of the Royal Commission on Historical Manuscripts (London, 1891-3).

Report on the Manuscripts of His Grace the Duke of Portland. Ten volumes (London, 1891-1931).

Report on the Manuscripts of the Duke of Buccleugh and Queensberry. Three volumes (London, 1899-1926).

Report on the Manuscripts of the late Reginald Rawdon Hastings. Four volumes (London, 1928-47).

Report on the Manuscripts of the Marquess of Downshire. Four volumes (London, 1924-40).

Supplementary Report on the Manuscripts of the Earl of Mar and Kellie (London, 1930).

Howell, T. B., ed. *A Complete Collection of State Trials and Proceedings for High Treason and other Crimes and Misdemeanors from the earliest period to the year 1783.* Twenty-one volumes (London, 1816).

Journals of the House of Commons (n.p., n.d.).

Journals of the House of Lords (n.p., n.d.).

Lambarde, W. *Archeion or, a Discourse upon the High Courts of Justice in England,* ed. C. H. McIlwain and P. L. Ward (Cambridge, Massachusetts, 1957).

Laud, W. *The Works of the Most Reverend Father in God, William Laud,* ed. W. Scott and J. Bliss. Seven volumes (Oxford, 1847-60).

Minsheu, J. *The Guide into Tongues* (London, 1617).

Nicholas, E. *Proceedings and Debates of the House of Commons in 1620 and 1621.* Two volumes (Oxford, 1766).

Nichols, J., ed. *Progresses, Processions, and Magnificent Festivities of King James the First, his Royal Consort, Family, and Court, collected from Original Manuscripts, Scarce Pamphlets, Corporation Records, Parochial Registers, etc. etc.* Four volumes (London, 1828).

Notestein, W., Relf, F. H. and Simpson, H., eds. *Commons Debates, 1621.* Seven volumes (New Haven, 1935).

Osborn, L. B. *The Life, Letters, and Writings of John Hoskyns 1566-1638* (New Haven, 1937).

Powell, T. *The Attourneys Academy* (London, 1623).

Raleigh, W. *The Prerogative of Parliaments in England* (London, 1657).

Relf, F. H., ed. *Notes of the Debates in the House of Lords, officially taken by Robert Bowyer and Henry Elsing, Clerks of the Parliaments, A.D. 1621, 1625, 1628,* Camden Society, third series, xlii (London, 1929).

Rotuli Parliamentorum ut et Petitiones, et Placita in Parliamento. Six volumes (n.p., n.d.).

Rushworth, J. *Historical Collections.* Seven volumes (London, 1659-1701).

Scott, W., ed. *A Collection of Scarce and Valuable Tracts, on the most interesting and entertaining subjects; but chiefly such as relate to the History and Constitution of these Kingdoms. Selected from an infinite number in print and manuscript, in the Royal, Cotton, Sion and other public, as well as private libraries: particularly that of the late Lord Somers.* Thirteen volumes (London, 1809-15).

— *Secret History of the Court of James the First.* Two volumes (Edinburgh, 1811).

Selden, J. *Of the Judicature in Parliaments* (London, n.d.).

— *The Priviledges of the Baronage of England when they sit in Parliament* (London, 1689).

Smith, L. Pearsall. *The Life and Letters of Sir Henry Wotton.* Two volumes (Oxford, 1907).

Smith, T. *Catalogus Librorum Manuscriptorum Bibliothecae Cottonianae* (Oxford, 1696).

Smith, T. *De Republica Anglorum,* ed. T. Alston (Cambridge, 1906).

Spedding, J. *The Letters and the Life of Francis Bacon.* Seven volumes (London, 1861-74).

Spelman, H. *Archaeologus in modum Glossarii ad rem antiquam posteriorem* (London, 1626).

The Parliamentary or Constitutional History of England; from the earliest Times to the Restoration of King Charles II. Twenty-four volumes (London, 1761-3).

The Proceedings of the Lords and Commons In the Year 1628. against Roger Manwaring Doctor in Divinity, (The Sacheverell of those Days) For Two Seditious High-flying Sermons, intitled, Religion and Allegiance (London, 1709).

Thompson, E. M., ed. *Chronicon Angliae* (London, 1874).

Whitelocke, B. *Memorials of the English Affairs, from the Suppos'd Expedition of Brute to this Island, to the End of the Reign of King James the First* (London, 1709).

— *Memorials of the English Affairs; or, an Historical Account of what passed from the beginning of the Reign of King Charles the First, to King Charles the Second His Happy Restoration* (London, 1682).

Williams, R. F., ed. *The Court and Times of James the First.* Two volumes (London, 1848).

— *The Court and Times of Charles the First.* Two volumes (London, 1848).

Wilson, A. *The History of Great Britain, being the Life and Reign of King James* the First, relating to what passed from his first access to the Crown, till his Death (London, 1653).

Winwood, R. *Memorials of Affairs of State in the Reigns of Q. Elizabeth and K. James I; collected (chiefly) from the Original Papers of the Right Honourable Sir Ralph Winwood*, ed. E. Sawyer. Three volumes (London, 1725).

Wotton, H. *Reliquiae Wottonianae* (London, 1651).

Yonge, W. *Diary of Walter Yonge*, ed. G. Roberts, Camden Society, xli (London, 1848).

2. Secondary sources: books

Adams, E. N. *Old English Scholarship in England 1566-1800* (London, 1917).

Aylmer, G. E. *The King's Servants; The Civil Service of Charles I 1625-42* (London, 1961).

Bellamy, J. G. *The Law of Treason in England in the Later Middle Ages* (Cambridge, 1971).

Bowen, C. D. *Francis Bacon* (London, 1963).

— *The Lion and the Throne; The Life and Times of Sir Edward Coke 1552-1634* (London, 1957).

Davies, G. *The Early Stuarts 1603-60* (Oxford, 1949).

Dodd, A. H. *The Growth of Responsible Government from James the First to Victoria* (London, 1956).

Elton, G. R., ed. *The Tudor Constitution* (Cambridge, 1962).

Erskine May, T. *A Treatise on the Law, Privileges, Proceedings and Usages of Parliament*, 13th edition (London, 1924).

Eusden, J. D. *Puritans, Lawyers, and Politics in Early Seventeenth-Century England* (New Haven, 1958).

Evans, J. *A History of the Society of Antiquaries* (Oxford, 1956).

Forster, J. *Sir John Eliot; a Biography*. Two volumes (London, 1872).

Fussner, F. S. *The Historical Revolution; English Historical Writing and Thought 1580-1640* (London, 1962).

Galbraith, V. H. *Studies in the Public Records* (London, 1949).

Gardiner, S. R. *The History of England from the Accession of James I to the Outbreak of the Civil War 1603-42*. Ten volumes (London, 1896-1901).

Gibb, M. A. *Buckingham 1592-1628* (London, 1935).

Goodman, A. *The Loyal Conspiracy; the Lords Appellant under Richard II* (London, 1971).

Hale, M. *The Jurisdiction of the Lords House*, ed. F. Hargrave (London, 1796).

Harcourt, L. W. V. *His Grace the Steward and Trial of Peers* (London, 1907).

Hill, C. *The Century of Revolution 1603-1714* (London, 1964).

Holdsworth, W. S. *A History of English Law*. Sixteen volumes (London, 1903-66).

Hulme, H. *The Life of Sir John Eliot 1592 to 1632* (London, 1957).

Jolliffe, J. E. A. *The Constitutional History of Medieval England from the English Settlement to 1485*, 2nd edition (London, 1948).

Judson, M. A. *The Crisis of the Constitution; an essay in Constitutional and Political Thought in England 1603-45* (New Brunswick, 1949).

Keir, D. L. *The Constitutional History of Modern Britain 1485-1951*, 5th edition (London, 1953).

Kenyon, J. P., ed. *The Stuart Constitution* (Cambridge, 1966).

Maitland, F. W. *The Constitutional History of England* (Cambridge, 1963).

Mathew, D. *James I* (London, 1967).

McIlwain, C. H. *Constitutionalism: ancient and modern*, revised edition (Ithaca, 1947).

— *The High Court of Parliament and its Supremacy* (New Haven, 1910).

McKisack, M. *Medieval History in the Tudor Age* (Oxford, 1971).

Mirrlees, H. *A Fly in Amber* (London, 1962).

Mitchell, W. M. *The Rise of the Revolutionary Party in the English House of Commons 1603-29* (New York, 1957).

Moir, T. L. *The Addled Parliament of 1614* (Oxford, 1958).

Morgan, I. *Prince Charles's Puritan Chaplain* (London, 1957).

Neale, J. E. *Elizabeth I and her Parliaments*. Two volumes (London, 1953, 1957).

— *The Elizabethan House of Commons* (London, 1954).

Notestein, W. *The House of Commons 1604-10* (London, 1971).

— *The Winning of the Initiative by the House of Commons* (London, 1962).

Pallister, A. *Magna Carta; the Heritage of Liberty* (Oxford, 1971).

Pike, L. O. *A Constitutional History of the House of Lords* (London, 1894).

Pocock, J. G. A. *The Ancient Constitution and the Feudal Law; a Study of English Historical Thought in the Seventeenth Century* (Cambridge, 1957).

Pollard, A. F. *The Evolution of Parliament* (London, 1920).

Prestwich, M. *Cranfield; Politics and Profits under the Early Stuarts* (Oxford, 1966).

Reinmuth, H. S., ed. *Early Stuart Studies; Essays in Honor of David Harris Willson* (Minneapolis, 1970).

Roberts, C. *The Growth of Responsible Government in Stuart England* (Cambridge, 1966).

Ruigh, R. E. *The Parliament of 1624* (Cambridge, Massachusetts, 1971).

Russell, C. *The Crisis of Parliaments; English History 1509-1660* (London, 1971).

Salmon, J. H. M. *The French Religious Wars in English Political Thought* (Oxford, 1959).

Steel, A. *Richard II* (Cambridge, 1962).

Stephen, J. F. *A History of the Criminal Law of England*. Three volumes (London, 1883).

Stubbs, W. *The Constitutional History of England in its Origin and Development*. Three volumes (Oxford, 1874-8).

Tanner, J. R., ed. *Tudor Constitutional Documents, A.D. 1485-1603, with an historical commentary* (Cambridge, 1922).

Tawney, R. H. *Business and Politics under James I; Lionel Cranfield as Merchant and Minister* (Cambridge, 1958).

Taylor, A. J. *The Jewel Tower, Westminster*, 2nd edition (London, 1965).

Thorne, S. E. *Sir Edward Coke 1552-1952* (London, 1957).

Tout, T. F. *Chapters in the Administrative History of Mediaeval England*. Six volumes (Manchester, 1920-38).

Watson, A. G. *The Library of Sir Simonds D'Ewes* (London, 1966).

Wedgwood, C. V. *Thomas Wentworth, First Earl of Strafford 1593-1641; a Revaluation* (London, 1964).

Wilkinson, B. *Constitutional History of Medieval England 1216-1399.* Three volumes (London, 1948-58).

— *Studies in the Constitutional History of the Thirteenth and Fourteenth Centuries*, 2nd edition (Manchester, 1952).

Willson, D. H. *King James VI and I* (London, 1962).

— *The Privy Councillors in the House of Commons 1604-29* (Minneapolis, 1940).

Wormuth, F. D. *The Royal Prerogative 1603-49* (Ithaca, 1939).

Zagorin, P. *The Court and the Country* (London, 1969).

Zaller, R. *The Parliament of 1621; a Study in Constitutional Conflict* (London, 1971).

3. *Secondary sources: articles*

Anderson, C. B. 'Ministerial Responsibility in the 1620s', *Journal of Modern History*, xxxiv (1962), 381-9.

Aston, M. 'The Impeachment of Bishop Despenser', *Bulletin of the Institute of Historical Research*, xxxviii (1965), 127-48.

Ball, J. N. 'Sir John Eliot at the Oxford Parliament 1625', *Bulletin of the Institute of Historical Research*, xxviii (1955), 113-27.

— 'The Impeachment of the Duke of Buckingham in the Parliament of 1626', *Melanges Antonio Marongiu; Studies presented to the International Commission for the History of Representative and Parliamentary Institutions*, xxxiv, 35-48 (Palermo, 1968).

Barratt, D. M. 'The Library of John Selden and its later History', *Bodleian Library Record*, iii (1951), 128-42, 208-13, 256-74.

Bellamy, J. G. 'Appeal and Impeachment in the Good Parliament', *Bulletin of the Institute of Historical Research*, xxxix (1966), 25-46.

Bond, M. F. 'Clerks of the Parliaments 1509-1953', *English Historical Review*, lxxiii (1958), 78-85.

— 'The Formation of the Archives of Parliament 1497-1691', *Journal of the Society of Archivists*, i (1957), 151-8.

Butt, J. 'The Facilities for Antiquarian Study in the Seventeenth Century', *Essays and Studies*, xxiv (1938), 64-79.

Chrimes, S. B. 'The Constitutional Ideas of Dr John Cowell', *English Historical Review*, lxiv (1949), 461-87.

Clarke, M. V. 'Forfeitures and Treason in 1388', *Fourteenth Century Studies*, ed. L. S. Sutherland and M. McKisack, 115-45 (Oxford, 1937).

— 'The Lancastrian Faction and the Wonderful Parliament', *Fourteenth Century Studies*, ed. L. S. Sutherland and M. McKisack, 36-52 (Oxford, 1937).

— 'The Origin of Impeachment', *Fourteenth Century Studies*, ed. L. S. Sutherland and M. McKisack, 242-71 (Oxford, 1937).

Edwards, J. G. '*The Anonimalle Chronicle 1333-81*', *English Historical Review*, xliii (1928), 103-9.

Flemion, J. S. 'The Dissolution of Parliament in 1626; a Revaluation', *English Historical Review*, lxxxvii (1972), 784-90.

Foster, E. R. 'Procedure in the House of Lords During the Early Stuart Period', *Journal of British Studies*, v (1966), no. 2, 56-73.

— 'The Procedure of the House of Commons against Patents and Monopolies', *Conflict in Stuart England*, ed. W. A. Aiken and B. D. Henning, 57-85 (London, 1960).

Galbraith, V. H. 'Thomas Walsingham and the Saint Albans Chronicle 1272-1422', *English Historical Review*, xlvii (1932), 12-30.

Hazeltine, H. D. 'Selden as legal historian; a comment in criticism and appreciation', *Harvard Law Review*, xxiv (1910-11), 105-18, 205-19.

Hulme, H. 'The Leadership of Sir John Eliot in the Parliament of 1626', *Journal of Modern History*, iv (1932), 361-86.

Johnson, R. C. 'Francis Bacon and Lionel Cranfield', *Huntington Library Quarterly*, xxiii (1960), 301-20.

Lambrick, G. 'The Impeachment of the Abbot of Abingdon in 1368', *English Historical Review*, lxxxii (1967), 250-76.

Leonard, H. H. 'Ferrers' Case; a Note', *Bulletin of the Institute of Historical Research*, xlii (1969), 230-4.

Lewis, N. B. 'Article VII of the Impeachment of Michael de la Pole in 1386', *English Historical Review*, xlii (1927), 402-7.

Lomas, S. C. 'The State Papers of the early Stuarts and the Interregnum', *Transactions of the Royal Historical Society*, new series, xvi (1902), 97-132.

Palmer, J. J. N. 'The Impeachment of Michael de la Pole in 1386', *Bulletin of the Institute of Historical Research*, xlii (1969), 96-101.

Plucknett, T. F. T. 'Impeachment and Attainder', *Transactions of the Royal Historical Society*, fifth series, iii (1953), 145-58.

— 'The Rise of the English State Trial', *Politica*, ii (1937), 542-59.

— 'State Trials under Richard II', *Transactions of the Royal Historical Society*, fifth series, ii (1952), 159-71.

— 'The Impeachments of 1376', *Transactions of the Royal Historical Society*, fifth series, i (1951), 153-64.

— 'The Origin of Impeachment', *Transactions of the Royal Historical Society*, fourth series, xxiv (1942), 47-71.

Plumb, J. H. 'The Growth of the Electorate in England from 1600 to 1715', *Past and Present*, no. 45 (1969), 90-116.

Pollard, A. F. 'The Authorship and Value of the *Anonimalle Chronicle*', *English Historical Review*, liii (1938), 577-605.

Rabb, T. K. 'Parliament and Society in Early Stuart England; the Legacy of Wallace Notestein', *American Historical Review*, lxxvii (1972), 705-14.

— 'Sir Edwin Sandys and the Parliament of 1604', *American Historical Review*, lxix (1964), 646-70.

Resneck, S. 'The Early History of the Parliamentary Declaration of Treason', *English Historical Review*, xlii (1927), 497-513.

Richardson, H. G. and Sayles, G. O. 'The Parliaments of Edward III', *Bulletin of the Institute of Historical Research*, viii (1930), 65-82; ix (1931), 1-18.

Snapp, H. F. 'The Impeachment of Roger Maynwaring', *Huntington Library Quarterly*, xxx (1967), 217-32.

Snow, V. F. 'The Arundel Case 1626', *The Historian*, xxvi (1964), 323-49.

Sparrow, J. 'The Earlier Owners of Books in John Selden's Library', *Bodleian Quarterly Record*, vi (1931), 263-71.

Styles, P. 'Politics and Historical Research in the Early Seventeenth Century', *English Historical Scholarship in the Sixteenth and Seventeenth Centuries*, ed. L. Fox, 49-72 (London, 1956).

Wernham, R. B. 'The Public Records in the Sixteenth and Seventeenth Centuries', *English Historical Scholarship in the Sixteenth and Seventeenth Centuries*, ed. L. Fox, 11-30 (London, 1956).

Zebel, S. H. 'The Committee of the Whole in the Reign of James I', *American Political Science Review*, xxxv (1941), 941-52.

INDEX

Abbott, George, archbishop of Canterbury, 76 and n., 97, 121, 154, 158, 159n., 162, 173, 207, 215

Abergavenny's case, 81n.

Abingdon, abbot of, imprisonment at instigation of townsmen (1368), 11-12

Addled Parliament (1614), 74 and n.; dissolved, 80

Admiralty Court, 80-1

Alford, Edward, 50, 51, 76, 88, 124, 126, 136-7, 180

Annals (Stow), 27

Anonimalle Chronicle, 27 and n.

Antiquaries in reign of James I, 28-36

Anyan, Dr Thomas, Master of Corpus Christi College, Oxford, case of (1624), 156, 173, 175-6

Appeal of treason or felony, 13, 22-3, 28, 38

Appello Caesarem (Montague), 207

Arundel, Thomas Howard, earl of, 113n., 132

Attainder, 16, 60, 72n., 212-13, 216

Aubrey, Christopher, 111, 112n.

Audley, Sir Mervyn, 75

Bacon, Francis: correspondence with Selden, 36; and Thornborough's case, 58; and Cowell's case, 61 and n.; and Mompesson's case, 97, 98n., 100, 103; on question of referees, 100-1; attacked as referee, 103 and n., 104n.

his case (1621), 1, 31, 35, 44, 52, 78, 110-18, 124, 133, 140, 144, 145, 157, 161n., 162, 165nn., 167, 168, 171, 199, 206, 214n.; evi-

dence against him, 110-12, 136; conference between Lords and Commons, 113; evidence before Lords committees, 113-15; his submission, 115-16; sentenced by Lords, 116; Commons invited to come to demand judgment, 116-17

Bancroft, Richard, archbishop of Canterbury, 62

Bayly, Lewis, bishop of Bangor, 207n.

Bill, proceedings by, 14, 38, 194-6, 209, 210n.; *see also* Petition

Bennet, Sir John, judge of the prerogative court of Canterbury, 31, 48, 111n., 131n., 140, 144, 145; his case (1621), 133-5, 157n.: accused of corruption, 134; expelled by Commons, 134; conference with Lords, 135; both Houses lose interest, 135

Bowyer, Robert, Clerk of the Parliaments, 56 and n.

Bracton, Henry de, 24, 191

Briefe Discourse Concerning the Power of the Peeres and Commons . . . (Cotton), 30

Bristol, earl of, 188-9, 196n., 197, 199, 201

Brooke, Christopher, 105, 152, 155, 173

Buckeridge, John, bishop of Rochester, 211 and n.

Buckingham, George Villiers, duke of, 1, 80, 92-3, 99-101, 103, 104, 108n., 110, 127, 134n., 141, 147, 153, 171, 172n., 176, 208; and Bacon's case, 111, 114 and n., 116, 118n.; and Yelverton, 118, 121-2; and Michell's case, 132;